# ᴅᵹ THE ROYAL WHORE ᵹᴅ

*CHILTON BOOK COMPANY*
*Philadelphia · New York · London*

# THE
# ROYAL
# WHORE

*Barbara Villiers, Countess of Castlemaine*

*by ALLEN ANDREWS*

TO MY LADY

*pour tout' autre que vous, vous motes tout désir*

# Contents

1 / *I will live and die loving you*  1

2 / *Whosoever I find to be my Lady Castlemaine's enemy
in this matter, I do promise upon my word
to be his enemy as long as I live.*  34

3 / *Cuckolds all a-row,
the old dance of England.*  73

4 / *You damned jade
meddling with things
you have nothing to do with.*  94

5 / *Venereal pleasures, accompanied with looseness,
debauchery and prophaneness, are not such heinous crimes
and crying sins, but rather they do mortify the flesh.*  162

6 / *I wonder that so inconsiderable a Person
as you will contend with a Lady of my Quality.*  202

7 / *Madam, all that I ask of you, for your own sake,
is Live so for the future as to make the least
noise you can, and I care not who you love.*  233

8 / *Now all things of gallantry are at an end
with you and I.*  254

*Appendix*  267

*References*  278

# Biographical Notes

ANNE  Queen Anne of Great Britain (1665–1714). Anne Stuart, niece of Charles II, second surviving daughter of James, Duke of York, afterwards King James II, and Anne Hyde, Duchess of York and daughter of Lord Chancellor Clarendon. Anne was rigorously brought up as an Anglican though her father was a Catholic, and she acquiesced in 1688–9 when James was deposed in favor of Anne's elder sister Mary and her husband, William of Orange. Anne succeeded William as sovereign in 1702. She married Prince George of Denmark and bore him seventeen children of whom none survived infancy.

ARLINGTON  For Lord Arlington see Sir Henry BENNET.

ARRAN  Earl of Arran. An ambiguous title held simultaneously by Richard Butler, second son of the Marquis of Ormonde (with reference to the isle of Aran off Galway, Ireland) and as the courtesy title of the eldest son of the Duke of Hamilton (with reference to the isle of Arran off Bute, Scotland). Richard Butler, Earl of Arran, cheerfully lied to the Duke of York in 1660 that he had already seduced the Duchess. James

Douglas, Earl of Arran, son of the third Duke of Hamilton, fathered Charles Hamilton, the illegitimate son of Barbara Fitzroy, who was the illegitimate daughter of Barbara Villiers and John Churchill, Earl of Marlborough (later Duke.) James Douglas became the fourth Duke of Hamilton.

BENNET    Sir Henry Bennet (1618–1685). Fought for the Royalists, joined Charles II in exile, and became his ambassador in Madrid. After the Restoration he became Secretary of State (1662–1674) and a member of the Cabal. He became Baron Arlington in 1663 and Earl of Arlington in 1672. His heiress-daughter Isabella was married to Henry Fitzroy, third child of Charles II and Barbara Villiers.

BERKELEY    Sir Charles Berkeley (1630–1665) was a contemporary and favorite of Charles II, whom he served in exile, and a favorite of James, Duke of York, whom he tried to rescue from the marriage with Anne Hyde by falsely saying that he and others had seduced her. At the Restoration he became a courtier, Keeper of the Privy Purse, and, it was said, the King's pimp. He was on terms of equal familiarity with Charles II and Barbara Villiers and was rumored to have fathered one of her children. He was made Viscount Fitzharding in 1663 and Earl of Falmouth in 1664. He married Mary Bagot and was killed at the side of the Duke of York in the naval battle of Lowestoft next year.

BUCKINGHAM    George Villiers (1628–1687), second Duke of Buckingham, brought up with the children of Charles I after his father's assassination, was a venturesome, erratic, unscrupulous and witty man never long out of the affection of Charles II. He was a first cousin of, and in the main a consistent enemy to, Barbara Villiers. He married Mary Fairfax, daughter of the Parliamentary commander-in-chief, but maintained a scandalous liaison with the Countess of Shrewsbury, whose husband he killed in a duel.

BUTLER    The Butlers were an influential noble family with great estates in Ireland, and took their name from the Hereditary Butler of Ireland. James Butler, generally called the Marquis of Ormonde though in reality he was twelfth Earl and first Duke of Ormonde, was Lord Lieutenant of Ireland intermittently for eighteen years under Charles I and Charles II. A son was Richard, Earl of Arran. A daughter, Lady Elizabeth Butler, was second wife of the Earl of Chesterfield.

CARNEGIE   See Lady Anne HAMILTON.

CHARLES   King Charles II of Great Britain (1630–1685). Second son (his elder brother was born prematurely and died after a few hours) of King Charles I and Henrietta Maria of France. Charles was under fire at the battle of Edgehill at the age of twelve and had his own command within three years. After his father's execution he invaded Scotland from France and marched south, but was defeated by Cromwell at Worcester and went into exile for nine more years. After his Restoration on his thirtieth birthday, in 1660, he married Catherine of Braganza. He had no legitimate issue but acknowledged thirteen bastards, namely:

*By Lucy Walters:* James, Duke of Monmouth, b. 1649.

*By Elizabeth Killigrew, Lady Shannon:* Charlotte, Countess of Yarmouth, b. 1650.

*By Catherine Pegge, later Lady Green:* Charles, Earl of Plymouth, b. 1657; Catherine, b. 1658.

*By Barbara Villiers, Mrs. Roger Palmer, later Countess of Castlemaine, later Duchess of Cleveland:* Anne, Countess of Sussex, b. 1661; Charles, Duke of Southampton, b. 1662; Henry, Duke of Grafton, b. 1663; Charlotte, Countess of Lichfield, b. 1664; George, Duke of Northumberland, b. 1665.

*By Nell Gwyn:* Charles, Duke of St. Albans, b. 1670; James, b. 1671.

*By Louise, Duchess of Portsmouth:* Charles, Duke of Richmond, b. 1672.

*By Moll Davies:* Mary, Countess of Derwentwater, b. 1673.

King Charles II was succeeded by his brother James, Duke of York, as King James II.

CHESTERFIELD   Philip Stanhope (1633–1713), second Earl of Chesterfield and first seducer of Barbara Villiers, married Lady Anne Percy, eldest daughter of the tenth Earl of Northumberland, and after her death Lady Elizabeth Butler, eldest daughter of the Marquis of Ormonde, and after her death

Lady Elizabeth Dormer, by whom he had his surviving son,
father of the fourth Earl who wrote the famous letters to his
(natural) son.

CHURCHILL    Arabella Churchill (1648–1730), daughter of Sir
Winston Churchill and sister of John Churchill was maid of
honor to the Duchess of York and speedily became mistress of
James, Duke of York, to whom she bore four children includ-
ing James, Duke of Berwick. Later she married Colonel
Charles Godfrey by whom she had two daughters.

John Churchill (1650–1722), son of Sir Winston Churchill,
was page to the Duke of York and began a career in the Army
at the age of seventeen. His liaison with Barbara Villiers, the
issue of which was the Lady Barbara Fitzroy, lasted for some
eight years after which he secretly married Sarah Jennings and
entered the orbit of Princess, later Queen, Anne. He was
created Baron Churchill in the Scottish peerage in 1682 and
in the English peerage in 1685, Earl of Marlborough in 1689
and Duke of Marlborough in 1702.

CLARENDON    Edward Hyde (1609–1674), first Earl of Clarendon, was a lawyer whose first, brief marriage connected him
with the Villiers family so that he called Barbara "cousin."
He was a principal adviser to Charles II through his exile, and
Lord Chancellor from before the Restoration until he was dismissed in 1667. In exile he wrote the great history of the
Civil War and after.

CLEVELAND    The last Earl of Cleveland, a Royalist general, died
in 1667, and the title was revived for Barbara Villiers as
Duchess of Cleveland in 1670.

DUKE    "The Duke," when used without a territorial title, refers
generally to James, Duke of York.

FALMOUTH    For the Earl of Falmouth see Sir Charles
BERKELEY.

FITZHARDING    For Viscount Fitzharding see Sir Charles
BERKELEY.

FITZROY    The children of Charles II and Barbara Villiers were
at first given the surname Palmer, and later the surname
Fitzroy. Barbara's child by John Churchill was also carelessly
surnamed Fitzroy, but Charles II never acknowledged her.

The five Fitzroy children are listed among Charles's bastards under the heading CHARLES.

GRAFTON   For the Duke of Grafton see Henry Fitzroy under CHARLES.

GRANDISON   The second, third and fourth Viscounts Grandison of Limerick were William Villiers, cousin of George Villiers, second Duke of Buckingham and father of Barbara Villiers, died 1643, and his brothers (Barbara's uncles) John, died 1659 and George, died 1699. Barbara used George as her legal trustee to handle many of her gifts from Charles II.

HAMILTON   The Hamiltons were and are an extensive Scottish noble family which branched into Ireland.
Lady Anne Hamilton was the daughter of William Hamilton, Second Duke of Hamilton. She married Robert, Lord Carnegie, and later became Countess of Southesk.
Anne Duchess of Hamilton was the aunt of Lady Anne Hamilton and succeeded Lady Anne's father as Duchess of Hamilton in her own right.
Elizabeth, George and James Hamilton were descended from the Hamiltons, Earls of Abercorn. The brothers were soldiers and courtiers personally attached to Charles II. Their sister Elizabeth (1641–1708) was married in 1663 to Count Gramont after some persuasion by James and George.
Charles Hamilton (1691–1754) was the illegitimate son of James Douglas, Earl of Arran, and Barbara Fitzroy, who was the illegitimate daughter of John Churchill and Barbara Villiers. He stayed with his grandmother until her death after which he went into Europe and developed as a historian. He was styled Count of Arran.

HENRIETTE ANNE   Princess Henriette Anne (1644–1670), youngest daughter of Charles I and Henrietta Maria, was brought up in France and was married to Philippe, Duke of Orleans, brother of the French King Louis XIV. Though he saw very little of his sister Charles II was extraordinarily attached to her; he constantly referred to her as "Minette."

HENRIETTA MARIA   Queen Henrietta Maria (1609–1669), youngest daughter of King Henri IV of France and Mary de Medici, was consort of Charles I and mother of Charles II and James II.

HYDE  For Anne Hyde see the Duchess of YORK.
For Edward Hyde see the Earl of CLARENDON.

JAMES  For King James II see the Duke of YORK.

JERMYN  Henry Jermyn, Senior, (1604?–1684) was master of
the horse to Queen Henrietta Maria and during her exile
became an indispensable household and state servant, and was
reputedly her morganatic husband. At his mother's request
Charles II created him Earl of St. Albans just before his Restoration. Within days of Jermyn's death Charles created his
son Charles, by Nell Gwyn, Duke of St. Albans.
Henry (Harry) Jermyn, Junior, (1636–1708) was the nephew
of the Earl of St. Albans, a wild joker and rake who was made
Earl of Dover in 1685.

LICHFIELD  For the Countess of Lichfield see Charlotte Fitzroy
under CHARLES.

LOUIS  King Louis XIV of France (1638–1715), a full cousin
of Charles II, succeeded to the throne at the age of five and
began his personal, despotic government in 1661 at the age of
twenty-three. Throughout the lifetime of Charles II the
French king had brilliant success both politically and militar-
ily. The waning of his influence was emphasized by the Protestant invasion of England by William of Orange and the
subsequent great series of military defeats by the Duke of
Marlborough.

MARLBOROUGH  For the Duke of Marlborough see John
CHURCHILL. .

MARY  Queen Mary II of Great Britain (1662–1694). Princess
Mary, eldest surviving daughter of James, Duke of York, and
his Duchess, Anne Hyde, was married at the age of fifteen to
William of Orange, her first cousin. Unhappy and childless,
she reacted to the dethronement of her father in 1688–9 with
unfilial delight and succeeded him with her husband as joint
heirs.
For Princess Mary of Orange see Princess ROYAL.

MINETTE  For Minette see Princess HENRIETTE ANNE.

MONMOUTH  James, Duke of Monmouth (1649–1685), the
eldest illegitimate son of Charles II, was rescued as an illiter-
ate from his mother, Lucy Walters and brought up at Queen
Henrietta Maria's frugal court. He came to England in 1662.

He was greatly loved by his father but was finally involved in a plot against the King's life. On the accession of James II Monmouth attempted a Protestant insurrection but was defeated and speedily executed.

MONTAGU  For Edward Montagu see the Earl of SANDWICH.
Ralph Montagu (1638–1709), an accomplished libertine, was intermittently over many years Charles II's ambassador to Louis XIV, and it was in Paris that he had his calamitous affair with Anne, Countess of Sussex. Ralph Montagu's sister was Lady Harvey, alternate friend and enemy of Barbara Villiers and her daughter. A shrewd politician with the knack of bouncing aptly, Ralph eventually became Duke of Montagu with a greatly envied town house which is the site of the British Museum.

NORTHUMBERLAND  The Earls of Northumberland were for long the ancient family of Percy but after three centuries the line began to fail. Algernon Percy, tenth Earl, married one of his daughters, Lady Anne Percy, to the Earl of Chesterfield and her sister, Lady Elizabeth Percy (who wrote to Chesterfield greatly concerned about his chastity) to the Earl of Essex. Algernon's second wife, Lady Elizabeth Howard, daughter of the Earl of Suffolk, became the formidable Countess of Northumberland with power to control the marriage of her granddaughter, Lady Betty Percy. Elizabeth Howard's son was Josceline, eleventh Earl of Northumberland, who died in 1670 at the age of twenty-six without a male heir. He had married Lady Elizabeth Wriothesley, daughter of the Earl of Southampton, who gave birth to Lady Betty Percy, heir to Josceline's wealth and some of his titles but not to his earldom, which became extinct. Elizabeth Wriothesley was the Countess of Northumberland who married Ralph Montagu as her second husband, and by that marriage was deemed to have relinquished the control over her daughter Lady Betty Percy, who was eventually married three times before she was aged sixteen. The territorial title of Northumberland was allocated to George Fitzroy, son of Charles II and Barbara Villiers, who became Duke in 1683 but died without issue in 1716. Northumberland became a Percy title once more when the son of Lady Betty Percy, Algernon Seymour, seventh Earl of Somerset, became Earl of Northumberland, and the son-in-law who succeeded him took the name of Percy.

ORLEANS   For the Duchess of Orleans see Princess HENRIETTE ANNE.

ORMONDE   For the Marquis of Ormonde see the family of BUTLER.

PALMER   Roger Palmer (1634–1705) was the son of Sir James Palmer by his second wife Catherine Herbert, daughter of the first Baron Powis and widow of Sir Robert Vaughn. Roger married Barbara Villiers soon after his father's death in 1657. Barbara's five children by Charles II were all at first baptized under the name of Palmer, although Roger knew only two of them. He was fond of those he knew, and made Anne, Barbara's eldest daughter, the trustee of his will.

RICHMOND   Stuarts very closely connected with the royal house of Stuart, being descended from Mary Queen of Scots and Darnley, held the joint dukedom of Lennox and Richmond. One Duchess of Richmond was Mary Villiers, sister of George, Duke of Buckingham and cousin of Barbara. Her son was succeeded as Duke in 1660 by Charles Stuart, sixth Duke of Lennox and third Duke of Richmond, who eloped with the distant cousin of his and the King's, Frances Stuart. After his death in 1672 the dukedom was vacant, and it was re-created for the son of Charles II and the Duchess of Portsmouth.

ROYAL   The Princess Mary, sister of Charles II, was known by her English title as the Princess Royal and by her Dutch title as Princess of Orange. She married Prince William, who became Dutch Stadtholder in 1647. He died in 1650 when Mary was pregnant with the son who was to be William of Orange, King William III of Great Britain.

SANDWICH   Edward Montagu (1625–1672), a Commonwealth naval commander, was created Earl of Sandwich when he went over to Charles II just before the Restoration. He was a kinsman of Samuel Pepys and briefly a lover of Barbara Villiers. He was blown up in his flagship in the battle of Sole Bay.

SHREWBURY   Francis Talbot, eleventh Earl of Shrewsbury, was killed by the Duke of Buckingham in 1668 in a duel prompted by the liaison between Buckingham and the Countess of Shrewsbury. The son of the Earl and Countess, Lord John Talbot, was killed in a duel by Henry Fitzroy, Duke of Grafton, in 1686.

SOUTHAMPTON Thomas Wriothesley (1607–1667), fourth Earl of Southampton, was the son of Henry Wriothesley, third earl, Shakespeare's "onlie begetter" of his sonnets. Thomas's daughter Elizabeth married first the tenth Earl of Northumberland and second Ralph Montagu. When the title lapsed on Thomas's death it was annexed by Barbara Villiers as her own subsidiary title as Duchess of Cleveland. Her son Charles Fitzroy bore the courtesy title Earl of Southampton, which was later converted into the actual title of Duke of Southampton.

SUSSEX For the Countess of Sussex see Anne Fitzroy under CHARLES.

YORK James (1633–1701), Duke of York, second surviving son of Charles I, was heir to the throne throughout the reign of Charles II, and the fact that he was a declared Catholic from 1673 was the biggest single factor in English politics thereafter. He succeeded his brother as King James II in 1685 and was expelled by the Glorious Revolution of 1688.

James married as his first wife Anne Hyde, daughter of Charles's Lord Chancellor, and as his second, Maria d'Este (Mary of Modena.)

*National Portrait Gallery, London*

*Barbara Villiers, Duchess of Cleveland. After Sir Peter Lely.*

BARBARA Villiers and Lady Anne Hamilton lay in bed together in the lees of the morning light conceded to the Duchess of Hamilton's modest house in the City of London, giggling as they schemed how to fix an assignation that day with their mutual lover the Earl of Chesterfield. If the laughter was at times theatrically forced, there was justification. Barbara was sixteen, a maiden libertine, and an alliance with Anne in a joint approach to the wild nobleman Chesterfield was an early concession to cynicism in the pursuit of love.

For the length of a year, during which the young Mistress Villiers had known that she was already beautiful and was sought honorably and dishonorably, she had been touched by the fever of attraction for Chesterfield: a Royalist cosmopolitan widower of the world who had suffered for the King and was, at twenty-three, compactly notorious for drinking, gaming, dueling and debauchery. They met, and at first challenge she feinted girlishly with would-be wounding taunts. He parried, deflecting scorn with an accomplished pass of devotion: "Is it not a strange magic in love which gives so powerful a charm to the least of your cruel words that they endanger to kill a man at a hundred miles distance? But why do I complain of so pleasant a death, or repine at those sufferings which I would not exchange for a diadem?"[1]

Soon Barbara knew that she had not only lost her heart but that she had also abandoned her discretion. Stung by the humiliations that youth is heir to, and by constant competition from the idle, rootless, Royalist young ladies cooped up in Commonwealth London, she began to expose herself in the ache of a passion whose pathos she was never known later to inspire or repeat, even for the King. "I would fain have had the happiness to have seen you at church this day," she wrote to Chesterfield, "but I was not suffered to go. I am never so well pleased as when I am with you, though I find you are better when you are with other ladies. For you were yesterday all the afternoon with the person I am most jealous of, and I know I have so little merit that I am suspicious you love all women better than myself. I sent you yesterday a letter that I think might convince you that I loved nothing besides yourself, nor will I ever, though you should hate me; but if you should, I would never give you the trouble of telling you how much I loved you, but keep it to myself till it had broke my heart."[2]

She had been in the habit of going to Chesterfield at his lodgings in Lincoln's Inn Fields. Now, in naked conference with Anne Hamilton, she devised a more public rendezvous. Flirtatiously they composed and despatched a joint note: "My friend and I are just now abed together a-contriving how to have your company this afternoon. If you deserve this favour you will come and seek us at Ludgate Hill about three o'clock at Butler's shop, where we will expect you. But lest we should give you too much satisfaction at once, we will say no more. Expect the rest when you see. . . ." And they wrote their signatures.[3]

But Lady Anne's mother discovered the liaison, banished her daughter to Windsor and forbade any communication from Chesterfield. Anne wrote a last note begging him, "Give me some adieus with your eyes, since it is to be done no other way."[4] Chesterfield answered with jocular ambiguity: "You, that were the soul of this little world, have carried all the life of it with you, and left us so dull that I have quite left off the making love to five or six at a time, and do wholly content myself with being as much as is possible Yours, C."[5]

All the parties in the affair knew that no such remission was intended. Barbara told her lover with happy insincerity, "I am so sorry to hear that the having a kindness for you is so great a crime that people are to suffer for it,"[6] and she sped on to savor the consummation of her triumph in words whose assurance is monumental against the tentative virginity of her previous declarations. "The joy I had of being with you last night," she confided, "has made me do nothing but dream of you. And my life is never pleasant to me but when I am with you or talking of you. Yet the discourses of the world must make me a little more circumspect. Therefore I desire you not to come tomorrow, but to stay till the party be come to Town. I will not fail to meet you on Saturday morning."[7]

The censorious "discourses" of the outside world might

have been expected to induce circumspection. The year was
1657, the zenith of the authoritarian Puritan interregnum.
His Highness, Oliver Cromwell, was Lord Protector of the
Commonwealth of England, Scotland and Ireland, and a
shabby, hungry young man—generally called Charles
Stuart—was in turn writing begging letters to gentlemen he
did not know* or disconsolately trying to get himself shot in
a minor battle across the Channel.[9] Merry England was
officially dead, and nowhere more formally than in London,
under the very eyes and heels of the saints and levelers who,
fascinated and terrified by the irrepressibility of sexuality,
had erected the barricades of ordinance and persuasion
against every identifiable expression of suspect human con-
gress—the tavern, the theatre, the sweaty old sports, dancing,
lyric music and poetry, and the singing, mutual sight and
contact of the flesh.

For every old festival there was now only the substitute
sad Sabbath. Yet the missionaries had failed, not only on
Barbara's Saturday mornings but in church on Sunday, too.
Barbara Villiers, who within three years, at the age of nineteen, was to begin her reign as what Andrew Marvell called
"the Royal Whore"[10] and Oldmixon, "the lewdest as well as
the fairest of all King Charles's concubines,"[11] was not baptized into dissipation by the excesses of the Restoration
Court, but by practice in Puritan London.

Nor did the entourage of Charles II catch debauchery by
infection from the French—the time-honored English scape-
goats in matters venereal. During his eleven years' "travels"

---

*Typically, to an English colonel by personal messenger, who was
empowered to give a receipt: "I am so much informed of your good
affection to me that I cannot doubt of your readiness to assist me with
the loan of an hundred pounds, which I will repay to you as soon as I
am able. . . ."[8]

Charles spent altogether five years in France, sometimes incognito, often uncomfortable, when even his mother could not afford a fire and he had to limit himself to one meal a day.[12]

His visits to the staid French Court can be measured in days, and during a considerable part of his second stay in Paris his fourteen-year-old cousin, King Louis XIV, was actively engaged in quelling a civil war. It is true that the ennui of poverty in Paris set Charles on a rare, reckless bout of drinking and womanising along the fringe of his society[13]—he was not naturally a drunkard and his tendency was to capitulate to women rather than to ravish them. But it was later, from Spanish-dominated Brussels, that a horrified Commonwealth spy led his list of the King's crimes with the fact that he took his sister to the theater on Sundays. (Princess Mary of Orange had traveled from The Hague to bring him some pocket money and teach him the steps of the latest dances.) "I think I may truly say," the agent enciphered in his despatch to Cromwell's secretary of state, "that greater abominations were never practised than at Charles Stuart's Court.* Fornication, drunkenness and adultery are esteemed no sin amongst them."[15]

But the delights of debauchery were not confined to the Continent, and libertinism was only one of a number of contemporary expressions of the revolt against authoritarianism, which was indeed one of the springs of Protestantism. Literary pornography sprang fully armed from the head of individualism in 1650, and within ten years the mines of the

---

*In 1656. The "Court" was officially at Bruges, save for those of its members who still could not leave the last caravanserai, Cologne, because of unpaid debts. One of Charles's "courtiers," the Earl of Norwich, was embarrassed because he had frequently to retreat into a cave or behind a bush to mend his breeches.[14]

main assault against the established conventions of the family, religion and society through explosive amoral carnality were substantially laid.[16] During the same period— 1648–1660—the Invisible College was meeting at Oxford: the gathering of cultured men who spurned the current ideological controversies to devote themselves to practical inquiry and research into the real world, testing every theory by repeatable experiment. This body took more formal shape with the Restoration, and in 1662 received Charles's charter and became the Royal Society. It was the philosophical prime mover, which by its individualist questioning spirit shifted the milieu of universal man and matter from the skittle alley of an arbitrary God, working through illogical miracles and the sanctions of myth and superstition, to "its own true channel of natural causes* and effects."[17]

In the formative years before the Restoration there were other signs of the rejection of authoritarianism. On the side of dignity was the mighty abstract of the emergence of the supremacy of law over the arbitrary will of executive men. On the side of impudence was the homely fact that children moved towards achieving a certain independent status which encouraged bringing them up as individuals. There are occasional, astonishing records of the independence of young girls. Mary Boyle, daughter of the Earl of Cork, refused at the age of fourteen to marry the man of her father's choice, a noble heir with £8,000 a year; but soon afterwards she accepted the proposal of Charles Rich, later Earl of Warwick, after he had spent two hours on his knees by her bedside "handsomely expressing his passion." (She had measles,

---

*But originally the founders did not intend to question religion. The Society's historian wrote: "These two subjects, God and the Soul, being only foreborn: in all the rest they wander at their pleasure."[18]

and her sister-in-law kept intruders at bay.) She promptly implemented her consent, oblivious of the measles. "Thus we parted, this evening," she recorded, "after I have given away myself to him, and if I had not done so that night I had been, by my father's separating us, kept from doing it at least for a long time." For she was promptly sent to Hampton Court and ordered to see no young man. But she was married privately, giving her age as eighteen although she was really fifteen. Her husband was twenty-five. She lived her life as a very pious woman.[19]

The fact that Barbara Villiers was about the same age as Mary Boyle when she earnestly lost her virginity to a man of twenty-three may seem to confirm a pattern of sexual maturity among girls in seventeenth-century England which clashes with what is known about the onset of puberty in northern countries.[20] What enabled Barbara Villiers, Anne Hamilton and Mary Boyle to go to bed so nonchalantly, so adequately and so young? They were all of "good" family, amply nourished—which is a great aid to sexual maturity—and enjoyed the zest of a sophisticated upbringing. It gave them a physical and mental development which then made privileged families stand out from the rest in far greater contrast. In the case of Barbara and Anne, and many of their contemporaries among the gentility, there was an additional factor. They were war babies.

Like many girls living just three hundred years later, Barbara Villiers was born in '40, her father was killed in the war in '43, her mother married again in '48 and eventually brought Barbara from the country to her stepfather's house in town. She was comparatively poor, precociously beautiful, and the set she moved among had fluid moral standards.

She was a Villiers, "one of the race of the Villiers," a member of an ancient family which in two generations produced a most unequal progeny: luminous and unscrupulous men like the two Dukes of Buckingham; nonentities of perpetual oblivion like the first Duke's two brothers, whom he drew into the peerage with him by a sort of osmosis; or simple, loyal gentlemen of justice and integrity like Barbara's father, William Villiers, second Viscount Grandison.

George Villiers, first Duke of Buckingham, was the second son of a second marriage by a Leicestershire knight whose family had come over with the Conqueror. Masterfully managed by his widowed mother, George was introduced in youth to the court of James I—who was, at forty-seven, a prematurely senile, fat and fidgeting homosexual. James fell in love with the ripe youngster, made him a Knight of the Garter and promoted him through three ranks of the peerage in three years, explaining his passion with the words, "Christ had his John, and I have my George."[21]

All Buckingham's family received honors from the King. One half-brother became ambassador to Bohemia and was created Viscount Grandison of Limerick in the peerage of Ireland. Full brothers became Viscount Purbeck and the Earl of Anglesey, and even his mother received a personal title. Buckingham was assassinated in 1628, and his months-old son, George, the second duke, was brought up with the royal family. He became the evil genius of Charles II and a dangerous court enemy to his cousin, Barbara Villiers.

Grandison's son, the second viscount, married a fourteen-year-old heiress to £180,000, Mary Bayning, and their only child, Barbara Villiers, was born next year and was christened in St. Margaret's Westminster on November 27, 1640. Early in 1642 Charles I left London, only to return for his trial and execution seven years later; and Grandison followed him, never to return. He was handsome, honorable and "of that rare piety and devotion that the court or camp could not show a more faultless person,"[22] said Edward Hyde, later Charles II's Lord Chancellor, who loved Grandison and learned to hate his daughter—for which she exacted satisfactory revenge. Grandison's devotion to the King was unquestioning. "If I had not understanding enough to know the uprightness of the cause," he used to say, "nor loyalty enough to inform myself of the duty of a subject, yet the very obligations of gratitude to the King on behalf of my house are such as my life is but a due sacrifice."[23] And he duly offered his life.

At the outset of the Civil War he brought all his surviving brothers into the struggle, and himself raised a regiment for the King. His cavalry raided Nantwich, occupied it and commandeered all the rebel gentlemen's horses.[24] Isolated at Winchester, he was captured by the Parliamentarians. He escaped and fought at the battle of Edgehill, where an officer of his regiment recaptured the royal standard taken from the dead Sir Edmund Verney.

In July, 1643, Grandison was commanding a division of three thousand foot at Prince Rupert's siege of Bristol. After two days' bombardment the infantry stormed the walls at three in the morning and enabled the pioneers to blow up the fortifications sufficiently for Rupert's cavalry to enter.[25] The Parliamentary forces surrendered and marched out amid blows and jeers from Royalist soldiers shouting raucously, "Where is your King Jesus?" But young Lord Grandison had no part in the triumph. He had received a shot in

the thigh and the medicine of the time could not save him.
He was carried to Oxford and died there after many weeks.
He was buried in Christ Church where he is still commemo-
rated by a white marble monument erected by Barbara in
her maturity as Duchess of Cleveland.

But in September, 1643, his daughter was a landless baby
in a seething country, the charge of an eighteen-year-old
mother whose own family estates—largely in Essex and
Suffolk—were under the firm control of Cromwell's Eastern
Association. There was much other property which was
slowly disappearing under the rising tide of war. Ten thousand pounds of Lady Grandison's money had been lent in
peacetime to the Earl of Cleveland on the security of a
mortgage on the Earl's manors of Stepney and Hackney.
Another sum of £18,000 had been similarly lent to the Duke
of Lennox. When Barbara was only a month old her father
was suing in the House of Lords concerning these debts. He
raised the matters annually until he died, and then the
family suit was prosecuted by Lady Grandison's brother-
in-law on her behalf. The estates which were security for the
loans were sequestrated by the Roundhead victors. After
years of litigation the King was beheaded and there was no
House of Lords to appeal to. The matter was suspended,
but never forgotten, and resentment over this poverty
imposed by her own class may well have been a black fami-
ly-grudge excessively clouding Barbara's childhood, and some
explanation both of her later rapacity for land and property
and an infantile preoccupation with certain noble titles.[26]

Lady Grandison, after five years' widowhood, agreed to
marry her husband's cousin, Charles Villiers, the second Earl
of Anglesey. Anglesey had also lost his estates and was

living in the City of London, by Ludgate Hill. For a time Barbara was boarded in the country but eventually she came to town. With her auburn hair and blue eyes she was already beautiful, though conscious of her plump, babyish face about which she was at first teased and which she speedily reduced. When she first came to London "she appeared in a very plain country dress; but this was soon altered into the gaiety and mode of the Town, which adding a new lustre to that blooming beauty of which she had as great a share as any of her sex, she became the object of divers young gentlemen's affections."[27] Among these young gentlemen was Philip Stanhope, second Earl of Chesterfield.

Stanhope, the grandson of the first earl, was another fatherless child whose mother had married again and gone abroad as governess to Charles II's sister the Princess Royal, Princess Mary of Orange, subsequently the mother of William III. During the Civil War, when the boy was between ten and fifteen, he spent much time at the Princess's Court at The Hague and at the bare Court of Charles I's exiled Queen Henrietta Maria in Paris. At the age of sixteen he fought the first of his many duels, wounded his opponent and left Paris for Italy. One year later he returned to England and married Lady Anne Percy, the eldest daughter of the Earl of Northumberland. When she died of smallpox after childbirth, he again went abroad, and an uncle gained a decree in Chancery against him and seized his estate for an alleged debt of £10,000. But, on the death of his grandfather in September, 1656, he succeeded to the title and estates of the Earldom of Chesterfield, came home and composed his quarrel with his uncle, and took an appraising look at Commonwealth England.[28]

He was a good-looking young man, too appreciative of his fine hair to hide it under a wig, witty though mannered, resourceful, undoubtedly brave . . . and a tosspot, a rake and a bully with his sword. What the godly Cromwell saw in this Royalist rinse-pitcher it is now difficult to assess—but he sought him for his son-in-law. Chesterfield, who had no reason to lie, wrote later in his manuscript, *Life*: "The Protector Oliver Crumwell* was extremely civil to me and proffered me his daughter with twenty thousand pound in marriage and the choice of what command I would desire, either in the Fleet or the Army. But my refusal of this offer turned all his kindness into hatred."[31]

In the same year Chesterfield came so close to marriage with Mary Fairfax (daughter of Lord Fairfax who was commander-in-chief of the Parliamentary army at Naseby), that the banns were called three times in St. Martin-in-the-Fields.[32] (George Villiers, second Duke of Buckingham, temporarily abandoned his exiled king to marry Mary within a few months and thus regained his estates, which Parliament had given Fairfax for his military services.) In this same year, too, Chesterfield became involved with Barbara Villiers, who was fifteen when he returned to England,

---

*Except for significant passages, spelling and punctuation are modernized throughout this work, but Chesterfield's pronunciation is interesting. The daughter Cromwell offered is said to have been Frances. There is credible evidence[29] that early in 1657 Cromwell was considering marrying her to Charles II and achieving the Restoration in Oliver's own lifetime. Frances might understandably have agreed to this match, but she would almost certainly have refused Chesterfield. She was a spirited young girl, charmingly self-willed and defiant of Puritan conventions. She refused the final suitor proposed by Cromwell that year, and persuaded her father to let her marry the man she loved, Robert Rich, a nephew of Mary Boyle's Charles Rich. She won her way, insisted on music and dancing at her festivity, and "was given a wedding that scandalised the Puritans."[30]

and with Lady Anne Hamilton, about the same age.* A Cromwell, a Fairfax, a Villiers and a Hamilton in one season: for a repatriated traveler this was a notable amatory record.

But a wilder year was to follow. Chesterfield challenged Lord St. John, a kinsman of Barbara's, to a duel. The meeting came to the notice of the authorities before swords could be drawn, and Chesterfield was arrested and confined. He gained his release and added Lady Elizabeth Howard, the young daughter of the Earl of Berkshire, to his string, running her concurrently in his stable with Barbara, Anne and others whose mementoes he preserved. When scandal linked his name with Elizabeth's too damagingly he dropped her, and she wrote him a pathetic plea: "I am not guilty of anything you lay to my charge, nor will I ever alter from the expressions I have formerly made. Therefore I hope you will not be so unjust as to believe all that the world says of me, but rather credit my protestation of never having named you to my friends, being always careful of that for my own sake as well as yours; and therefore let it not be in the power of any, nor of your own inclinations, to make me less Your very humble servant. If you will meet me in the Old Exchange about six o'clock I will justify myself."[35]

*Lady Anne's circumstances were similar to Barbara's. Her uncle James, the first Duke of Hamilton, escaped from Windsor after Charles I's execution but was recaptured and beheaded six weeks after his king. Her father, William, the second duke, died of wounds after the battle of Worcester and was succeeded by her cousin (also Anne) as Duchess of Hamilton in her own right. The Commonwealth then moved against the family estates. William's property was entirely forfeited, his widow being allowed only £400 a year for the support of herself and her four daughters: so she remarried.[33] The duchy was diminished until, by 1658, a Scot was writing: "Our noble families are almost gone. Lennox has little in Scotland unsold. Hamilton's estates, except Annan and the Barony of Hamilton, is sold."[34]

Whether the Lady Elizabeth was pregnant, or reputed to be pregnant, and whether Chesterfield was the cause, is not now known.* But certainly the town linked a gentlewoman's name with Chesterfield's. His dead wife's sister wrote to him from the country, "where I know very little of what is done in the world: I hear so much of your exceeding wildness . . . You treat all the drinking lords, you swear, you game and commit all the extravagances that are incident to untamed youths . . . And the worst of all is I hear that there is a handsome young lady (to both your shames) with child by you."[36] To this Chesterfield replied equivocally, "Your ladyship knows that the world is strangely given to lying . . . only forbear censuring on my account one of the most virtuous persons living."[37] (The phrase "on my account" is a touch of whitewashing genius: "The lady may indeed be pregnant, but if she is do not blame me, for my experience with her leads me only to believe in her virtue.")

His sister-in-law's reprimand did not halt his "exceeding wildness". By his own account (and transcribing his own rendering of the French language), "a young lady having drawn me for her Valentine, I presented her with a porcelain chamber pot and a looking glass fitted to the bottom of it with the inscription

*Narcissus se mirent en l'onde*
*vit la plus belle chose du Monde*†

† Spellbound Narcissus, rapt by his own worth,
Saw in the stream the loveliest thing on earth.

which was ill resented, and I had a quarrel with Captain

*Abortion was an accepted upper-class resort. Lady Elizabeth had her first acknowledged child after her marriage to the poet John Dryden, whose patron Chesterfield eventually became.

Whaley, who in a duel I wounded and disarmed, for which I was sent prisoner to the Tower by the Protector Oliver Crumwell."[38] Captain John Whaley was member of Parliament for Nottingham and Shoreham and Cromwell determined to extract a life for a life. Chesterfield's sister-in-law wrote anxiously to him in the Tower, from which he jauntily replied, thanking her for her "concern for my little disaster," which "would enable me to overcome a much greater than this that has happened to me by the wounding of Captain Whaley, whose life (if he dies) the Protector has engaged shall be satisfied with mine, but I think there is now little danger of it, and therefore I suppose my confinement in the Tower can only last till the next quarter sessions."[39]

Chesterfield was certainly contributing his scot and lot to the social turbulence of the times. In addition, throughout all this activity he ostentatiously advertised his Royalist sympathies, and suffered temporary imprisonment almost by routine as the officers of the dissolving Commonwealth strove more and more feverishly to strangle the Royalist plots they continually uncovered. In one period of twelve months he was arrested and confined six times, not only in the Tower of London but in Derby, the nearest jail to his country estate at Bretby in the Peak District.[40] How he managed to conduct, at increasing heat, his love affair with Barbara Villiers can be regarded as a striking testimonial to the resilience and determination of a Chesterfield—and of a Villiers. For, though it was unlikely to be a matter of dynastic concern to Philip Stanhope, there was now a serious rival in the field. His name was Roger Palmer, and he became Barbara's titular husband.

Roger Palmer, a year younger than Chesterfield, was born

in 1634 at Dorney Court, near Windsor—where the Palmers still live—to an affluent family with strong connections at the Stuart court. His mother, a widow, and a second wife when she married Roger's father, was the daughter of William Herbert, first Baron Powis, a prominent Roman Catholic; and the Catholic influence, not at first acknowledged, was strongly to affect Roger's later career. His father, Sir James Palmer, had been a courtier of James I and a personal friend of Charles I and was still titular Chancellor of the Order of the Garter. Like all the Cavalier Palmers, he had suffered under fines and sequestrations and was particularly irked—the old man was an amateur artist—at being pillaged of some rare Breughel miniatures which found their way into the hands of Colonel William Webb, the Commonwealth's Surveyor General.[41] Roger Palmer was educated at Eton College and King's, Cambridge, and after a gentlemanly interval he was admitted a law student of the Inner Temple in October, 1656, when Chesterfield was newly sniffing the air of England.

Roger may have known Barbara Villiers before he went to the Temple. He may have followed the fashionable study of the law—he was never called to the bar—in order to cultivate this London acquaintance. Certainly his passion for the fascinating lass of Ludgate Hill was so keen, and so strongly declared, that it seriously alarmed his father, who at seventy-three had only a few months to live. An observer declared that Sir James, "having strong surmises of the misfortunes that would attend this match, used all the arguments that paternal affection could suggest to dissuade his son from prosecuting his suit in that way, adding that *if he was resolved to marry her he foresaw he should be one of the most miserable men in the world.*"[42] It is tolerably certain

that Roger, and possibly his father, knew of the link between
Barbara and Lord Chesterfield, for after an initial hesitancy
she herself seems always to have scorned being a dissembler
in her love affairs, and London society was then a small
world.

Roger at least deferred to his father during his lifetime.
But eventually he had his way, and on April 14, 1659, the
Earl and Countess of Anglesey rid themselves of their troublesome daughter by witnessing her marriage to Roger
Palmer at the church of St. Gregory by St. Paul's: a chapel
then physically attached to the old cathedral like a wart on
its southwest corner. Barbara was eighteen years old, her
husband was twenty-four.

Marriage did not damp the liaison with Chesterfield, but
rather fanned it, for the period immediately after it is the
time of their most fiery correspondence. Very quickly Barbara offered to elope with his lordship. "Since I saw you,"
she said, "I have been at home and I find the mounser* in a
very ill humour, for he says that he is resolved never to bring
me to Town again and that nobody shall see me when I am
in the country. I would not have you come today, for that
will displease him more. But send me word presently what
you would advise me to do. For I am ready and willing to
go all over the world with you and I will obey your com-
mands, that am, whilst I live, Yours."[43]

To this Chesterfield replied in the warmest terms that he
ever permitted himself to be remembered by in relation to
Barbara. (He preserved more passionate, and some more
gently affectionate, letters to other women.) Almost always
he had addressed her by the formal "Madam," whatever the

*monsieur: Roger Palmer.

suggestiveness of the following text. Now he abandoned reserve sufficiently to write to her as, "My Dearest Life," in one of a succession of lamenting notes; though by the side of Barbara's simple language the grief seems rather forced. He wrote:

My Dearest Life
After having dreamt the short time of my sleep of the horror of your absence, and after apprehending much more a separation from you than from this insignificant being, pardon the importunity of these repeated messages which come like the short breathing of a dying man, who fain would force his fate to obey his will, and lengthen out the destined period of his last into a line of perpetuity.
Madam I fear it is decreed, and that necessity will force obedience. Therefore accept a heart for legacy you long had only right to, and receive the inviolable profession of my ever being

Dearest Life
Your C.[44]

The unpleasant problem of skirting around the suggested elopement was solved for Chesterfield in a fortuitous way. Barbara caught smallpox, and it was Chesterfield who left town. Believing that she was dying, and careless by now of the circumstances, Barbara wrote what she thought might be her last words:

My Dear Life
I have been this day extremely ill, and the not hearing from you hath made me much worse than otherways I should have been. The doctor doth believe me in a desperate condition, and I must confess that the unwillingness I have to leave you makes me not entertain

*the thoughts of death so willingly as otherways I should.
For there is nothing besides your self that could make
me desire to live a day, and if I am never so happy as
to see you more, yet the last words I will say shall be
a prayer for your happiness. And so I will live and die
loving you above all other things, who am,*

My Lord,
Your B.[45]

Letters of this nature addressed to Chesterfield had to
jostle for priority with the crisscross of the Royalist plotting
and counter-plotting communications which sped between
England and the Netherlands, many of them having been
assiduously opened, copied, deciphered, resealed and delivered by the spies on either side. "The bearer will inform you
of our plans," the King in Brussels wrote to Chesterfield in a
letter which never passed out of the hands of its original
postman. "And I am confident that when it is seasonable
that we should meet you will manifest your affection."[46]
Chesterfield had been nominated—not so secretly as the
King had hoped—one of his county commissioners to act for
him after a rising until the Sovereign came. Intermittent
imprisonment—surprisingly mild by modern standards
because it *was* so intermittent—as Commonwealth agents
unraveled details of Chesterfield's plans and pledges, had to
be reckoned among the distractions which prevented him
from giving Barbara the fullest regard during her illness.

She recovered from the smallpox, unmarked and jubilant
in the assurance that she was now immune from the disease.
When he knew that she was getting better, Chesterfield
wrote with his more conventionally phrased devotion excus-
ing himself from coming to London to see her. His business
was elsewhere. The plots for the restoration of King Charles

were multiplying and coordinating. Oliver Cromwell was dead, Richard Cromwell had been dismissed, and the army had issued a general order that all Papists and Cavaliers should remove twenty miles from London. No Cavalier of any caliber took great notice of it. At Dorney Court on the Thames, five miles outside the limit,—and in the center of the city, too—Roger Palmer was engaged in "promoting the royal cause at the utmost hazard of life and great loss of fortune," as he later veraciously reminded Charles.[47] Barbara was caught up in the excitement. One of her kinsmen was Sir Allan Brodrick, a leader of the devoted inner core of Cavaliers which called itself the Sealed Knot, and a man who had subsisted throughout the interregnum on a razor edge of risk. He needed a reliable messenger to go to the King, and could not spare Roger, who was reserved for more individual responsibility. He asked that Barbara might go. And so the arrangements were made which were to bring together the king and the concubine.

Lord Chesterfield was on the run. A grossly mismanaged Royalist rising in August, 1659, had resulted in the usual arrests, and he had again been incarcerated in the Tower. This time he was in his greatest peril. He was accused of high treason and his estates were confiscated. Defending himself vigorously, he achieved his freedom after giving £10,000 as security.[48] As if he were constitutionally incapable of keeping out of trouble, he was quickly involved in another duel. The cause was characteristically trivial. He had seen an unknown gentleman from the Middle Temple riding a sprightly mare in Covent Garden, and sent his footman across to request the sale of the beast. The rider was Francis Wolley, a young man bearing a name perhaps too ominously reminiscent of Captain Whaley. A bargain was struck for eighteen pieces of gold, and the mare was handed over immediately. Chesterfield was soon discontented with her, and on coming out of prison positively disliked the animal. Three months after the sale he was riding in his coach when he accidentally passed Francis Wolley. He promptly asked him to take the mare back, and Wolley refused. At a further meeting a quarrel developed and Chesterfield challenged.\* The duel was fought at dawn "on the backside of Mr Colby's house at Kensington"[52] and Chesterfield quickly wounded Wolley's hand and then ran him straight through the heart. When Wolley's servant saw that his master was dead, he fired a pistol at Chesterfield's head. The shot missed and Chesterfield ran for Chelsea. He took a boat to a ship outward bound and escaped to France.[53] Samuel Pepys, out early in a coach with a pretty woman, commented wryly: "In our way to Kensington we understood how that my Lord Chesterfield had killed *another†* gentleman about half an hour before and was fled."[54] The Reverend Dr. Wolley, who had sought his son all night, found him dead on the field with his prayerbook in his pocket.[55]

---

\*His second was Philip Howard, one of Lady Elizabeth's brothers, so the Berkshire family's disapproval of Chesterfield seems to have eased. Lord Mordaunt, one of the coordinators of Royalism in England, said in Chesterfield's defense: "I must do him this right, never man suffered more than he did to shun fighting, but the insolence of Mr Woolley pulled the sad judgment on his head."[49] In view of the known characters of Chesterfield and Wolley this is an unlikely version, sent to the King next day to ease his wrath against Chesterfield for dueling—which Charles abhorred.[50] Sir John Grenville also wrote to Brussels asking that the King request Wolley's father, who had been a court preacher, not to proceed violently against Chesterfield in this critical revolutionary time.[51]

†Author's emphasis: possibly unfair.

The paths of Barbara Villiers, Lord Chesterfield and King Charles II now converged. The duel was fought on January 17, 1660. Chesterfield made his way to the court of the English Queen Mother in Paris. From there he wrote to Charles II at Brussels, conceding that his body was forfeit, but begging his life "to no other end than to venture it on all occasions in Your Majesty's service and quarrel."[56] On the very day that he wrote this plea Barbara Palmer was in the King's company and Roger Palmer was at the most crucial stage of his cloak-and-dagger career in England.

On February 3 Sir Allan Brodrick wrote excitedly to the King: "Sir, It hath pleased Almighty God to vouchsafe me an opportunity, almost equal to my prayers, for the advancement of Your Majesty's service in discovering the Councils of State." He disclosed that Henry Darell, a Royalist, whose brother had married Roger Palmer's eldest sister Catherine, had been accepted as a principal clerk in the Council of State, "who hath already delivered to me all the intercepted, with whatever secrets have been hitherto in debate, and will so continue to do from time to time." In addition, Brodrick's kinsman Roger Palmer was confirming the correspondence by passing over to Brodrick duplicates of the intercepted letters in case the originals miscarried. Brodrick described Darell and Palmer to the King as "persons of great worth and fidelity, hereditary servants to your Crown, by a long series of ancestors, and the present service so important, that your Majesty may in more than ordinary expressions of kindness own this meritorious act of theirs."[57]

The King wrote enthusiastic thanks to the two young men. To Roger Palmer he said:

*I hear from a good friend of yours how much I am be-
holding to you in several respects, and how much you
have contributed to the doing me a very signal service,
which I can hardly value or ever reward enough, and yet
I will do what I can towards it.*

*You have more title than one to my kindness, and you
may believe I am very well pleased to find so much
zeal and affection to run in a blood. You shall find that
I have a full sense of it and that I will always be*

*Your affectionate friend.*[58]

"You have more title than one to my kindness," the king
had told Roger Palmer, following the model of Hyde's draft
letter; and at this instant the faces of both King and Chancellor are turned away from Clio so that we do not know
how broad was their smile or how extreme their irony.
Charles was already familiar with Barbara Palmer and, if he
had reached the ultimate familiarity, Hyde would have been
pretty sure to have known about it. For, while they still lived
in poverty in their meager quarters in Brussels, Hyde's office
and bedspace was in the room immediately below the King's
bedchamber, which fortuitously gave the Chancellor the
most effective observation post possible.[59] Hyde was certainly curious about the relationship, as he was about Barbara Palmer herself, and in his reply to Brodrick's letter of
February 3 he twitted him about his reticence: "What sense
the King hath of yours to him, and of the service you do
him, you [will under]*stand by what himself says to you, as
your [fri]*ends will by what His Majesty hath sent to them
... I suppose one of them is the husband of our Cousin Villiers, though I could never get so much information from

*Original letter now dog-eared: conjectures within brackets.

you, upon several questions I have asked you, and it seems the King knows more of it than I do, for he told me this day that she had had the smallpox."[60]

There was at that time a scare about smallpox in Brussels, and Hyde had mentioned to the King that he ought to take precautions about it. When the King pooh-poohed Hyde's concern on the grounds that Mrs Palmer had had the disease, the Chancellor was disingenuously amazed: "Of what interest could that person's immunity be to anyone but her husband?"[61]

It was a month before Charles replied to the petition of Lord Chesterfield, which he said had been long in reaching him. He then wrote cordially, forgiving him. The King's spirits were high with the near certainty of his approaching restoration, and he ended his letter: "I hope the time is at hand that will put an end to our calamities. Therefore pull up your spirits to welcome that good time, and be assured I will be always very kind to you as Your most affectionate friend, Charles R."[62]

Chesterfield had now spent several weeks at the Queen Mother's court in the Palais Royal. It had been over ten years since his last attendance there, and a striking new personality had blossomed in his absence. The Princess Henriette Anne, who had been a baby before, was an enchantingly delicate and lively girl of fifteen and the darling of the Court. She had never known her father, for she had been conceived when Henrietta Maria had brought her husband arms and money from Holland after the battle of Edgehill; war had separated the Queen from Charles I when she was seven months pregnant, and when the baby was three weeks old Henrietta Maria had fled with her to France after the defeat of Marston Moor. The princess had lately captivated her brother Charles II—who himself had not seen her for years—to such an extent that an affection quickly sprang up between them so close that it was to be slandered as incestuous, although it was maintained after the Restoration only by assiduous correspondence, save for one family reunion and the auspicious meeting which led to the Treaty of Dover. Between this appealing, forward princess and the errant Lord Chesterfield there grew up a relationship which the rake later thought fit to conceal.

When he received the King's friendly acquittal Chesterfield determined to pay his personal homage, and by this decision possibly precipitated the first occasion when Barbara, Chesterfield and the King were in simultaneous orbit. Chesterfield traveled to Breda, the Dutch border town to which the King had moved from Brussels in April, 1660, in order not to be based on the soil of a country (Spain), which was at war with Commonwealth England. The King granted his full pardon and Chesterfield returned to Paris. If Barbara was then in Breda—and she had no further tasks to do in England, where her husband was contesting a seat for the Convention Parliament—her lover would have sensed a difference in her welcome. Whether she was then in Breda or not, Chesterfield heard of her cultivation by the King.

There is no commentary, except his own innuendo, on the next episode in Chesterfield's life, and it is recorded literally as he set it down in later years. (The reference to Henriette Anne as the Duchess of Orleans is a slip made in writing the account long after the event. She did not marry Philippe, duc d'Orléans, the perverse brother of Louis XIV, until the next year. Chesterfield usually gave his subjects their later rather than their contemporary titles.)

Chesterfield wrote in his manuscript, *Life*:

> I went into France and from thence in to Holland and waited on the King at Breda where I had his Majesties pardon, from thence I went back again through Flanders into France where I stayed some time at Paris and waited on Queen Mother and her Daughter the Dutches of Orleans who when I took my leave

from Paris I went to Bourbon, and after the having taken the waters there, I went to Callis [Calais] and meeting the King as hee was comming from Holland on the sea I went into his Majesties ship and waited on him to England.[63]

This author has deciphered the coded entry as:

ᚼᛘᚼᛁᛉᚴᛘᛘᛁᛈᛘᚢᛉᚱᚼᚵᛈᚼᛉᚼᛘᚴᛉᚼ

D E S I R E D   M E T O F O R G I V E H E R

FRE DOMS & I N D I SCRETI CNR

V PON SO SMALL ACQVAI NTAACE & TH

AT I WOVLD NOT HAVE THE   WORS OP

I N I ON   NOF HRE &

Allowing for corruptions in enciphering, this may read:

"[The Duchess of Orleans] *desired me to forgive her free-*
*doms and indiscretions upon so small acquaintance and*
*that I would not have the worse opinion of her, and from*
*Paris I went to Bourbon. . . ."*

Henriette Anne was a princess concerning whose character
most historians* have followed G. M. Trevelyan, who called
her "the lady of whom nothing but gentle was ever
reported."[65] Chesterfield's account excites conjecture
mainly because he enciphered it, and long after the lady, as
well as his next two wives, was dead, though he enciphered
nothing concerning Barbara Villiers; also because the event
follows a visit to Charles II which may have left him with a
sexual grudge against the King. Did he take revenge by
seducing the King's sister? A prudent brother, familiar with
psychology and astrology, as Charles was, might have forecast that the proximity of a pert girl of fifteen—a favorite
age of the earl's—and a roué of Chesterfield's propensities
would be an unfortunate conjunction of heavenly or of
earthly bodies.

---

*Not all historians. Hester Chapman sums up "Minette" as,
"accomplished, quick and a little precocious . . . She developed so early
as sometimes to give the impression of brilliance. Her intelligence was
of the type now described as silly-clever."[64] Gilbert Burnet, a partisan
anti-Papist, said she "was thought the wittiest woman in France, but
had no sort of virtue, and scarce retained common decency."[64A]
Evidence for this is meager.

When Louis XIV was one year married and Henriette Anne was the
bride of his transvestite and sodomite (but virile) brother, Philippe,
duc d'Orléans, the two fell in love. To cover the infatuation the Duchess prompted the King to pretend he was courting one of her ladies,
Louise de La Vallière. He adopted the ploy too enthusiastically and
soon made Louise his *maîtresse en titre*, legitimizing the two of their
five children who grew to maturity (and six children by Athénaïs de
Montespan). Burnet perpetuated the innuendo of an incestuous relationship between Charles II and his sister.

Whatever seduction occurred at that time was quickly regretted. In all the selections from his correspondence—which Chesterfield copied for gratification in his old age—he generally noted simply the year of writing. Two letters only are dated with any precision. One is the letter written to him by Charles II extending the royal pardon for dueling, dated April 2, 1660. The other is dated April, 1660, the month he went to see the King, returned to the King's sister, and then left for the south. The letter is addressed "To the Lady —— in France," and it ends:

"But why do I write to one that I shall see no more, and perhaps disturb her peace with storms of my unruly thoughts?

"Forgive, forgive, and what is more forget, him who can only love, but not procure either your happiness or his own."[65A]

The Earl journeyed from Paris to Bourbonne-les-Bains, in the foothills of the Vosges, where he took the spa waters. From this resort he wrote to Barbara, gracefully conceding her victory and asking for a keepsake: "The news I have from England concerning your ladyship makes me doubt of everything, and therefore let me entreat you to send your picture, for then I shall love something like you and yet unchangeable."[66]

It was a new experience for Chesterfield to cast himself in the role of the abandoned, rather than the deserting, lover. Perhaps, in spite of her poor dowry and lack of title, he should have taken her when he could: if it was fidelity he wanted, he judged wrongly in the case of his second, aristocratic wife whom he had to frogmarch ignominiously from the Court of Charles II to remove her from the King's brother. It is difficult to assess the depth of Chesterfield's feeling. Was it sincerity, melancholia or a sense of style that made him write to Barbara:

> Vous motes tout espoire, pour vous belle inhumaine
> Et pour tout autre que vous, vous motes tout desir?
> (Beautiful savage, you starve me of hope
> And for all others extinguish desire.) [67]

On April 13, 1660, Brodrick, in England, wrote to Hyde, in Breda, that Roger Palmer was donating to the King £1,000 which he could ill afford, and asked Hyde to see that Palmer got his reward after the Restoration: "644.291.42.-570.12.37.225 [Roger Palmer] had provided 830.849.597 [one thousand pounds] for his [the King's] service had he been forced to the extremity of the sword, which he will deliver me to transmit the next week with his most humble duty, there being now no such use of it on the place: But with it I must presume to whisper to your lordship his condition, a gay wife and great expense to a slender fortune in possession, the main of his estate being in lease for some years yet to come, and in jointure, which I hope your lordship will so consider as to vouchsafe your intercession hereafter without any mention of it at present."[68]

Hyde needed no reminder of Barbara Palmer's gay nature, which had already been established at Charles's court. Palmer himself was physically unable to protect himself—or Barbara—at Breda, and it may have been a complete surprise to him when the Monarch summoned the gay wife to his bed in Whitehall on the first night of the Happy Return. On the day Brodrick wrote, the first parliamentary elections in twenty years were in progress and Palmer was elected for the borough of New Windsor. The Convention Parliament

met on April 25 and was in comparatively busy session thereafter.

At Breda the rhythm was steadily quickening. Ambassadors began to call, in the sudden realization that the
pauper puppet their governments had discounted for so
long had been proclaimed in his own capital, by heralds and
king-at-arms, *Carolus Rex*, by the grace of God King of
Great Britain—France—and Ireland.

At first Charles received them without pomp, for he and
his courtiers still wore the shabbiest of dress. Then presents
of money began to come in: some officially voted by Parliament and the Dutch States-General, some calculatingly
given as laid-out talents, and a little shaken from shrunken
purses by Royalists who still genuflected in their hearts when
they spoke of "His Sacred Majesty." Much of the funds
came in bills and the Dutch financiers haggled over the
exchange, but a portmanteau of £10,000 in gold pieces was
brought by fourteen London merchants, and the King called
in his brother and sister to marvel at the glowing sight. The
Court moved to The Hague, now needing seventy-two
coaches-and-six to carry it. The great ambassadors called:
French, Spanish, Austrian. Deputations from English commercial and Scottish ecclesiastical interests were at Charles's
antechamber door. Banquets were hastily organized.
Political emissaries hurried back and forth across the Channel. The Navy arrived to escort the king for whom they had
only tardily declared. Charles bade farewell to the continental mainland, and never saw it again in his life.

He came to Dover, where the white cliff tops were dark
with jubilant people, and he knelt on the land as he came

ashore. Canterbury ... Rochester ... Blackheath ... Deptford ... St George's Fields ... St Paul's. The elements of
the great procession steadily accrued until every component
was in place for the last march to Whitehall. The sheer
sound of the happiness of the ordinary people was a taxing
intensity to accept. There were bells sounding from more
churches than London can boast now. There were tapestries
and silk banners and golden decorations hanging from the
balconies. There really were the fabled flowers strewn in the
streets and fountains running with wine. Past Temple Bar
and down the Strand to Westminster the cavalry trotted in
silver and scarlet, the tough, brown pikemen marched, and
the English incongruity of massed dignitaries proceeded—fat
aldermen in gold and lace, lean, tabarded heralds, mayor and
marshal, all encased by the cuirassed arrogance of the Life
Guards. Then the King himself—God deliriously bless
him—came riding on his horse so gravely, but doffing his
plumed hat so graciously to the cheers from every balcony,
aware that, after all the endearing spontaneity, he still had
hours of excruciating formal sycophancy to endure before he
was free.

There were ten thousand men in the official cortège of
welcome, and not a single woman. The contrast, in the arms
of Barbara Villiers that night, was a silken relief. Charles
had been fifteen hours on display, well over half of them in
the saddle. If he was tired, he said so—Charles was not
ashamed to declare that he was too sleepy for lovemaking.[69]
For his mistress, any climax to that tumultuous day would
be an overwhelming memory. But there are some women
who, as if by the application of joy or ambition, can infallibly seal a high occasion with a physical trophy. On the
night of the Restoration—or as near to that night as makes

no historical difference[70]—Barbara Villiers conceived her first child, in the palace and in the embrace of the King of England.

Chesterfield had written to her after she had first met the King: "You starve me of hope And for all others extinguish desire." She had told Chesterfield, "I will live and die loving you above all things." The declarations may well have been true. But the stream of life was separating them with its tide. Perhaps, now that one was older—nearly twenty—loving, like truth, was not really important compared with the realities of property, position and title. In the great procession which had brought the King home that day the old Earl of Cleveland had led a force of a thousand gentlemen, uniformed in buff laced with silver.[71] The gray Cavalier had borne himself nobly, but time was short for he was clearly near to death. Within five weeks of the King's return the House of Lords was again considering the debt of £10,000 owed with twenty-six years' interest by the Earl of Cleveland to the mother and aunt of Mrs. Barbara Palmer.[72] The case of the Duke of Richmond, Duke of Lennox, Earl of Lichfield would follow.

## 2 ◁ *Whosoever I find to be my Lady Castlemaine's enemy in this matter, I do promise upon my word to be his enemy as long as I live.*

KING Charles II was, in 1660, a lean, athletic and maturely lined man of thirty, six feet tall, with shining black hair falling in long, natural curls which no periwig could better. He was alert, affectionate, garrulous, self-indulgent and cynical. His keenest instinct was to survive, as a person and a sovereign; and the frustrated love he was to lavish on his thirteen bastards[1] as the only fruit of his flesh—even though the eldest plotted to kill and supplant him—is some symbol of this.

For Charles II, survival demanded cynicism. He had known enough of shame and beggary to discard any illusion that divinity hedged a king. His father's mutilated head had been stitched back to the body after execution—"Like sewing up a goose" was the ribald comment of the Oxford surgeon who did it[2]—but the axe had eternally severed any conviction of godhead in his successors. Charles I died in the sincere belief that he was a martyr "for the laws and liberties of the land and for the maintenance of the Protestant religion."[3] The freedom and liberty of the people, he had declared in his last hours, "consists in having government . . . It is not in their having a share of the government; that is nothing appertaining to them. A subject and a sovereign are clean different things."[4]

The father had died an immutable authoritarian; the son saw security in being a variable politician. In dismissing his first Parliament, and giving no indication of when he would call the next, Charles II told them that, although he would govern by direct rule and the decisions of his privy councils, his one guiding criterion would be: " 'What is a Parliament like to think of this action or this council?' and it shall be want of understanding in me if it will not bear that test."[5] Previously he had assured them: "Never King valued himself more upon the affections of his people than I do; nor do I know a better way to make myself sure of your affections than by being just and kind to you all; and whilst I am so, pray let the world see that I am possessed of your affections."[6]

Within the Court the King demanded more than a general affection. In personal relationships he seemed to search for mutual devotion, committal and surrender. He failed in his quest, through poverty of judgment in nominating the devotees and because of the natural rhythmic brevity of most emotional dedication unbuttressed by the formal sanctions. Both Charles II and Barbara Villiers were supremely promiscuous people, but for different reasons. In the woman there developed, on the basis of an emotionally ardent nature, a massive sensuality combining conventional avarice with a technical, almost philosophic but always physical interest in eroticism, whether with monarch, footman, archbishop or ropedancer from a public fair. In experimentation she was almost worthy of the Royal Society. The King, though not denying himself the flagrant titillation of court gallantry, sought more the calm of commitment, perhaps what the parallel pilgrim Lawrence called "the peace of fucking,"[7] which Don Juan never could achieve.

Affection was his compensating need. If for his political security he relied on being a weathercock, emotional reassurance demanded the best in constancy that could be obtained in an unstable time. Recognition and status for his concubine were therefore almost as essential as love, and the semiofficial court appointment of *maîtresse en titre*, hitherto unknown in England, became accepted as an unwritten clause in the Restoration Settlement. Publicly dependent on his subjects, and privately on his mistress, the dark man settled himself on his splintered throne, with rueful geniality acknowledging both his obligations:

> *Of a tall stature and of sable hue,*
> *Much like the son of Kish\* that lofty Jew,*
> *Twelve years complete he suffered in exile*
> *And kept his father's asses all the while.*
> *At length by wonderful impulse of Fate*
> *The people call him home to help the State,*
> *And what is more they send him money too,*
> *And clothe him all from head to foot anew;*
> *Nor did he such small favours then disdain,*
> *But in his thirtieth year began to reign.*
> *In a slashed doublet then he came to shore,*
> *And dubbed poor Palmer's wife his Royal Whore.*[8]

\*Saul, son of Kish, was "a choice young man and a goodly . . . from his shoulders and upward he was higher than any of the people." Reference to the passage in 1 Samuel IX, then better known, sets the brilliance of this introduction.

"Poor Palmer" was not entirely destitute now that the King had come home and the financial persecution of the Royalists was ended. Roger had taken a town house convenient for Parliament in King Street, between Whitehall Palace and Westminster Hall. It was next to the house of Admiral the Earl of Sandwich, second cousin and patron of Samuel Pepys. The close connection of Sandwich and Pepys, as a member of the Navy Board and the Earl's deputy on the Privy Council, entailed many visits to King Street, and to Sandwich's gossiping wife and housekeeper, which gave the diarist a keyhole insight into the affairs of Palmer's wife, for whom Pepys displayed a notable fascination. Working late in King Street one night that summer, he was so distracted in his letter writing by the music from a party next door that he finally capitulated and stood by the outer door for some time listening to the fiddles. "The King and Dukes there," he noted, "with Madame Palmer, a pretty woman that they have a fancy to, to make her husband a cuckold."[9]

The King had not publicly committed himself yet to Barbara, and the camouflage that the two randy dukes, his brothers, were interested was not unwelcome. This amorous pair—the outwardly wooden James, Duke of York, then aged twenty-six, and the witty and susceptible Henry, Duke of Gloucester, just twenty-one—had been marked by the public within a week of the Restoration as noticeably "haunting" St. James's Park,[10] where the monkey parade of gallants regularly took up formation. But before autumn Henry was swiftly dead of the smallpox, and the King, hammering out the politics of his resettlement while wearing purple mourning for his brother, could not find the time to bury him, but sent James as chief mourner.[11] Three weeks later—when Barbara was included in the royal party at Sunday service in the chapel at Whitehall—while the King yawned at a dull sermon and laughed at a clumsy anthem, the alert Pepys "also observed how the Duke of York and Mistress Palmer did talk to one another very wantonly through the hangings that part the King's closet and the closet where the ladies sit."[12]

The flirtatious Duke of York was coupling his wantonness with some public camouflage on his own account. He was in serious domestic and dynastic trouble over a secret marriage, the contract of which fashionable London said he had signed with his blood,[13] but which his mother and a mixed bag of courtiers were making every effort to have canceled. The struggle was watched shrewdly from the side by Barbara, who assiduously applied its lessons to her own career.

The lady in the affair was Anne Hyde, the daughter of a highly embarrassed Sir Edward Hyde, newly confirmed Lord Chancellor of England. Hyde had been the bosom friend of Barbara's father and was already a political enemy of the daughter: the restoration of monarchy after eleven years' republicanism had opened frontiers to unprecedented spoils, and in the gold rush to allocate offices and places under the Crown far too many appointments were pressed on the King by "the cabal that met at Mistress Palmer's lodgings."[14] Hyde resisted these appointments, which, incidentally, brought Barbara Palmer much money as well as an apprenticeship in court intrigue,* but he had to pass far more than he approved.

---

*It was normal for office seekers to pay bribes while striving and a present or fee when successful. An additional perquisite was the habit of the King to present a favorite with power to recommend the creation of a baronet or two, for which the Restoration market price was £500 a time.[15]

Sincerely, if self-importantly, toiling as Charles's prime
minister,* Hyde was backing his sovereign and offending
the Cavaliers by a merciful conciliation of the country, the
disbanding of the army, and, above all in his own eyes, the
triumphant reestablishment of the Anglican Church. At the
peak of his heavy labors the Lord Chancellor was informed
that his daughter was eight months pregnant by the Duke of
York.

It was a matter of some personal chagrin that the man
who tried to keep his finger on the pulse of the nation, and
had made it his business to know the King's amours and mistresses from the time he had listened to the creaks from
Charles's room above him in Brussels, was unaware of the
condition of his daughter and ignorant that she had had a
long liaison with the King's brother.

Anne Hyde was a pleasant, intelligent girl of twenty-two.
Her friends did not swear she was pretty. (But Charles said
that his brother was sent his mistresses as a penance.) Anne
was more often described as a cow. She certainly inherited
her father's plumpness, which she increased by overeat-
ing—"a pleasure to watch and a blessing to see her," said a
courtier who disapproved of the current slimming
trends[17]—until the satirists took over and declared that her
flunkeys did not mount behind her carriage, but vaulted
onto her own projecting buttocks:

With Chanc'lor's belly, and so large a rump,
There, not behind the coach, her pages jump.[18]

*He clung to the office of Lord Chancellor and refused the novel
post of working as the King's first minister as "a title so newly translated out of French into English that it was not enough understood to
be liked, and every man would detest it for the burden it was attended
with."[16]

She had been, for some years before the Restoration, maid of honor to the Princess Royal, the King's sister, Mary of Orange, who had been a widow at The Hague since she was nineteen. She had met her mistress's second brother at the court of the Queen Mother in Paris, and James, stiff, reserved and stuttering—except when game was sighted —had pursued her ardently. Anne Hyde had been sufficiently in control of the situation to get James to sign a marriage contract in August, 1659,[19] following which they lived intermittently and secretly together as man and wife.

After the Restoration Hyde sent to The Hague for his daughter, whom he now intended to marry to a young English nobleman. Though he was on excellent terms with her, he was so much deceived by her girth and good nature that he still failed to notice that she was pregnant or that she enjoyed any particular intimacy with the Duke of York. The Princess Royal now decided to make a state visit to England, and it could be calculated that her woman's eyes would be sharper than the Chancellor's. Under the pressure of events James stole into the Chancellor's home, Worcester House in the Strand, with his Church of England chaplain and was privately married to Anne at midnight on September 3, 1660.

James then went to the King, threw himself on his knees, and in a flood of tears disclosed his situation with Anne Hyde. He begged permission to marry her publicly, and declared that if Charles would not give his consent he must go immediately into permanent exile: a strange, proposed exodus for the heir apparent to the throne three months after the restoration of the monarchy.

A puzzled Charles asked Hyde's friends, the Marquis of

Ormonde and the Earl of Southampton, to bring the Chancellor to Whitehall and to break the news to him. Hyde was a portly man of fifty-one, disabled by gout, sententious in phrase, and mainly irritating in the patronizing way in which he expressed his undeniably high principles. The disclosure of his daughter's condition took him completely aback. He declared passionately that as soon as he got home he would turn his strumpet daughter into the street. When it was suggested that the couple might be already married, Hyde ranted that he would much rather have his daughter the Duke's whore than his wife, and if she were really married she should immediately be committed to a dungeon in the Tower and an Act of Parliament be passed to behead her. "And I shall be the first man to propose that to Parliament," he concluded.[20]

At this moment the King came into the room, but could not soothe the maddened Chancellor. Hyde went back to the Strand and imprisoned his daughter in her room: which did not prevent his wife, who now knew the details of the marriage, from quietly admitting the Duke of York to pass the nights with her.

The Princess Royal arrived from Holland, and immediately the situation changed. James broke off all contact with Anne. Court gossip was encouraged to repeat that the whole affair was over. The Queen Mother wrote to Charles from France that she was traveling hotfoot to England "to prevent so great a stain and dishonour to the Crown." In addition a gang of courtiers intrigued to convince the gullible James that Anne Hyde was worthless as a wife because they had all had the ultimate favors from her already. The Earl of Arran declared, with defamatory wit, that once at Hounslaerdyke, where James and Anne had become engaged, she had left a game of ninepins on the pretext of feeling faint and he had followed her to a private room, cut her laces, and "exerted himself to the best of his ability both in succour and consolation."[21] Harry Jermyn and Richard Talbot offered additional spurious reminiscences. Tom Killigrew, a licensed wit who had decided that the matter was not yet clinched, contributed a masculinely diverting but completely imaginary account of how "he had found the moment of his happiness in a certain closet which was constructed above the water to quite another end than relieving the pangs of love. Three or four swans," he added, "had been the witnesses of his good fortune, and he had no doubt that they had witnessed the good fortune of many others in the same closet, since Miss Hyde resorted there often, and seemed indeed inordinately fond of the place." In conclusion Sir Charles Berkeley, with touching charity, assured the Duke of York that he, too, had had Anne Hyde, and was not too impressed with her now, but was willing to marry her in order to do the Duke a favor.

Almost alone in the Court, the King behaved with magnanimity. He assured Hyde that all the slanders on his daughter were false and would be exposed. The time came for Anne's child to be born and he sent trusted ladies of the Court to be with her in her trouble. (The Bishop of Winchester also attended, and took it upon himself to demand of Anne in the middle of her pangs, "Whose child is it of which you are in labour? Have you known any man other than the Duke of York?"—a brutal enough procedure, but an ordeal which, once passed, told wonderfully in favor of the lady.)

The Queen Mother arrived with Princess Henriette Anne from France, breathing fire against Chancellor Hyde as a suspected upstart wishing to marry a worthless woman into the royal family: Charles listened to her fulminations all the way from Dover, and the night he got to Whitehall signed a warrant creating Hyde a baron—and gave him £20,000 to sustain the honor—so that next morning, when the Privy Council formally congratulated the Queen Mother on her return to England they were led by the Chancellor in his new peer's robes.

Within a short time the Princess Royal was attacked by the smallpox, and on her deathbed expressed her repentance over the campaign against James's marriage, in which she had played too large a part herself. The shock of Mary's death—the second of the King's family to be taken in three months—put York himself in such gloom, and generally sobered the Court to such an extent, that Sir Charles Berkeley was moved to confess that his and his cronies' stories of infidelity with Anne Hyde were impure invention. The volatile Duke promptly sent a note to Anne saying he would visit her immediately, ending it, "Have a care of my son," and he rushed to tell the King all about it.

Both the King and his brother called on the newly acknowledged Duchess of York at her father's house. The Queen Mother was still shouting wildly from the palace, "Whenever that woman is brought into Whitehall by one door I go out by another, never to return." But eventually she made her peace, first with her son and then with his wife. And she took her daughter back to France to be married to another King's brother—who was rather less reliable as a fighting general than the competent James, but never went into battle before applying full cosmetic make-up.[22]

Barbara Palmer stayed in the background throughout this crisis, though Harry Jermyn and Charles Berkeley were of her acquaintance. She was new to the Court and not at ease with the family; also she was pregnant and whiningly discontented with her condition. She never recognized any of these handicaps again. In the next great royal family quarrel she was the cause and center of the upset, a political and public nuisance whose name alone was on the protagonists' lips, and she let her pregnancy tap her body and spirit so little that she swore she would be delivered of the King's bastard in the royal bed at the time of the royal honeymoon.

For the moment she merely indulged in the shrewish temper which was developing within her. Chesterfield was married again: she reserved revenge on his new kinsfolk and loosed an idle dart at him. The marriage, to the twenty-year-old Lady Elizabeth Butler, daughter of the Marquis of Ormonde, had been in course of arrangement for a whole year from September, 1659, by negotiation between Chancellor Hyde and Lady Ormonde with a dowry fixed at £6,000.[23] The Ormondes were added to her list of enemies and she broke with Chesterfield. He seemed genuinely troubled at first. "After so many years' service, fidelity and respect," he wrote to her, "to be banished for the first offence is very hard."[24] But he soon accommodated himself to a more conventional and witty contemporary tone, and wrote again: "Let me not live if I did believe that all the women on earth could have given me so great an affliction as I have suffered by your displeasure. 'Tis true, I ever loved you as one should do Heaven, that is, more than the world, but I never thought you would have sent me there before my time . . . Do not suffer one to perish who desires only to live on your account. Besides, naturally I hate dying, and it is one of the last things I would willingly do to show my passion."[25]

In early February, 1661, Barbara's stepfather, the Earl of

Barbara Villiers, Duchess of Cleveland, in her later years. After Sir Godfrey Kneller.

*Barbara Villiers in one of her more flamboyant portraits.*

Barbara Villiers with one of her children. After Sir Peter Lely.

A youthful Barbara Villiers, Countess of Castlemaine. After Sir Peter Lely.

Anglesey, died of smallpox and was buried in St. Martin-in-the-Fields. Not only did he leave no property to Barbara, but his estate was taken by his widowed sister Anne, Countess of Sussex—and Sussex became another title noted for future reference in Barbara's mind. On February 25 Mistress Palmer bore her first child, whom she named Anne, and whom she was to see, at the age of thirteen, Countess of Sussex. Roger Palmer was still officially living with her, and the girl temporarily took his surname, until the King gave the name Fitzroy to his children by Barbara.

The rhythm of events now quickened towards the intricate arrangements for the King's coronation. Charles maintained the extraordinary energy of his early years on the throne. When the light permitted, he was up by five for his "morning physic" at tennis,[26] or to ride in the park or to scull or swim in the river at Chelsea. At court, walking fast for exercise between council and committee meetings, he was jostled by petitioners, he retreated to experiment in his chemical laboratory, he arranged his afternoon theater visits and he touched for the "King's Evil" of scrofula—no monarch ever effected so many cures as he was reputed to have done. The lighter innovations of Restoration life were becoming evident: organ music and ritual in the churches, women acting on the stage, a gaming house in Lincoln's Inn Fields, and black beauty patches worn tentatively by the court ladies and more timorously by citizens' wives.

In politics Roger Palmer had made his last mark as a member of the Convention Parliament by voting to the King an income from the Excise, of which thousands of pounds were to be used in personal grants to Barbara. A selection of the regicides had been publicly hanged, drawn and quartered "looking as cheerful as any man can in that condition," and their limbs displayed on the battlements. A crazy insurrection of religious men who believed the end of the world was at hand raised the cry "King Jesus and the heads upon the gates," scattered the city trainbands and routed the King's Life Guards before they died hard awaiting God's descent, and by the military effect of their impetus seriously alarmed those who thought the King was being too easy on his ideological enemies. Somewhat defiantly the bodies of Cromwell and his lieutenants were dug up in Westminster Abbey and exposed and reburied at Tyburn. The small scale of any bloody reprisal against Commonwealth leaders strengthened the political acceptance of the monarchy by permitting trimmers to be accepted into the establishment, but it also gave opportunities for brutal malice at court. Cromwell's daughter Mary, always a Royalist, was a member of the Court with her husband, Lord Falconberg. During the time that Cromwell's body hung at Tyburn a courtier told her: "Madam, I saw your father yesterday." "What then, sir?" she countered warily. The courtier yawned: "He stunk most abominably." "I suppose he was dead, then?" said Lady Falconberg. "Yes." "I thought so," she commented, "or else I believe he would have made you stink worse."[27]

On the Saturday before his coronation King Charles dubbed sixty-eight Knights of the Bath to ride robed with their esquires in his procession, and in a ceremony at the banqueting hall promoted to earldom six noblemen including Baron Hyde, who advanced to the dignity of Earl of Clarendon. In the evening he took Barbara to the Cockpit Theater within Whitehall Palace where, the Duke of York being publicly attentive to his Duchess in the same box, the King demonstrated "a great deal of familiarity" with Mistress Palmer.[28] On St. George's Day the King was crowned, amid great pageantry and a certain amount of confusion at the banquet, which ended with a pitched battle between the corps of barons and the King's footmen for possession of the canopy which the barons had held over the King's head. In the melee the bishops (who were not yet restored to the House of Lords) and the judges took the opportunity to advance their official precedence, and sat down at the upper tables reserved for the barons.[29] Elections for the new Parliament (the Cavalier Parliament, which sat from 1661 to 1679) had already been held, and as soon as he met them officially Charles announced his projected marriage to the Infanta Catherine of Braganza, the daughter of the Queen Mother and virtual tyrant of Portugal.

It was a political marriage. It opened up India and the Mediterranean to the English by the cession of Bombay and Tangier, and to the satisfaction of Louis XIV—who had spent £100,000 to encourage the match[30]—it aligned Great Britain with Portugal opposite France's enemy Spain, against whom the Portuguese were struggling for independence.

A year was to pass before the marriage was consummated, and that year was Barbara's consolidation. She spent it gaily and expensively to such effect that the town, now accepting her as the great beauty of the day, was also soon talking of "the lewdness and beggary of the Court."[31]

There was now no public masking of the fact that she was the King's mistress.[32] But she still lacked the permanent status of a noble title, and though the King might well be persuaded to pay her public honor, a much more reliable lever was the concern he felt for their offspring. In the week that she suspected she was pregnant for the second time the King ordered his secretary of state to prepare a warrant for Roger Palmer to be made an Irish earl: and to underline who was really being ennobled, he ordered that succession to the title was to be restricted to children "gotten on Barbara Palmer, his now wife."[33]

Three weeks later Barbara had decided on her title. The warrant was for the earldom of Castlemaine and barony of Limerick. Barbara's father had been Viscount Grandison of Limerick, and her uncle had succeeded him. Lady Castlemaine, showing her extraordinary preoccupation with territorial style, had ensured that her unborn son would bear the courtesy title of Lord Limerick.

There were difficulties in getting the final authority for the honor. Normally, when a warrant was signed by the King it would be taken personally to the Lord Chancellor for a patent to be prepared and sealed by "passing the Great Seal," after which it registered an effective act. In the same way any official grant of money would need to pass the Lord Treasurer.

The Lord Chancellor, now ennobled as Earl of Clarendon, and his close friend and colleague the Lord Treasurer, the Earl of Southampton, had combined against Mistress Palmer in a formidable alliance. Clarendon admitted that he was "an implacable enemy to the power and interest she had with the King, and had used all the endeavours he could to destroy it"[34]—and the lady knew it.

Jointly with Southampton, Clarendon resolved never to ask the mistress to suggest any course of action to the King (though at the time such tactics could be the quickest way to get political decisions approved) and never to let any document pass in which her name was mentioned.[35] They kept this pledge for the seven years of their partnership, and Lady Castlemaine's name appears on no English state document before 1667, and on no treasury precept. Clarendon, in fact, stopped the grants made to her by the King,[36] and all the money she acquired over this period had to come from the King's privy purse and from the bribes she received for using her influence.

It was because she knew that no warrant for an earldom would pass the Great Seal that Barbara Palmer accepted from the King an Irish title which could bypass the supervision of the Lord Chancellor of England. But she still had no certainty that her husband would accept the honor. Roger was in no doubt of the reason for his ennoblement, and hesitated over the shame of acceptance. He did not finally flout the King, but delayed assuming his title and never claimed his right to sit in the Irish Parliament. Barbara styled herself Lady Castlemaine from the moment the King signed the warrant, but she cautiously kept the paper for months in the pocket of her petticoat, and did not send it to Ireland for official registration until she had pulled the strings that would remove any opposition either from Roger or the Irish chancellery.[37]

In the traditional folly deliberately revived at the turn of the year the King attended the last great masque ever given for the Lincoln's Inn revels, and on Twelfth Night he threw the dice to open the court gaming—and quickly lost the £100 he had set himself.[38] He was no gambler, and he was sorry to see that the ladies whom he would eventually be called upon to succor from his privy purse were far deeper in than he: but it was customary for the King to play to open the Epiphany festivities.

The great bout of revelry subsided into an aftermath of

sour scandal. The climax of the new year was to be the arrival of Catherine, already publicly prayed for as Queen, and her subsequent marriage to Charles which, because communications with Portugal were very poor, was intermittently expected for three months from February.

Lady Castlemaine's position in the reconstituted royal circle began to be the subject of jealous gossip.[39] It had been assumed that she was a temporary light-o'-love, serving while the King was disengaged. Her ennoblement and her obvious fresh pregnancy projected the situation into a debatable future. What status was she to take when the new Queen arrived?

The imbroglio was made the more delightfully intriguing by the arrival of a new beauty at Court, virtually consigned from France on personal recommendation to the King. Princess Henriette Anne sent over from her own entourage Frances Stuart, a strikingly attractive, fifteen-year-old distant kinswoman of the King, "to be one of the maids of honour of the Queen your wife," Minette recommended. "Had it not been for this purpose, I assure you I should have been very sorry to let her go from here, for she is the prettiest girl imaginable and the most fitted to adorn a Court."[40]

Fifteen years was a dangerous age in the English court, but the persistent virginity of Frances Stuart was to become a leading theme in its annals. She certainly attracted immediate attention: "So admired and so rich in clothes and jewels," said a generous lady who observed her, "that she is the only blazing star."[41] She outshone Barbara, whose pregnancy made her ill,[42] but at the St. Valentine's Ball she missed the highest distinction. The King kept to the old custom of choosing his valentine by lottery instead of nomination, and drew the Duchess of Richmond. Lady Castlemaine drew him,[43] which at least assured her a handsome present. The Duke of York spent £800 on a valentine token, but the Duke was at the chase again, for the Duchess was seven months pregnant.*

The clash over the King's valentines produced a rowdy sequel. The Duchess of Richmond was Mary Villiers, thirty-seven years old and already twice widowed but a powerful figure at court as the eldest sister of the Duke of Buckingham. Although she was a first cousin of Barbara Villiers, she bore her no affection, but headed the court faction who were "in envy of my Lady Castlemaine,"[44] and in a resounding verbal scuffle with the reigning favorite "calls the latter Jane Shore, and did hope to see her come to the same end."[45] (Jane Shore, mistress of King Edward IV, was disgraced and died miserably.)

Instinctively aware that the best military defense of a position is to attack from within its cover, Barbara paused merely to note for the future that the Duchess of Richmond was in her subsidiary titles Countess of Lichfield and the lady of the manor of Grafton. Then she continued with the prosecution of her main, bloody-minded assault against Clarendon, against the clerics who preached meaningfully to the King on adultery,[46] and against the high civil servants who sought to undermine her status. She did not hesitate to challenge Charles himself when she thought she saw him yielding. In a climactic quarrel as the King's dignitaries left to welcome Catherine at Portsmouth she announced that for the imminent birth of her child she intended to lie in at

---

*Their first child, a son, had died. Their daughter, Mary, was born on April 30, 1662. The active Duke sired sixteen legitimate children and five illegitimate, but far healthier, offspring. The only legitimate issue to reach maturity were Mary and Anne, who both became sovereign queens of Great Britain, and James, the "Old Pretender."

Hampton Court Palace, where the King and Queen were to begin their married life.[47]

Charles's reaction to an attitude which, estimated at its minimum valuation was a coquettish tantrum and, at its gravest, sheer, blazing presumption, was outstandingly complaisant. He went to Barbara's house and dined and took supper with her for six days running, although in the middle of the sequence Queen Catherine had already landed at Portsmouth and all London's bells were officially rung and bonfires lit to celebrate her arrival. But, although almost every other resident in King Street built a bonfire, Barbara pointedly did not even though the King was within; instead the King and the mistress cheerfully publicized their own *entente cordiale*. After a rueful or petulant complaint at the size to which the King's child had swollen her they sent for a pair of scales and weighed each other, and Barbara proved her point by declaring that she was the heavier.

The King's attitude is all the more revealing when it is compared with his reaction to Catherine's revolt which followed almost immediately. All his life he maintained that he was never ruled by women, and it was a delicate point of honor with him that he would not brook from a woman "defiance for the decision of supremacy and who should govern."[48] Yet, under the assault of Barbara Castlemaine he clearly capitulated. It is a measure of the influence which this fiery and determined woman wielded over him, not only domestically but, in the cloudy political times which lay ahead; decisively, when the mistress became the paid agent of the King of France.

On Whitsunday, May 18, 1662, the King, delayed in

London by a profusion of bills which Parliament wished to have passed before it was prorogued, attended divine service—receiving the sacrament on his knees, which was still considered novel in Restoration England—and kept the clerks hanging about Whitehall until eleven at night while he discussed the impending legislation with the Privy Council.[49] Parliament detained him in town until nine next evening, when he drove with a Life Guards escort to Guildford, slept very briefly, and went on to Portsmouth. He found Catherine in bed with a fever and could only give her a first English kiss. (The English were a kissing nation and when Charles was traveling the country gentlewomen artlessly gave him their mouths to kiss, which he did not consider *lèse-majesté*. But the Duke of York, sent ahead to greet the shy Catherine, had saluted the Queen more formally.)

Charles was therefore eased of a recurring preoccupation over his potency; though impatient at the long delay in London, he had pushed a scribbled note to Clarendon across the table of the council chamber: "I shall have one conveniency in it too, that if I should fall asleep too soon when I come to Portsmouth I may lay the fault on my long journey."[50] Now he wrote at greater length to Clarendon: "It was happy for the honour of the nation that I was not put to the consummation of the marriage last night; for I was so sleepy by having slept but two hours in my journey as I was afraid that matters would have gone very sleepily."[51]

But circumstances gave him some days after the wedding ceremony to brace himself. He wrote to his sister: "I was married the day before yesterday, but the fortune that follows our family is fallen upon me, car Monr. Le Cardinal m'a fermé la porte au nez, and though I am not so furious as Monsieur* was, but am content to let those pass over before I go to bed with my wife, yet I hope I shall entertain her at least better the first night than he did you."[52]

As for Barbara Castlemaine, she celebrated the day of the royal wedding by ordering a great laundering of all her underclothes, and had them set out to dry in the palace grounds, delighting the voyeurism of Pepys: "And in the Privy Garden saw the finest smocks and linen petticoats of my Lady Castlemaine's, laced with rich lace at the bottom, that ever I saw; and did me good to look at them."[53] That night he went to the theatre and was sentimentally moved to see the lady sitting, dejected, in the audience, and he fancied she was already experiencing public contumely. All now depended on the King's relations with the Queen. If he were pleased with her, that, "I fear, will put Madam Castlemaine's nose out of joint."[54]

Catherine of Braganza was a small, frail woman of twenty-three of no particular beauty, her hair at first dressed in tight corkscrews projecting like saucers from her ears so that "at first sight," Charles confided to a crony, "I thought they had brought me a bat, instead of a woman."[55] Her upper front teeth projected to distort her upper lip, which Charles generously ignored, telling his Chancellor: "Her face is not so exact as to be called a beauty, though her eyes are excellent good, and not anything in her face that in the least degree can shock one. On the contrary, she has as much agreeableness in her looks altogether as ever I saw: and if I have any skill in physiognomy, which I think I have, she must be as good a woman as ever was born ... I am confi-

---

*Minette's husband, the Duc d'Orléans.

dent never two humours were better fitted together than ours are ... I cannot easily tell you how happy I think myself; and I must be the worst man living (which I hope I am not) if I be not a good husband."[56]

Charles seemed to evince a genuine intention to live lovingly with his wife. He had told Clarendon that, after marriage, "I will contain myself within the strict bounds of virtue and conscience,"[57] and both before and after his wedding he declared he had banished Barbara from his bed.[58]

Lord Chesterfield, who had been appointed Chamberlain to the Queen and was in constant attendance on her—perhaps applying his previous knowledge of Barbara—was unconvinced. After describing the Queen in flattering terms to a friend, he added: "Yet I fear all this will hardly make things run in the right channel; but if it should, I suppose our Court will require a new modelling, and then the profession of an honest man's friendship will signify more than it does at present."[59]

Sir John Reresby, who was at Portsmouth with Chesterfield, declared roundly that Catherine "had nothing visible about her capable to make the King forget his inclinations to the Countess of Castlemaine, the finest woman of her age."[60] If Catherine was no blazing star, her entourage did even less to prepossess people in her favor. She had been brought up in a Catholic convent, and was despatched to England with a train of rather dirty monks and a corps of lady attendants whom the Court dismissed as monsters and even Clarendon called "old, ugly and proud."[61] They insisted on wearing the old-fashioned farthingales, with skirts draped over the frames of pregnancy-baskets. They were excessively concerned with their virtue, which they declared was in danger even if they slept in a bed which had at any time previously been occupied by a man; and they took understandable objection to the unembarrassed sanitary habits of the English.

"Yesterday," Chesterfield reported, "they complained that they cannot stir abroad without seeing in every corner great beastly English pricks battering against every wall, and for this and some other reasons they are speedily to be sent back to their own country."[62]

The "other reasons" for the quick return of the Portuguese attendants were Charles's reprisals against his wife for her rejection of Lady Castlemaine. It was but one of many violent actions which marked the honeymoon period of the new, model court during what were, even for the stormy Barbara, some of the most turbulent weeks of her life.

The King had underrated both the sophistication and the spirit of Catherine. He had also promised Barbara too much. Charles imagined that the libertine carillon of his infatuation for Lady Castlemaine, even if the score ever reached Lisbon, would not be jangled before the convent-conditioned ears of the Infanta. But the masterful Queen Regent of Portugal not only knew the whole affair but had bluntly repeated it to her daughter, and had made her promise that she would never tolerate Castlemaine's presence at her court in England. This was a difficult pledge for Catherine to keep, since at the same time Castlemaine was making the King promise that she would be appointed a personal attendant to the Queen as a lady of the bedchamber.

The war between the Queen and the Miss—the new court name for a kept woman[63]—was over more than the comparatively trivial issue of who should or should not bear an archaic and comic court title. The position of lady of the bedchamber tokened for the holder an assured status in the eyes of the King and Queen. It was the second in precedence of the very few royal posts which could be given to a woman, and it had the additional attraction of being new-minted, for it could not be bestowed while the King was still a bachelor. Until the Queen was in residence in England and had approved the appointment, no formal royal honor could be paid to a woman except incidentally by ennobling her husband.*

On Barbara Castlemaine's side, therefore, the main incentive to grab the honor was to achieve status and esteem in a jealous court. On Queen Catherine's side the distaste for the appointment concerned both status and intimacy. She had no wish to honor her husband's whore and even less inclination to accept her proximity as a personal attendant on whom she would have to lean in many delicate matters confronting a new and foreign consort. To the King what began as a matter of status and reparation for Barbara rose dangerously to defense of the personal prestige of a sovereign and was further complicated by two emotional factors: the interest and affection he felt for his new child by Barbara, and a certain semipublic humiliation in the fact that he had failed to keep out of Barbara's bed for more than a fortnight although he had assured some of his friends and counselors that he would.

The counselor most concerned–and most unwillingly

---

*This was not the case in France, where Henri IV—Charles's grandfather—had begun the practice of ennobling his mistresses and legitimizing their offspring. Charles eventually made his mistresses peeresses in their own right, but always referred to their offspring as his "dear and natural children" without legitimizing them. Had he sired elder legitimate heirs of his own body, so that the succession to the throne was unchallenged, he might have given his bastards that additional respect, besides making them dukes. But none of their descendants among the hereditary noblemen of England today seems particularly ashamed of his origin.

concerned—was Chancellor Clarendon, whom Charles appointed as his ambassador to the Queen when the intensity of the war demanded negotiations more subtle than his angry pride would allow him to voice as husband to wife. Clarendon had to plead the case for a woman whom he pathologically loathed to such a physical extent that he seems unable to pronounce or formulate or write her name. In the autobiography which he composed in exile—having had to flee the country to escape impeachment and execution, as he believed because the schemer and coordinator of his enemies was Lady Castlemaine—never once in the course of many thousands of words about her can be specifically mention her. He begins his account of her in words of general doom, like the prelude to an ancient myth:

> There was a Lady of youth and beauty, with whom the King had lived in great and notorious familiarity from the time of his coming into England, and who, at the time of the Queen's coming or a little before, had been delivered of a son whom the King owned . . . When the Queen came to Hampton Court she brought with her a formed resolution that she would never suffer the Lady who was so much spoken of to be in her presence.[64]

And so the story of the Lady unrolls, not only to recount the bedchamber crisis but also the ensuing years of "implacable enmity" between the woman and Clarendon which he considered led to his downfall: yet, by a curious literary nausea, the name of the "Lady" is never set down.

The Court moved from Portsmouth to Hampton after two additional days of irksome delay, while fresh coaches were sent for because the farthingales of the Portuguese

ladies would not allow anyone to sit beside them.[65] The
Queen was queasily and feverishly sick and, having been
bled, did not move out of doors. There was a curious hiatus
in the continuity of appointments to her household. No
ladies of the bedchamber had been named except the First
Lady, who was also Mistress of the Robes and Keeper of the
Privy Purse to the Queen. She was the Countess of Suffolk,
and she held an invidious position in the struggle for power,
for she had been born Barbara Villiers, the sister of Lady
Castlemaine's father, and the King when in difficulty with
his mistress sometimes applied to Barbara's aunt to intervene
with an affectionate influence which it is not clear that she
really held.

Matters hung in uneasy abeyance. In effect the Court was
counting down the last days of Barbara's pregnancy. The
turbulence of the minor whirlpools in the Court correspond-
ingly increased. Lord Cornbury, who as Clarendon's son
secured a rare early appointment to the Queen, told the
Marchioness of Worcester: "No other office is yet visibly disposed of, though I think there are forty pretenders to every
one; and they are all here, both men and women, expecting
their doom, and I am sure they will not all be pleased.
There are twenty little intrigues and factions stirring, but
with those I do not meddle, and therefore will not venture
to give you any account of them; only thus much I will tell
you, that there are great endeavours used to make— ———,
you know who, a Lady of the Bedchamber, but it is hoped
by many they will not take effect; a little time will show us a
great deal, I will say no more of this for fear of burning my
fingers."[66]

The King and Queen came to Hampton Court on

Charles's birthday, May 29, 1662. There had been as yet no trial of strength between them and neither doubted that the matter of which they were both aware could be smoothly handled. Charles was well enough pleased with Catherine and she was, after a week of his gentle attention, willfully and passionately in love with him.

Lady Castlemaine was a dozen miles away in King Street, Westminster, where the Monarch had persuaded her to await the birth of their child. Roger Palmer was also at King Street. It was his home for the fortnight that the King was away. It was an ironically short time since this ardent man had been fighting with all the passion of youth for two dreams: to see his king restored, and to win Barbara Villiers from Lord Chesterfield and to marry her. Now he knew along with the rest of the town, that his wife was the King's trollop and he was miserably reminded every day of the details of his humiliation by the sight of her belly and the sound of his title.

At this time Roger acknowledged the Roman Catholic faith. It was less a conversion than an acceptance of beliefs with which he had long been familiar through his mother and her family.

Lady Castlemaine had her child. It was a boy and she called him Charles.

The King hastened from Hampton to visit her, not telling the Queen.

When the King had left, Lord Castlemaine, in a twisted gesture of futile and irrational shame, took the child whom the King acknowledged and who bore the King's name and had him baptized by a Roman Catholic priest.

Lady Castlemaine learned immediately of the baptism. Raging, she sent a messenger to Hampton Court Palace.

The King came back from Hampton. With him were the Countess of Suffolk, Barbara's aunt, and Aubrey de Vere, Earl of Oxford. They called for Lady Castlemaine at King Street and drove her and the child to St. Margaret's Westminister. There they had the boy christened by an Anglican minister. The record still declares:

*1662 June 18. Charles Palmer L$^d$ Limbricke*
*[Lord Limerick] s. to y$^e$ right honor$^{ble}$*
*Roger Earl of Castlemaine by Barbara*

"He is my son," the King confirmed, only temporarily assigning him to another father. And Charles drove back to his palace at Hampton very keenly aware that he could no longer postpone fulfilling the promises he had made to the boy's mother.

Lady Castlemaine was driven to Hampton Court.

Queen Catherine, sitting in her room in the palace amid a large company of the lords and ladies who were still jostling for positions in her household, looked up to see the King come in with a lady on his arm: auburn-haired, composed, strikingly gowned. The Queen smiled and rose to her feet. The King presented the newcomer: "My Lady Castlemaine." The Queen pleasantly extended her hand to be kissed by the tall woman. Then in a surge of emotion she realized who this was. She sat down, very shaken. Her face was white. Without a sound of sobbing but as if they were erupted, tears gushed from her eyes. Her nose bled, and she fell in a faint. Courtiers carried her into a more private chamber stood silent and ill at ease with their eyes on the King, then tiptoed away. The King had not gone in to the apartment. The great crowd that had been in the presence

Queen. His brown face, with the deep-set lines, was tight in anger as he escorted Lady Castlemaine to her coach. "She has publicly defied me, I am the governor," he said of the Queen. It was an extreme interpretation of what others might describe as an uncontrollable physical reaction to the shock of a situation long feared.

The matter was now not only in the open between husband and wife, when before it had not been pressed to a decision; it was also public to the extent that there had been a cloud of witnesses within the court. Charles privately reproached Catherine for her behavior, and perceived no penitence. He more formally put Lady Castlemaine's name on the list he proposed for the ladies of the bedchamber, and the Queen decisively pricked it out.

The breach was clear, and Charles ostentatiously abandoned Catherine within the Court. He spent his evenings with a set—Harry Killigrew, Charles Berkeley, Harry Jermyn—who were his genuine friends but, being younger and far more confirmed in general debauchery than the King, could be relied upon to support the glorification of his mistress. Indeed, they drew to his attention the "glorious example"[67] of his maternal grandfather, King Henri IV of France, who obliged his Queen to receive his mistresses at court. They avoided the specific mention that his paternal grandfather, King James VI of Scotland and I of England had done the same with his male favorites.

Charles made one more determined effort to overcome Catherine's resistance. He swore to her that he had had no familiarity with Lady Castlemaine since Catherine's arrival at Portsmouth and that he would never court her again. Catherine, quite out of control, merely spat words against him in incoherent rage. The King decided that he would have to turn to Chancellor Clarendon.

Clarendon, who avoided prolonged stays at Hampton but had his son as a reliable informant, somewhat incredibly told the King that the whole situation was new to him, and this sudden declaration of intent to give further honor to Lady Castlemaine filled him with horror for "the hardheartedness and cruelty in laying such a command upon the Queen." He declared boldly to his master that whatever might be the practice in the Court of France "where such friendships were not new in the Court nor scandalous in the Kingdom," the thought in England was that a woman who prostituted herself to the King was as contemptible to any lady of honor as if she were a common whore. Here the King, who had borne the reproof patiently enough, burst out in angry protest. Clarendon went on to remind the King that already his light mode of living had lost him much support in the country, and to continue it would be only to aid those who desired the destruction of the monarchy.

The King then committed himself to a notable statement of his position as he saw it then.

"I have undone this lady," he said, "and ruined her reputation, which was fair and untainted till her friendship with me, and I am obliged in conscience and honour to repair her to the utmost of my power. I will always avow a great friendship for her, which I owe as well to the memory of her father as to her own person; and I shall look upon it as the highest disrespect to me in anybody who shall treat her otherwise than is due to her own birth and the dignity to which I have raised her.

"I like her company and conversation, from which I will not be restrained, because I know there is and will be all innocence in it. My wife shall never have cause to complain that I broke my vows to her if she will live towards me as a good wife ought to do, in rendering herself grateful and acceptable to me, which it is in her power to do. But if she continues uneasy to me I cannot answer for myself that I shall not endeavour to seek content in other company.

"I have proceeded so far in the business that concerns my Lady Castlemaine, and am so deeply engaged in it, that she will not only be exposed to all manner of contempt if it succeeds not, but my own honour will suffer so much that I shall become ridiculous to the world and be thought too in pupillage under a governor.

"And therefore I shall expect a conformity from my wife herein which shall be the only hard thing I shall ever require of her and which she herself may make very easy. For my Lady Castlemaine will behave herself with all possible duty and humility unto her, which if she fails to do in the least degree she shall never see my face again. And I shall never be engaged to put any other servant about her without first consulting with her and receiving her consent and approbation.

"Upon the whole I will never recede from any part of the resolution I have taken and expressed to you. And therefore I require you to use all those arguments to the Queen which are necessary to induce her to a full compliance with what I desire."

Clarendon went to the Queen to put the case which the King had so sternly made. She was disabled by wounded pride to such an extent that she dissolved in uncontrollable tears and he had to retire. Next day she sent for him and asked him to forgive her emotion. "Do not blame me," she begged him, "if, having greater misfortune upon me and struggling with more difficulties than any woman in my condition, I sometimes give vent to passion that is ready to break my heart."

The Chancellor, an unsympathetic confidant for any young person and at his worst when dealing with a woman, tactlessly remarked that the Queen, coming from hot-blooded Portugal, ought to be more familiar with "the follies and iniquities of mankind" which were so much more frequent there than in the cooler climate of England. But even here young men were lustful. "I cannot believe," he told her, "that you are so utterly ignorant as to expect that the King your husband, in the full strength and vigour of his youth, is of so innocent a constitution as to be reserved for you whom he had never seen, and to have had no acquaintance or familiarity with the sex." He then passed on the King's pledge of future fidelity. He assured her "All former appetites are now expired, and he has dedicated himself entirely and without reserve to you. If you meet his affection with the warmth and spirit of good humour which you well know how to express you will live a life of the greatest delight imaginable." Catherine was innocently pleased, and asked Clarendon to thank her husband for his goodness and ask his pardon for "any passion or peevishness I may have been guilty of, and assure him of all future obedience and duty."

Clarendon observed that after such an assurance of obedience the Queen would doubtless accept the Countess of Castlemaine as a Lady of her Bedchamber.

Catherine's response was of fiery rage which burned away the tears. "The King's insistence upon that particular," she cried, "can proceed from no other ground but his hatred of my person. He wishes to expose me to the contempt of the world. And the world will think me deserving of such an affront if I submit to it. Before I do that I will put myself on board any little vessel and so be transported to Lisbon."

"You have not the disposal of your own person," the Chancellor coldly reminded her. "You cannot go out of the house where you are without the King's leave. Do not speak any more of Portugal, where there are enough people who wish you to be." More mildly he advised her at least to be conciliatory with the King. If she persisted in rejecting Lady Castlemaine at least she should not provoke her husband to anger, "for his passion will be superior to yours." He left her and went to the King. He unconvincingly assured Charles "Her unwillingness to obey you in this one particular proceeds only from the great passion of love which she has for you," and he advised that the Queen should be left in peace for a day or two.

But the King could not be held off. In a noisy quarrel within their apartments which was heard outside and swiftly relayed through the palace he put the list to the Queen once more. She made the inevitable threat to go home to Portugal.

"You will do well first," stormed the King, "to know whether your mother will receive you. I shall give you a fit opportunity to know that by sending to their home all your Portuguese servants. I shall forthwith give order for the discharge of them all, since they behave themselves so ill—for to them and their counsels I impute all your perverseness."

There was more than pique in this reprisal. The extraordinary courage which the Queen had shown in confronting her husband needed some buttress of support and advice, from her spiritual confessors as well as her ugly ladies-in-waiting. The order to deport them caused the virtual isolation of Catherine and the erosion of her obeliscal resistance. But it was also a political spur to the Queen Regent of Portugal, who had gambled on omitting to consign half Catherine's dowry, but was in the weaker position because she still needed the physical presence of an expensive British army and navy.

Clarendon had dodged court life for two or three days, and came back to find the situation nearing its worst. The King was making an almost childish display of gaiety while the Queen sat dumb in despair. She went to bed and he did not follow her, but caroused in the palace all night, coming back to their chamber in the small hours, for at this point he tenaciously maintained his caprice of never sleeping in any other room. He sent Clarendon once more to the Queen, reminding him "I will gain my point and never depart from that resolution."

The weeping Queen admitted that she had said much to the King for which she would willingly ask his pardon. The Chancellor pushed to the heart of the conflict. "I do not justify or defend the proposition that has been made to you concerning my Lady Castlemaine as just or reasonable," he told her. "But tell me, do you think it in your power to divert it, or that it is not in the King's power to impose it on you?"

"I will not dispute the King's power, what it may impose, being sure that I cannot rescue myself from it."

"Then submit cheerfully," he urged her. "For you cannot resist."

"My conscience will not give me leave to consent," said Queen Catherine.

The Chancellor's expression hardened—he always regretted that he did not have a diplomat's face and could never dissemble his feelings. It was a brave but unfortunate thing to say to the militant Anglican Clarendon, who fundamentally doubted whether a Catholic, and particularly a Catholic queen, could have a conscience unless it was the voice of the keeper of her conscience, the Queen's confessor.

"The King may do as he pleases," Catherine continued. "But I shall not consent to it."

Clarendon reported this to the King and asked to be dismissed from any more involvement in an affair in which he had been so markedly unsuccessful. The King let him go, but sent a last shot after him discouraging him from permitting gossip or intrigue about the bedchamber affair and its implications, whether it were in Worcester House, Whitehall or even Ireland. There was discontent in significant circles. Sir Allan Brodrick, the Royalist conspirator who only two years previously had asked the Chancellor to persuade the King quietly to reward Roger Palmer for his generosity,* had been appointed Provost Marshal of Munster. Brodrick was talking, and others might echo.

The tone of the King's letter to Clarendon is formidable and revealing:

"I forgot when you were here last to desire you to give Brodrick good counsel not to meddle any more with what concerns my Lady Castlemaine and to let him have a care how he is the author of any scandalous reports; for if I find him guilty of any such thing I will make him repent it to the last moment of his life.

"And now I am entered on this matter I think it very necessary to give you a little good counsel in it, lest you may think that by making a further stir in the business you may divert me from my resolution, which all the world shall never do.

"And I wish I may be unhappy in this world and the world to come if I fail in the least degree of what I have

_____
*See page 30.

resolved: which is of making my Lady Castlemaine of my wife's Bedchamber; and whosoever I find use any endeavour to hinder this resolution of mine (except it be only to myself) I will be his enemy to the last moment of my life.

"You know how true a friend I have been to you. If you will oblige me eternally, make this business as easy as you can, of what opinion soever you are. For I am resolved to go through with this matter, let what will come of it: which again I solemnly swear before Almighty God.

"Therefore, if you desire to have the continuance of my friendship, meddle no more with this business, except it be to bear down all false scandalous reports and to facilitate what I am sure my honour is so much concerned in.

"And whosoever I find to be my Lady Castlemaine's enemy in this matter, I do promise upon my word to be his enemy as long as I live . . .

Charles R."[68]

At this point Roger Palmer, Earl of Castlemaine, showed the steel to declare himself also an enemy of Lady Castlemaine's. In a quarrel on the grand scale Barbara stormed out of the King Street house, not as a refugee but as a pirate. She took away every article of value: all the plate, the jewels and the pick of the furniture. She took all the linen and even every servant, except one porter left to guard the looted house. She went only ten miles, to Richmond Palace, where her uncle Colonel Edward Villiers, Knight Marshal of the Royal Household, had his residence. Roger Castlemaine shrewdly and promptly declared himself not responsible for his wife's debts. He obtained a bond from Viscount Grandison and the Earl of Suffolk, two of Barbara's uncles, indemnifying him to £10,000 for debts existing or to be incurred by his wife or her agents.[69] As soon as this virtual deed of separation was signed Barbara found herself free to come back to King Street. She returned the furniture and servants, but for the moment stayed in Richmond. For Richmond was only four miles from Hampton.

The King sent for Barbara. In effect he also sent for Catherine. Lady Castlemaine kissed the Queen's hand, and the Queen, in obedience to the King, permitted it. "I cannot say there was no discomposure," wryly reported an onlooker.[70] But soon the distance of four miles proved too far. The King brought Barbara to Hampton Court Palace and set her up in apartments there.

Queen Catherine was now alone. All her Portuguese attendants except a blind, sick gentlewoman had been sent home. They had gone without even the grace of parting presents, for Charles–short on his dowry—withheld from the Queen the money she might have spent on them.

When the King and Queen sat in the great hall at Hampton he did not talk to her. He had his mistress by his side and friends laughing around him, while she sat unregarded, unable to expel Lady Castlemaine from her vision or her thoughts.

If the Queen rose and left the room, one or two courtiers would have the heart to accompany her while the rest pressed closer round the King to make jokes about his wife. Even her servants, catching the mood of the planned ordeal, and understanding where the gratuities lay, showed "more respect and more diligence to the person of the Lady than towards their own mistress, who they found could do them less good."[71]

The King was a naturally affectionate man, and in his general intercourse would be taking a hand, caressing a shoulder, and would not be denying himself a light kiss—as Catherine remembered from her own brief bliss. Day after day she watched it all, and when she went to bed heard the mirth rise higher, until the King came back in the summer dawn.

And the Queen's spine snapped. Unexpectedly she capitulated to Lady Castlemaine, ingratiating herself with an obsequiousness that was pathetic in its totality: "The Queen on a sudden let herself fall first to conversation and then to familiarity, and even in the same instant to a confidence with the Lady; was merry with her in public, talked kindly of her, and in private used nobody more friendly."[72] Soon the Queen and her lady were the sight of the common people, laughing together as they shared a coach with the King. And when the Queen went to the first Mass allowed her by the marriage treaty, her attendant was Lady Castlemaine.

In a context other than Restoration England it would have been the end of an undergraduate game. A young woman of twenty-three had been outplayed by a girl of twenty-one. But this was the end of Catherine as a character. The Court was never to be influenced by her, except in a taste for masquerades, dancing and cards, in which she became something of a pioneer, so that a satirist wrote of her:

> Ill-natured little goblin, and designed
> For nothing but to dance and vex mankind,
> What wiser thing could our great Monarch do
> Than root ambition out by showing you?
> You can the most aspiring thoughts pull down,
> For who would have his wife to have his crown?[73]

Henceforth the King kept her for breeding, and she failed

at that. In her weakness perhaps she was surer of his affection—he was memorably gentle to her when he thought she was dying. But, for Charles, the encounter had been a deluding victory, not really worth any laurels, even if he had demonstrated with accuracy that an enemy of my Lady Castlemaine was an enemy of the King.

# 3 ᴏᴈ *Cuckolds All A-row,*
## *the old dance of England*

IN the early years of his estrangement from his wife, Roger, Earl of Castlemaine, found one major inconvenience. Whenever Lady Castlemaine was pregnant—which was not infrequent—Lord Castlemaine was expected to be in England, and preferably in London, as near to the computed date of conception as hindsight would allow; and he was tacitly expected to stay there with a show of concern until the birth of the child. Virtually this was to provide a retrospective alibi for the King. Protocol at the English court did not yet permit married women resident in Whitehall Palace to produce without censure children who could not broadly be ascribed to their husbands. The attitude to unmarried ladies was even more unfeeling. However, the activities of the Monarch made it convenient soon to change this rule.

Barbara Castlemaine and her husband met publicly for the last time in August, 1662, on a gallery overlooking the

Thames at Whitehall. The King and Queen were making their state entry into London by river from Hampton Court, and Castlemaine had secured a box from which the children and the servants could watch the spectacle. It was disconcerting that both master and mistress should decide to attend, and typical that Barbara arrived first. Roger took off his hat as he came into the enclosure, and Barbara politely bowed. From that time on they ignored each other, walking up and down in opposite directions as they waited. But they took it in turns to lift the new baby, Charles, from the arms of his nurse, and cradle and rock him for a little. Roger never bore a grudge against Barbara's children, and was to make the eldest, Anne, his heir.[1]

As the thousand gilded barges on which pageant masters and stage designers had been working for months came to touch the shore at the palace stairs, and the great guns boomed from Lambeth, a surge in the crowd made a section of scaffolding sway and fall on the people packed in the street. None of the courtly ladies above took notice of the accident except Lady Castlemaine, who ran down among the rabble and nursed a child who had been hurt. Later a dismounted horseman, booted and spurred, kept her talking on the gallery for some time. Barbara had no headdress, and the wind was ruffling her hair. She took the riding hat from her escort and wore it with a natural air.[2] That was the last image Roger had of her, with a man's plumed hat over her auburn hair and her hand shading her blue eyes from the sun: Behind her her husband, and ahead of her the King, the Court, and any intermediate lover she fancied.

There was an early perverse tug of attraction for the young Duke of Monmouth. The King solved this by marrying off his son at the age of thirteen, and the mistress compensated for it by altering course towards Harry Jermyn, a courtier whose apparently meager physical equipment contrasted provokingly with his dazzling reputation as an amorist. Charles's eldest bastard, the son of Lucy Walters, the first and worst-reputed of all his mistresses, had been brought over from France by the Queen Mother as a good-looking boy with a plain name: James Crofts. The King became attached to him and he was attached to Barbara. In a scene of multiple reconciliation and amity in Somerset House the Queen Mother sat smiling with Queen Catherine, who smiled on Lady Castlemaine, now officially of her bedchamber, while the Queen Mother smiled on the Duchess of York, now altogether approved as her daughter-in-law, and Master Crofts, "a most pretty spark," smilingly doted and dallied with some concentration on Lady Castlemaine.[3] The public audience ended with a return to Whitehall Palace—where the Queen believed Lady Castlemaine had no private apartments but the King and Lady Castlemaine knew that she had[4]—and *en route* the loyal plebs were permitted to applaud the smiling King, Queen, King's mistress and King's sprig all intriguingly entangled within the same coach.[5]

In self-defense the King quickly set himself to negotiate a marriage between his forward lad and Lady Anne Scott, the ten-year-old heiress of the Earl of Buccleuch, meanwhile fencing him from indiscriminate attack by promoting him to be Duke of Monmouth,[6] with precedence immediately behind the Duke of York. In his own self-defense the Duke of York asked his brother the King for security that the young lad would not eventually hopscotch over him in precedence to become the heir to the throne if the Queen failed to bear children—an assurance which for long the King would not specifically give. The only immediate reaction which the Duke could control was to engender another child,[7]—at which, within wedlock, he was more adept than the King.

It was the King's diversion to pretend to his mother that his wife was pregnant. "You lie," she would answer,[8] at first blushing with pleasure at his playfulness but inevitably responding more bitterly as the months passed by. There was never such indecision with Barbara. But the regular discovery of her condition still regularly entailed the problems of protocol.

When courtiers whispered that Barbara was pregnant again in October, 1662, they recognized that Roger Castlemaine, who had been itching to go into Europe, would not be given his pass to leave the country. The man who first passed the news from London to the provinces added a gossiping corollary evincing the virility of the putative father: "It's said Hazelrigg's daughter is with child by him that I dare not name."[9] The newscaster was timid but Hazelrigg's daughter was brasher. She dared to name both the King and the Duke of York as possible fathers of her child.[10]

The King, who never sponsored more than one regular mistress at a time[11] but permitted himself occasional extracurricular studies, would not acknowledge authorship, being to the best of his memory—though sorely teased by Mistress Frances Stuart—concerned with taking, *en passant,* only Mistress Win Wells.

Winifred Wells, one of the Queen's maids of honor, was described by a courtier as "a big, splendidly handsome creature" marred only by "a certain air of indecision which gave her the physiognomy of a dreamy sheep." Coming from an ultra-Royalist family, she was not a girl to present the King with great difficulties, for, "as her father had faithfully served Charles I she thought it would ill become his daughter to decline to be served by Charles II."[12]

The Duke of York for his part, a very proficient huntsman, believed that unless he had been misled by false scent—which in this case was, for personal reasons, not credible—he had been at the relevant time (though he had now moved on), in pursuit of Mistress Middleton: Jane Middleton, married at fifteen in the year of the Restoration, was the most outstanding for stamina of all the beauties at the Court of Charles II. She retained her visual charms for a generation. Her disability was "carrying about her body a continued sour base smell that is very offensive, especially if she be a little hot," a condition inelegantly versified as

*Middleton, where'er she goes,*
*Confirms the scandal of her toes.*[13]

In spite of this drawback Mistress Middleton had at that time two fresh suitors: the glamorous Comte de Gramont, who had been expelled from the French court for pursuing a temporary mistress of King Louis XIV but whom Charles had gaily welcomed to Whitehall; and Harry Jermyn, recovering from serious wounds he had received in a duel and somewhat involved with Barbara Castlemaine, yet with the ambition to hunt fresh quarry.

The situation in autumn, 1662, was, therefore, that Lady Castlemaine was pregnant—she said by the King, who was interested in Win Wells, but was quite severely persecuting anyone who told the Queen details of his behavior with

Lady Castlemaine.[14] Unknown to the King, Lady Castlemaine was more than curious about the capability of Harry Jermyn. Jermyn was not rejecting Castlemaine but still wished to conquer Jane Middleton. Middleton was busy on her own account after having been relinquished by the Duke of York, who was now rather indiscreetly ogling Lady Chesterfield—he was known as "the most reckless ogler of his day."[15] Lady Chesterfield was flirting outrageously with James Hamilton, partly to encourage the Duke of York, partly to extract the last ounces of gratification from James Hamilton. Hamilton was anxious to crown his seduction of Lady Chesterfield with a further triumph over Lady Castlemaine. Lord Chesterfield, painfully aware that he was not dancing in this particular capriole but was reduced to picking up ladies in St. James's Park,[16] was nervily jealous of all who approached his wife.

The second Lady Chesterfield was Elizabeth Butler, daughter of the Duke of Ormonde and sister of the Earl of Arran, twenty-two years old, fair-haired, with enormous blue eyes usually flashing indecent invitations, and altogether a remarkably vivacious, if shallow, girl. She had been married by arrangement with the Earl when he was still infatuated with Barbara Palmer, and she had learned to return his coldness without acquiring his possessiveness. The man she had in her sights along with the Duke of York—though he in his turn coupled her as target with Lady Castlemaine—was her first cousin James Hamilton. Although young, he was colonel of a regiment of foot, Groom of the Bedchamber to the King, handsome and witty, and claimed to be the best dancer in the court and the most successful lover.

James Hamilton cultivated a friendship with Lord Chesterfield, confiding in him that he wished to seduce Barbara

Castlemaine and needed the advice of his lordship as the
only man who had ever really gained the lady's heart.
Chesterfield was flattered by this attention, and did not per-
ceive that it gave Hamilton extra opportunities to see Lady
Chesterfield, who gladly confirmed her capitulation to the
young soldier. Lord Chesterfield reciprocated by confiding
to Hamilton his suspicions of the Duke of York and his wife.
Consequently, Hamilton himself paid more attention to the
exchanges between Lady Chesterfield and the Duke of York,
and interpreted them as highly questionable. When he
reproached Lady Chesterfield with this, she indignantly
declared that Hamilton was her only lover.

One of the fashions that King Charles had brought over
from the Continent was the playing of the guitar. The
Duke of York played passably, but Lady Chesterfield's rendi-
tion was exquisite. When the Duke brought his instrument
to Lady Chesterfield's apartment to practice a difficult passage he found the virtuoso's husband there. But Chesterfield, who was chamberlain to the Queen, was sent for by
her Majesty—which temporarily convinced him that even
Queen Catherine was in a plot to further the Duke's seduction of his wife. But he had to leave the two together, since
the Queen was giving an audience to a group of the ambassadors from Moscow who were at that time visiting the
Court—dripping with jewels and lice in equal profusion. At
the end of the audience the ambassadors retired and the
King came into the chamber, not so much to see the Queen
as to talk to her maid of honor, Frances Stuart, who was
beginning to excite his attention more than formerly.
Shortly afterwards the Duke of York also came in and Chesterfield observed him darkly. Conversation turned to a

legend that all Russian women had beautiful legs, and the sequel to that remark reduced the moody Lord Chesterfield to a state of speechless rage which he could only relieve next day when he commandeered his confidant James Hamilton and took him for a private talk in Hyde Park.

The King, Chesterfield reported to Hamilton after a perfunctory inquiry about Lady Castlemaine, had declared that the finest legs in the world were in England, and the finest in England were Frances Stuart's. To back this statement La Belle Stuart made the appropriate demonstration. It was reputed that she was so naively concerned with her beauty that an ingenious courtier could strip her naked without her being aware of it, merely by mentioning the fine parts of other women. Frances now lifted her skirts above her knee to prove the King's point. And only the Duke of York contradicted the King's claim and her evidence. "Mistress Stuart's leg is too thin," he said confidently. "The most exquisite leg is plumper and shorter, and for its best advantage it should be seen in green stockings."[17]

Chesterfield groaned, and Hamilton had to smother his own groan—for he knew Chesterfield's conclusion and dared not say he knew. "What you don't know about Lady Chesterfield," said his lordship, "is that her beauty stops short at the waist. Her feet are ungraceful enough, but you cannot know that her legs are worse." Hamilton choked back a protest. "Lady Chesterfield's legs are short and thick," her husband continued, "and to make the best of them she almost always wears green stockings." His drawn face grew paler as he spat out his conclusion: "And now you know what caught the fancy of the Duke of York."

Hamilton hurried away to give vent to his own chagrin in a bitter letter to Lady Chesterfield, denouncing her infidelity to him. Next day at court she slipped a reply into his hand. In it she inveighed against the jealousy of her husband in inventing such a scandalous tale as that of the green stockings, and scorned the Duke of York as a putative lover. The only virtue of the whole episode, she declared, was that it diverted attention from Lady Chesterfield's infatuation for the fascinating James Hamilton.

Completely convinced, Hamilton went to his lodgings to write a tender retraction of all his suspicions. He bravely advised his mistress to show even more open regard for the ogling Duke if it would mask their own intrigue. As he was writing, Lord Chesterfield burst into his apartment crying that he had unmasked the adulterers. Hiding his love letter in confusion, Hamilton had no time to wonder by what means he had been betrayed—for Lord Chesterfield was raving about the Duke of York. "He was just now with my wife at a card party in the Queen's chamber," he howled. "They imagined they were cleverly hiding in the crowd. I do not know what had become of the Duke's hand, but I know very well that his arm had disappeared right up to the elbow. He turned round and saw me, and was so disconcerted by my presence that in drawing away his hand he came near to completely undressing Lady Chesterfield."[18]

This shocking revelation totally liberated James Hamilton from his allegiance to Lady Chesterfield, and he was free to devote himself entirely to Lady Castlemaine. Barbara herself had unwillingly publicized her early pregnancy by quickening while she was at dinner in distinguished company at Lord and Lady Gerard's, so that "all the lords and men were fain to quit the room, and women called in to help her."[19] But, clearly, Lady Castlemaine did not believe that her condition precluded dalliance, and her particular gallants did not consider themselves warned off. So assiduously obvious were the attentions of her man of the moment very shortly afterwards, that the King gave himself the notable embarrassment of banishing Harry Jermyn from Whitehall for courting Lady Castlemaine.[20]

The affair of the Duke of York in the card room was widely known at court. But when Lord Chesterfield also hurried his wife off to exile at Bretby in the Peak, and returned to glower at the courtiers, there was less sympathy for the Chamberlain who, it was thought, was committing the indecency of being publicly jealous of his wife. (What the Court did not then know was that Lady Chesterfield was four months pregnant.)

On the other hand, uxoriousness was not in favor in any fashionable sphere. When the Duke of York, trying in his own manner to make amends to the Duchess, put up a façade of affection at the theatre, even the bourgeois Pepys took offense at the "impertinent and, methought, unnatural dalliances there, before the whole world, such as kissing of hands and leaning upon one another."[21] Marital devotion seemed as indecent as husbandly jealousy, and when the King at the New Year's Eve ball at the palace called as his first country dance "Cuckolds All A-row, the old dance of England," his inspiration gave an immortal label to the mood of the age.[22]

At a court ball that Christmas season, "a child was dropped by one of the ladies in dancing, but nobody knew who, it being taken up by someone in a handkercher. The next morning all the Ladies of Honour appeared early at Court for their vindication, so that nobody could tell whose this mischance should be. But it seems that Mistress Wells fell sick that afternoon, and hath disappeared ever since, so that it is concluded that it was her."[23]

Win Wells, however, made no overt admission, and the dabbling philosopher-king coarsened the mishap in an extraordinary sequel. He had the foetus dissected in his closet, declaring with gay inaccuracy that in his opinion the child was a month and three hours old, and, since it was a boy, the person who was worst off from the abortion was himself, for he had lost a subject.[24]

Since Lady Castlemaine was first reported pregnant in October, 1662, but had no child until September, 1663, the pangs she experienced at Lady Gerard's in early December may have marked her own miscarriage, induced or otherwise, after which she may have gone to it again: the King was spending so many consecutive nights with her through the winter festival that even the sentries gossiped about his frequent furtive exits in the morning;[25] and if the banished Harry Jermyn had found opportunities to court Barbara effectively, their affair had inspired considerable ingenuity.

If the lady miscarried, she was in experienced hands. Sir Alexander Frazier, one of the King's physicians, had a poor reputation as a healer since he let Prince Henry of Gloucester die in 1660, but, possibly doing better as a pox doctor, he confidently ran his own department at court, being "so great with my Lady Castlemaine, and Stuart and all the ladies at Court, in helping to slip their calves when there is occasion, and with the great men in curing them, that he can do what he please with the King in spite of any man, and upon the same score with the Prince [Rupert]; they all having more or less occasion to make use of him."[26]

The reflection on Frances Stuart was typical of London opinion, but unsubstantiated by any court source, except the Comte de Gramont who would rather fashion a good tale than tell a dull one. Mistress Stuart was probably, forensically, a virgin. But that was now not for want of trying on the part of the King, and her virtue owed nothing to a certain overconfident slackness on the part of Lady Castlemaine. Before Christmas—it was said at the time that she had been trying to divert the King from too great insistence on a relationship between her and Jermyn—Castlemaine had been inviting Stuart to sleep in her bed. When the King came to greet her in the morning he found two tousled beauties where he had expected one, and grew to rely on the profusion.

In a zenith of recklessness one idle night Barbara began a frolic with Frances that they should act a charade of getting married. Their companions joined in and played out a mock marriage with priest, book and ring. Then they cut the ribbons from bride Frances's dress, put Barbara and Frances to bed and brought them their sack posset, and threw the bride's stocking to see who was next to be married: "but, in the close, it is said that my Lady Castlemaine, who was the bridegroom, rose, and the King took her place."[27]

After that frolic was reported it is small wonder that few people believed Frances Stuart was not the King's Miss.

In baffled admiration of Frances's persistence the King gradually appreciated the profound distinction between the two women. Frances Stuart was simple, undemanding—beyond the pension which maintained her she accepted no more than a few jewels from the King during her long stay at court—and uninterested in power. Barbara Castlemaine was scheming, avaricious, quarrelsome and, by contrivance of personality and studied expertise, the most accomplished whore of her class. "She has all the tricks of Aretin," was a courtier's grudging recommendation,[28] when Pietro Aretino's volume of illustrated sonnets on sixteen sexual postures was something rich and rare and already banned.

A cabal met regularly in Lady Castlemaine's lodging and she had already succeeded in securing her first backstairs political appointments; whereas the most ambitious constructive interest ever recorded of Mistress Stuart is that she was interminably seeking help in building houses of cards.

Barbara sought money through many channels, including gambling at which she often lost heavily. The King paid, and tried to keep down the stakes at court gaming by sending to Paris for trinkets to be purchased from the Saint Germain Fair and used for betting.[29] Lady Castlemaine came to the King for more than her gambling losses. He was indeed her only provider. The Muscovite ambassadors brought gifts from the Czar valued at £150,000, and the cautious Clarendon had cautioned Charles against giving them away: "There goes no extraordinary wit to beg this present before it comes ... I hope you have not given it away already."[30] The King replied that he needed the furs and treasure too badly himself. But the thwarted Barbara begged from him, and secured, every Christmas present given to the King by the peers, and promptly outshone both the Queen and the Duchess of York by the jewels she wore at court.[31]

Even if she had had a sweeter nature Lady Castlemaine could never, because of the position she held, have expected popularity among the women at court without the most careful cultivation. But she had no fear and she sought no favor. An early enemy was Lady Gerard, one of the Queen's ladies, the French wife of a veteran Civil War general who was Captain of the King's Guard. Lady Gerard invited the King and Queen to supper. Lady Castlemaine learned of the invitation and decided on a show of power. Charles and Catherine arrived at their host's, but before any meal was served the King excused himself and left the house. Within minutes it was known where he had gone. He had crossed to Lady Castlemaine's and he spent the night there. No keener stab by one woman against another could be contrived. Lady Gerard took the matter badly and spoke bluntly of the King. The King spoke more crudely of her. Lady Gerard then referred to Lady Castlemaine in the frankest terms while speaking with the Queen. And for this the King struck. At a court ball Lady Gerard had to request the King as partner for one of the figures of a dance. He led her out and, instead of exchanging ballroom inanities, summarily discharged her from her post as Lady of the Bedchamber to the Queen.[32]

This was not well received at court, where Lord Gerard, in particular, was well liked. For the second time in two months the King had had recourse to banishment for offenses against Lady Castlemaine, and once again he had trespassed on the Queen's prerogative regarding the choice of her own women. The autumn smiles were over and Charles was on the worst of terms with Catherine, not supping once with her over a three-months spell.[33] Barbara had insisted on complete public recognition, and Charles therefore gave her official lodgings in the palace, allocating rooms immediately above his own, with access by a private stair.[34]

With the coming of spring there was a quickening in the pace of the complicated farce now being played at court. The Comte de Gramont, who had been paying spectacular but time-consuming homage to Lady Castlemaine, had at the same time been courting the aromatic Mistress Middleton, not face to face but in a more delicate and star-crossed way. He had been writing daily letters which he bribed her maid to give her at her most yielding moments.

He was shocked to discover that the maid had kept not only his money but his messages, since she had no love letters of her own.

The Count complained to Mrs. Middleton, who was unresponsive since she was welcoming back from his first ambassadorship in France her lover, Ralph Montagu, strongly reputed to be the father of her daughter.[35] Considering that it would be pointless to appeal for the intervention of the hitherto inactive Mr. Charles Middleton, husband to Jane, Gramont cut his losses and looked afresh around a court which was entering one of its frequent periods of pageantry.

The King safely married the Duke of Monmouth to Lady Anne Scott, and pulled them out of bed after ten minutes because he considered the bride too young.[36] Still markedly remote from the Queen, he then drove from Windsor to Whitehall, proprietorially conducting Lady Castlemaine to her apartment. Once installed in her lodgings Lady Castlemaine cast her eye on Lord Sandwich as an intriguing contrast in maturity with Monmouth. Sandwich was flattered, and paid for his entertainment by gracefully losing £50 a time to Castlemaine at cards.[37]

Lady Chesterfield had a child at Bretby, and though Lord Chesterfield was uncertain whether he had become a father he saw that at least he had the decision on who should be godfather, and chose Lord Clarendon.[38] He comforted himself with the thought that he, Chesterfield, still wore among the courtiers the faint halo of the fathership of Lady Castlemaine's first child.

The Duchess of York had a son whose paternity nobody thought to question. Sir Charles Berkeley, who had falsely claimed he had seduced the Duchess and was now, as Lady Castlemaine's pimp,[39] high in favor with both the King and the Duke, was elevated to the Viscountcy of Fitzharding, in the Irish peerage, since Clarendon still guarded the English list from Castlemaine's creations.

Frances Stuart began to rise rapidly in the King's esteem and wishful imagination, and Barbara Castlemaine realized that she had overcultivated the bloom of an apparently vapid girl who was now a serious rival.

The Queen, aware of Frances's canny determination to stay a virgin, began to be more cheerful. When Barbara, as lady of the bedchamber to Catherine, questioned the time she took on her toilet with "I wonder Your Majesty can have the patience to sit so long a-dressing," the Queen replied "I have so much reason to use patience that I can very well bear with it."[40] It was a strong reminder of the light in which others saw the menace of La Belle Stuart. Barbara remembered the force of a sentence of exile, and banished Frances from her room. The King, who was taking supper with Barbara every night, said that if he did not find Frances there when he came the next evening he would never visit Barbara again.[41]

The claims of three women on the King were concentrated when the Comte de Gramont spent 2,000 louis in Paris on a custom-built calash and had it sent over to London as a present to Charles II. The calash (*calèche*) was a cutaway open carriage contrasting with the old-fashioned boxed coach, and it was greatly prized by beauties as a vehicle for revealing their charms as bountifully as possible when abroad in Hyde Park.

The Queen begged to be the first to use the calash, but Charles gave her little consideration. Lady Castlemaine had already requested it, having no qualms about the exhibition although she was noticeably pregnant. But then Frances

Stuart asked for its use on the same day. Lady Castlemaine declared that if she were not given the calash the shock to her tempestuous dignity would bring on a miscarriage. Frances Stuart swore that if the King denied her the calash he would lose all chance of provoking in *her* a miscarriage, or even a conception.[42]

It was the ace of trumps. Barbara stormed off to her sulking station, the residence of her uncle in Richmond Palace. Charles pretended to go hunting in Richmond Park next day, but got no farther than Barbara's room, and patched up the quarrel at least to the extent of persuading her to return to Whitehall.

But when the entire royal household rode on horseback in Hyde Park with the King affectionately holding the Queen's hand as they rode side by side, Lady Castlemaine was ignored by the courtiers and rode melancholily alone, while Mistress Stuart "with her sweet little eye" was supremely at ease among the group of ladies "talking and fiddling with their hats and feathers, and changing and trying one another's by another's heads, and laughing."[43]

Barbara decided on another demonstration of strength. This time it was the Duke of Buckingham who invited the King and Queen to an entertainment at his home. Barbara, hearing of it only at the house of her aunt, Lady Suffolk, declared grimly, "Well, much good may it do them, and for all that, I will be as merry as they." She swept back to King Street and ordered a great supper to be prepared. That night the King left the Queen and, with Lord Sandwich in his company, spent all the night at Lady Castlemaine's.[44]

The Court now moved to Tunbridge Wells, the waters of which, the Queen hoped, would be efficacious enough to cause her to conceive. Catherine's spirits were high as she raced on horseback to meet the King, come down late from London, and hugged him to her body.[45]

Lady Castlemaine was not at Tunbridge. She had proved, possibly more ostentatiously than she wished, that she had no need of the waters, and she was near her time for her third delivery. The waters were ineffective on the Queen, less surely so on her attendants. "Well may they be called *les eaux de scandale*," the observant French Ambassador reported to King Louis XIV. "For they nearly ruined the good name of the maids and the ladies (those I mean who were there without their husbands.) It took them a whole month, and some more than that, to clear themselves and save their honour; and it is even reported that a few of them are not quite out of trouble yet. For which cause the Court will come back in a week; one of the ladies of the Queen stays behind and will pay for the others."[46]

At Tunbridge the Comte de Gramont, rebounding from Mistress Middleton, fell in love with a cousin of Lady Chesterfield, the sister of Lady Chesterfield's lover, James Hamilton. Elizabeth Hamilton was one of the lovely women of King Charles's court captured in the series of "Windsor Beauties" painted for the Duchess of York by Sir Peter Lely. It is not certain that Gramont would have married her had it not been for the brotherly energy of James and George Hamilton, exerted first to ensure a contract of marriage and then to enforce it after consummation. For Gramont had omitted the ceremony, though Elizabeth had permitted the liberties, of the state of matrimony.[47]

On September 20, 1663, Lady Castlemaine gave birth in London to a son whom she called Henry. Two days later, the Queen, who had developed enough steel in her soul to be femininely cruel and maintained her official ignorance that Barbara had undergone childbirth, ordered her to ride with her to Oxford if she desired to remain a lady of the bedchamber. Barbara endured this considerable ordeal on horseback, and came to lodgings in Christ Church Meadow, where she had the consolation of being visited in bed each morning by the King.[48]

There was, in fact, a triumphant resurgence of their attachment once her baby was born. They came back to London, and in celebration Barbara gave her lover three successive suppers in King Street. When the Thames tide rose into her kitchen to disrupt the roasting of a chine of beef, "Zounds," she swore to her cook, "you must set the house on fire but it must be roasted."[49]

Suddenly Queen Catherine fell ill. After some days it was announced that she was dying. In genuine shock Charles knelt by her bedside imploring her to live. "Live for me, if you love me," he pleaded, never thinking, as a cynical courtier observed, that she would take him at his word.[50] And Catherine, who had never yet disobeyed him, lived. And the King went to take supper with Lady Castlemaine.

Later, sitting by his wife's bed as her fever ran its course, Charles heard her wonder in her delirium how she could have been brought to bed of a boy and yet have felt no pain. "But he is an ugly boy," she said. "No," said the King. "He is a very pretty boy." "If it be like you," said Catherine, "it is a fine boy indeed, and I would be very well pleased with it." And the King went to take supper with Lady Castlemaine.[51]

But it was at the end of this crisis that courtiers noticed

that the King's soft black hair was suddenly streaked with grey; and from this time on he wore a periwig. Next day Samuel Pepys had all his hair cut off and ordered two wigs for himself.[52]

No one had prayed harder for the Queen's full recovery than Barbara Castlemaine. She had become aware that if Catherine died it was the aim of a very powerful cabal to press the King to marry Frances Stuart: and the King needed no urging. The girl's fanaticism for virginity almost triumphed. Soon, when the novelty of his new baby by Barbara was dimmed, the King spent more and more time with Frances, to whom he had now allocated a special apartment, below his own. If he was not in her room he was toying with her in the open corridors, so "besotted that he gets into corners and will be with her half an hour together, kissing her to the observation of all the world."[53]

The Duke of York and the lords of state became so used to this that when they came into the palace on business they would ask, "Is the King above or below?" meaning in his own room or Mistress Stuart's.[54]

"There is nothing almost but bawdry at Court from top to bottom," moaned an English observer, while a French onlooker called down all the scorn of the gods on the abject way in which Englishmen showed themselves slaves to their mistresses.

But the Frenchman was the Comte de Gramont, hurrying home to Paris after receiving a message from King Louis XIV that the Count would again be welcome at the French Court. On the road to Dover he was overtaken by two gentlemen from the court of King Charles who approached him with drawn swords. The pursuers were James Hamilton and his brother George. "Have you forgotten anything?" they asked Gramont. "Why, yes, gentlemen," he replied, "I believe I have forgotten to marry your sister." Elizabeth Hamilton was, indeed, pregnant, and Gramont dutifully returned to Whitehall Palace and married her. The "Court of Cuckolds" had claimed another flunkey.

PIMP to the King and to Lady Castlemaine was, by
common repute in the Court,[1] Sir Charles Berkeley, later
Viscount Fitzharding and, later still when a warrant was
forced past Clarendon, Earl of Falmouth in the English
peerage. He was a young man in his middle twenties, of sufficient charm to win the deep affection not only of the King
but also of the Duke of York, in spite of the blatant lie he
had told of his early intimacy with Anne Hyde, James's
duchess: only Clarendon refused to condone this slur on his
daughter. Berkeley had sufficient nonchalant authority to be
able to call the King out of a council meeting because
Barbara had summoned him, and the King's sense of priori-
ties permitted him to obey.[2] But the effective council chamber was too often the lady's lodgings, and when meetings
were adjourned interested courtiers would sometimes watch
through the window Lady Castlemaine going to bed, with
Berkeley still in attendance.[3] In these lodgings, even before

the time of the King's marriage, gathered the clique who were intent on opposing Chancellor Clarendon.[4]

They were led by the ingratiating but irresolute politician, Sir Henry Bennet, later Lord Arlington: a tall man of forty-four, cultivating the air of a grandee after some years' service in Spain, his face given an odd hub by a narrow strip of black plaster which he constantly wore across the bridge of his nose to emphasize rather than mask an old sabre scar from the Civil War, and which did nothing to palliate the effect of his pale, protuberant eyes:

> Two goggle-eyes, so clear, tho' very dead,
> That one may see thro' them, right thro' his head,[5]

as a fellow-cabalist wrote of him.*

Potentially a far more competent confederate was Anthony Ashley Cooper, then Baron Ashley and Chancellor of the Exchequer at a time when that post was of minor importance, and later, Earl of Shaftesbury. Aged forty-one in 1662, he had not reached the full stature of the deviousness over which Charles II always puzzled as to whether it exceeded his own—the King had finally to content himself with the Scotch proverb: "At Doomsday we shall see whose arse is blackest."[6] Also temporarily in Barbara Castlemaine's salon was her thirty-four-year-old cousin George Villiers, Duke of Buckingham, the squandering, lecherous "chemist, fiddler, statesman and buffoon" who

> Laugh'd himself from Court, then sought relief
> By forming parties, but could ne'er be chief.[7]

*Buckingham. With the exception of Clifford substituted for Berkeley, the 1662 cabal had the same membership as the 1671 cabal.

The circle was completed by the Earl of Lauderdale, a giant, red-headed Scotsman of forty-six with an inflamed face and violent speech and manners.

Charles Berkeley was the youngest and in intellect the dimmest of the men in the Castlemaine cabal, but it would not have existed without him. He was the good-natured, physically attractive, amoral young man with an amateur military background—Berkeley was captain of the Duke's Guard—whom many monarchs have chosen as their court runabout-man to grease the slips of virtue. He was major-domo of the Charles-Barbara liaison, and from its inception controlled the political power of private access to the King. Harry Bennet had not been on good terms with Berkeley while they had been unconventional intimates of the King during the shiftless years before the Restoration. Accordingly, when in the spring of 1661 Bennet returned from his four years' labors as ambassador in Madrid, Clarendon tried to use him as a royal favorite who could oppose the influence of the objectionable Berkeley. Bennet accepted Clarendon's patronage until it had swiftly secured him a seat in Parliament, then summarily rejected the role of cats-paw to the Chancellor, who with belated clairvoyance growled that Bennet "knew no more of the constitution and laws of England than he did of China."[8]

Instead, Bennet made friends with Berkeley and painstakingly sought the favor of Barbara Palmer, as she still was. He could appeal to her strong sense of family regard by reminding her that at Oxford twenty-four years previously he had contributed a poem to a volume of verse by Christ Church men printed in memory of Barbara's uncle, Paul, second Lord Bayning.[9]

With these advantages Bennet promptly won the influential court post of Keeper of the King's Privy Purse, which Charles deliberately gave him as a warning cuff to Clarendon, who wanted it for a kinsman but had offended the King by opposing Charles's wish to extend toleration to Roman Catholics.[10] Barbara's first major political intrigue as the new Lady Castlemaine had been to try to persuade the King to appoint Bennet ambassador to France. Louis XIV had seen the proposed arrival at his court of a man so notably sympathetic to Spain as a threat to his policy of allying England with France and against Spain, which was already smoothly in action through the proposed marriage of Charles and Catherine. Louis had representations made to Clarendon, who persuaded Charles to quash the appointment and install Clarendon's nominee.[11]

In compensation, Lady Castlemaine cajoled the King to promise Bennet the extremely profitable office of Postmaster General. After some manoeuvring Clarendon had this appointment cancelled.[12] The chagrin in Lady Castlemaine's lodgings was extreme, and the cabal was confirmed as a standing anti-Clarendon committee for both personal and political motives.

Very shortly afterwards they registered a plain victory. They persuaded the King that one of his two secretaries of state should be displaced. They suggested it should be Sir Edward Nicholas, now approaching his seventieth year, who had stolidly served his sovereign since the days of Charles I. Berkeley and Bennet got an old courtier-friend of Nicholas to tell him that the King thought he had labored long enough and was willing to crown his retirement by the grant of a barony and £10,000 to sustain it.

Nicholas was touched by the King's generosity, although

he had hoped that he could pass the office over to his son. Finally he deprived his son both of the position and the peerage. For when Clarendon told him that it was all a plot, which he could hardly withstand but he should sell himself as dearly as possible, Nicholas asked—and got—£20,000 and no peerage. His post was immediately given to Sir Harry Bennet, and Bennet's post as Keeper of the Privy Purse passed to Sir Charles Berkeley, totaling a formidable increase in power for the Castlemaine set.

Whistling to keep up his spirits, Clarendon said jauntily at the time that, although the change had made a great noise at court, his own credit with the King had not diminished.[13] But his later summing up was: "From this time ... the Chancellor's interest and credit with the King manifestly declined ... Counsels were not so secret, and greater liberty was taken to talk of the public affairs in the evening conversation than had been before ... The King himself was less fixed and more irresolute in his counsels; and inconvenient grants came every day to the seal for the benefit of particular persons, against which the King had particularly resolved, and at last by importunity would have passed. Lastly, both these persons [Bennet and Berkeley] were most devoted to the Lady, and much depended on her interest, and consequently were ready to do any thing that would be grateful to her."[14]

While the King was either brazenly having it hollaed from Lady Castlemaine's window that he was within and wished to waylay from there his ministers proceeding to Committee, or at other times was seen stealing from Lady Castlemaine's door in a manner so furtive that it was judged "a poor thing for a Prince to do,"[15] Bennet and Berkeley established their control as the uncensorious bachelor-confidants of the King's pleasures as well as his business. They reached as far as Ireland to withdraw his favor from nobility who sneaked to the Queen of any details of the amour with Castlemaine.[16]

Bennet was Secretary of State within a fluid government format where the power of the office depended on the personality of its holder and his acceptability to the King. Dominating his companion secretary, Sir William Morrice, in both respects, Bennet became virtually foreign and colonial secretary, home secretary and director of the secret service. In addition he found himself, for his first few months, deputizing in the presidential position of "Grand Minister of State" which Clarendon himself always denied he was holding: for the Chancellor gave his new rival as much rope as could be spared, and took advantage of a genuine attack of gout to retire from routine activities until the spring of 1663. He was active enough to keep in touch with friends who held offices of state, including the Lord Lieutenant of Ireland, who complained frequently into a sympathetic ear of the absentee incompetence of Barbara's uncle, George, Lord Grandison.[17]

It was a convenient time for Clarendon to leave the limelight. He was bearing the main impact of the massive displeasure over England's decision to abandon the fortress of Dunkirk as a liability the country could not afford to retain. There was a deep popular and commercial protest at the loss of this military base (and merchantman's haven) in Europe.

There was also severe critical pressure from the government of Spain, for, although Cromwell had captured Dunkirk from the Spanish, Charles sold it to the French. Clarendon sardonically left that storm to be ridden out by a

Hispanophile minister while Charles, always wistfully impressed by the rare, physical sight of money, rode to the Tower of London to view the coins of the purchase price.[18] They had come promptly by ship from Calais, but Louis XIV was confidently assured by his ambassador to Whitehall that the five million livres (£400,000, three years' maintenance cost) he had spent on Dunkirk would soon return to France in payment for English purchases of the wines of Gascony.[19]

In home affairs the Chancellor also left to Bennet, under the King, the preservation of law and order, threatened by demonstrations, plots and uncoordinated armed risings, which were in protest against the narrow policy of the House of Commons rather than of the King in council. The Cavalier Parliament had insisted by its Act of Uniformity that the lately redesigned Church of England, its architecture purged of allusion either to the crude doric of Puritanism or any Corinthian excess of Romanism, must be imposed as a state religion; thus ensuring that opposition to the established church would entail danger to life or limb or property under the repressive legislation that was to follow as the Clarendon Code.

In a great intellectual massacre on Saint Bartholomew's Day, 1662, two thousand Presbyterian and Independent parsons of the old, broad Church of England—one-fifth of the establishment—resigned their livings and their livelihood because they could not affirm a required declaration. They took away with them all the biotic energy of intellectual controversy as well as addled scholasticism, and left the outwardly decent body of the Church to pass into a century of slow atrophy. Dissent in religion was forced into becoming a political attitude, of nonconformism rising sometimes into revolt.

Bennet sent the Life Guards clattering into the Presbyterian City of London "for show and to fright people"[20] and ordered a few exemplary hangings in the country "to justify that there was a plot, which few will believe."[21] It was to him part of the responsibility of government. He was not repressive by sympathy and he willingly drafted for the King—who sought toleration as a unifying and pacifying policy—a Christmastide Declaration of Indulgence, stating that the Sovereign would seek to influence Parliament to mitigate the disadvantages it had imposed on Dissenters and Roman Catholics.

It was all too clumsily done. Neither the King nor his Secretary of State were accomplished politicians enough to manage the extremely sensitive and reactionary Parliament on this issue. By coupling in the declaration relief for both Catholics and Dissenters they fired the virulent sectarianism of the Dissenters themselves, who seemed to prefer no toleration at all if the tender consciences being considered included those on the opposite religious wing.

The Church of England struck back through the bishops, who were now in Parliament again, and through its political leader, the Lord Chancellor. Clarendon arbitrarily decided that his illness no longer incommoded him, and came to the House of Lords to smash a bill which would give the King power to dispense penalties. It was a notable victory, ostensibly over the mismanaged "weak and unskilful"[22] toleration policy of Sir Harry Bennet; but it was even more clearly a decisive imposition on the King of the power of Clarendon.

The result was a new solidarity among the clique of ministers who opposed the Chancellor and had their best chance of influencing the King through the intimate relations they had with him at the evening gatherings in Lady Castlemaine's salon. Scandalous and frivolous as the Restoration court was, it was still the center of direct political power.

Gossips like Pepys—who was busy enough himself at the daily committees which ran navy affairs—emphasized the froth of the life at Whitehall, the seductions, corruptions, idle gambling and masquerades: all the social confetti which they heard about when they had not been there, though they did not hear of departmental deliberations at which also they had not been present.

The Court held workers as well as wastrels, but administration was always less lively to report than relaxation. Government was daily exercised. Because *everything* happened in Whitehall, and few councils were really executive until the King took his place at the table—with or without his dogs—the conduct and discussion of public affairs did not halt when the formal meetings adjourned, but clung to the person of this quick-witted, fast-walking monarch. As he strode from one appointment to another, he would take up a point with a civil servant passing in the galleries as often as he side-stepped an importunate petitioner or slyly brought a blush to a maid's cheek. When he came back to Barbara Castlemaine's rooms, the glass of wine and the sensuous encounter were there. But soon also there was dear Charles Berkeley, and the Harry Bennet with whom he had always discussed the latest dance steps in the same breath as the relief of Arras.[23]

Barbara Castlemaine, the alert, busy-minded hostess at these continuing conventions, was no political bluestocking but a self-centered courtesan. Yet, as a cultivated geisha and a woman accepted alone on terms of equality with mainly intelligent men, she promoted politics as well as personalities, affairs of state and culture* as well as of sexual provocation, in this prestigious series of after-supper conversations.

Occasionally she allowed herself a titillating exercise of power by presenting a newcomer to the circle. She encouraged the fifteen-year-old Frances Stuart, not recognizing the dangerous mistake she was making by that patronage. When Charles was meditating his Declaration of Indulgence she brought in the Earl of Bristol. If she saw this peer, an undisguised enemy of Clarendon's, as her hatchet man capable of securing the long-wished extinction of the Chancellor, it is an indication of Barbara's poor political judgement. The whole assay was a disaster.

George Digby, second Earl of Bristol, was an old friend of Bennet and of the King. He had been secretary of state to Charles II in exile, but he was converted to Roman Catholicism in 1658 and had to be deprived of his office. An endearing, impetuous and unreliable man, he could still assume no office on his return to England, but he appointed himself the political champion of the Roman Catholics.

He also made much of Lady Castlemaine. His enthusiastic partisan promotion of her cause during the bedchamber controversy increased Charles's affection for him. It was natural that Bristol should be deeply concerned with implementing the King's intention to secure some measure

*Lady Castlemaine's patronage—against current opinion—of John Dryden's first play, *The Wild Gallant*, obtained for it a number of additional performances at the Restoration court and earned her a verse tribute acknowledging the considerable and possibly crucial encouragement she gave to the young author.[24]

of toleration for Roman Catholics, and during the framing of the Declaration of Indulgence he was accepted more decisively as of the Castlemaine set. Clarendon effectively killed any parliamentary acceptance of toleration, and the irascible Bristol determined to bring the Chancellor down in a forlorn hope of foolish extremism. (At cards, dice and politics he was always an unsuccessful gambler.[25])

He was no mean orator—he had made a profoundly influential speech to the Lords, persuading them to support the King's policy of political appeasement by renouncing reprisals against all Commonwealth crimes except the regicide. Bristol now made the unorthodox step of going into the House of Commons to deliver a speech attacking the Chancellor. When the King asked later to see the speech, and told him it was seditious, Bristol burst into an extraordinary tirade against Charles himself, so completely dumbfounding the King in his own closet that, as Charles said afterwards, "I had not the presence of mind to call for the guard and send him to the Tower, as I ought to have done."[26]

Bristol was now paranoically alone and in danger. By the accidents of Barbara Castlemaine's private life she could not help him greatly. She was seven months pregnant, which she did not magnify into any monstrous disadvantage. She was then bearing the King one child a year, and had to learn to take gestation in her stride without conceding it too great an effect on her temperament if she was to maintain a dominating position among the men in her own salon. But she had momentarily lost that command. She knew the King's nature well enough to give Bristol strong advice to go no farther, but she could make no effective personal plea to the Monarch on his behalf. Bristol's suicidal gaffe occurred

at the end of the three-weeks' struggle in June and July,
1663, when Charles and Barbara were split over the status of
Frances Stuart.

The King had demanded that Barbara should continue to
invite Frances nightly to supper. Barbara, her sensitivity
increased by the contrast between La Belle Stuart's slim
taille and her own big belly, refused, sulked for some days
out of favor, stormed away to Richmond and was finally
wooed back.

During that week Bristol, with no influential support or
advice, went to the House of Lords and mounted his attack
not only against the Chancellor but, now, by implication
and by direct statement against the King, who had
appointed the Chancellor and still suffered him to continue.

Bristol went to the extreme of his privilege and called for
the impeachment of Clarendon for high treason. The
detailed articles of his charge were too feeble to sustain any
accusation of treason. They referred to the actions and neglect of the King rather than the Chancellor, so that the
gravamen of the prosecution was that it was by the King's
commissions and omissions that "his affairs grew every day
worse and worse and the King himself lost much of his
honour and the affection he had in the hearts of the
people."[27]

The House of Lords heard Clarendon's contemptuous
defense and ordered the articles of impeachment to be
examined by the judges for a decision on thir relevance to a
charge of high treason. They also ordered that a copy of the
articles should be sent to the King since he was "mentioned
so presumptuously in them." The judges threw out the
impeachment and the King threw out Bristol. He issued
warrants commiting him to the Tower, but allowed the Earl

to get adequate warning so that he could go into hiding. Eventually he escaped to France.

Bristol remained in the shadows for four years. On one occasion Barbara and Bennet persuaded the King to receive him privately, but he did not return to public life until after the Chancellor's fall.[28]

The affair of the Earl of Bristol did Barbara Castlemaine no good. Politically she was isolated, and socially she accepted the same segregation, staying in London for the last two months of her pregnancy while the Court made merry at Tunbridge Wells and Bath. Very promptly after the birth of her son, Henry, she joined the King again at Oxford, and with him at least she had regained the old relationship by the time of the Queen's serious illness. But her former cabal remained aloof, and Bennet joined the "committee" organized by the Duke of Buckingham to promote the King's marriage to Frances Stuart in the case of the Queen's death[29]—a proposal which Buckingham kept in his mind even when the Queen revived.

Consequently, Barbara Castlemaine was in a condition of comparative loneliness when in the autumn she began to take instruction in the Roman Catholic faith. At Christmastime she announced her conversion. Her kinsfolk were shocked—her cousin Buckingham stood politically (it is impossible to say by moral conviction) with the more extreme Protestants. But, when they asked the King to put obstacles in the way of the conversion, he made the leering reply that as far as the *souls* of his ladies were concerned he did not meddle with them.[30]

The Protestants slyly reported the comment of their divine, Edward Stillingfleet: "If the Church of Rome has gained no more by her than the Church of England has lost the matter will not be much."[31]

There is no known authentic explanation of the conversion. An anonymous, and often unreliable, privy councillor said that Barbara really knew that the King was a Papist at heart and she "had often been heard to say that she did not embrace the Catholic religion out of any esteem that she had for it, but because that otherwise she could not continue the King's mistress, and consequently Miss of State [*maîtresse en titre*]."[32]

With regard to the King's supposed Catholicism there are accounts[33] of both Charles II and Sir Harry Bennet acknowledging that faith together in 1659, but the only certainty is that both were reconciled to Rome on their deathbeds.[34]

With Barbara Castlemaine's conversion the King kept to his principle of outwardly not meddling, but at least Queen Catherine, in spite of an early suspicion that it was not done for conscience sake,[35] melted somewhat towards her lady of the bedchamber. She accepted an invitation to come with the King and sup at Lady Castlemaine's. The King was pleased enough at the gesture of reconciliation to mention the engagement disingenuously to his sister, Minette, as an excuse for breaking off a letter to her.[36]

They sat in those King Street apartments which had echoed with so much intrigue and were to embrace far more: a king "playing the good husband, abroad with my wife,"[37] gazing quizzically from one to the other of the women at his side—and dreaming of a third, Frances Stuart, whom he had never possessed, who allowed him so much and no more, and in so doing magnified his longing for her into the desire of the moth for the star, so that of all his women she became the only one whom he could not publicly say he loved[38] and who privately could not love him.

The relicts sat on his right and his left. He saw a barren Queen whose sterility was on the lips of every potboy and who was publicly and vainly exposed to the acrid waters of Tunbridge and Bath to make her fertile; a woman who with courage and shallow wit persevered not to be glum under her fate but could never be scintillating, a wife for whom he had a pitying affection and who maintained for him a combination of love and tolerance shiny with wear—enduring the shame of having to hesitate outside the door of her own dressing room while she listened to learn whether the King had taken a woman inside.[39]

And on his other hand the King saw a teeming mistress, a strong personality before bedtime and an omniscient witch afterwards, a woman for whom love stopped at the prepuce and clitoris and the only ecstasy was avarice, yet on the way and in the foothills of the nightly journey she first revealed, then stimulated and finally appeased the many itches she had learned to exalt into a memorable, meretricious splendor.

Only to Barbara Castlemaine, the attentive hostess in this complaisant yet restless, suffering trio, was the full irony of the evening apparent. The Queen was certain—and it was a half belief even with the King—that if she bore him an heir she would capture the man. All the medicines had failed, and instead she had almost died. Yet Lady Castlemaine had at that time her first indication that she was pregnant with a fourth child of whom, out of all his children by her, the King never could and never did question or deny the paternity.

She had passed a quiet autumn and she was ready for a more turbulent spring. Harry Jermyn had become detached from her, and was courting a Stuart heiress, kinswoman of the King, whom he abducted and would have forcibly married if she had not escaped and come galloping into Whitehall Palace yard to beg the King's protection.[40]

Barbara, grudgingly conceding to the King his right to cultivate his idealistic passion for Frances Stuart, consoled herself with the company of James and George Hamilton, Lord Sandwich and Charles Berkeley, now Lord Fitzharding.[41] But she would not lose face in polite society, which was humming again with gossip that the King had rejected Barbara for Frances. At the theatre where the King was expected she installed her party early in the box next to his. When the King came in, she first attracted attention by leaning across her lady companions to whisper to him for some time. Then she left her box and came into the King's, sitting down on his right between the King and the Duke of York.[42]

It would have been a magnificent demonstration that she was the Miss of State if the audience had not been able to mark the glower of displeasure which settled on Charles's face at this public "defiance of the decision of supremacy and who should govern." Yet the King never kept his rancor long, and could not keep away from their children. Even at midnight he would look in on Lady Castlemaine's nurses, ask them to bring out the children, and dandle them in his arms.[43]

Charles spent the night of his thirty-fourth birthday with Lady Castlemaine, bringing his fiddlers for a dance that lasted almost till dawn at her new court lodgings in the Holbein Gate, near enough the public thoroughfare for "all the world coming by taking notice of it."[44]

The new apartments were in the gatehouse built across Whitehall by Henry VIII and the suite had been used by him as a study. The move from her former lodgings in the Palace—always subsidiary to the house taken by Roger which she still kept up in King Street—was made necessary by a fire in her rooms,[45] but it brought the mistress rather nearer to the Queen's own apartments.

And all through the night of the twenty-ninth of May the Queen Catherine, shut away from her husband's festivities, stirred as the high violins occasionally awakened her, and looked at the lamp burning inside the clock by her bedside that told her the time all night, all the nights, until it pleased the King to take his formal place in her company.[46]

The fiddlers brought by Charles to his birthday ball were French musicians who had outlived the unpopularity falling to them at first when the King replaced his English band with "the French music."[47] The King occasionally lent them to the French Ambassador, the Comte de Cominges, to play in the embassy's chapel at Exeter House, where they additionally attracted many people to the Mass said there regularly. A new visitor to the chapel was Lady Castlemaine, "whom," the Ambassador reported to Louis, "I mean to regale as well as I can."[48]

Barbara was being increasingly courted for her influence with the King in the diplomatic manoeuvres which were becoming intensified in London as the English prepared themselves for war against the Dutch.

The object of the proposed war was plunder, on every material scale from a privateer's booty to company exploitation overseas. The Dutch had emerged as a great maritime and commercial power based on the products of their own colonial possessions, on the carrying trade they conducted within Europe and from the great empires of Spain and France, and on the dominating position held by Amsterdam as the world's money market. Commercial interests in England, and the national restless adventurism, considered that an agreeable share of all these advantages could be gained by declaring war on the "stinking Dutchmen."

Clarendon opposed this sentiment, desiring a close alliance with France. But after the Portuguese marriage and the sale of Dunkirk, which were steps towards such an alliance, he had to swallow the rebuff of witnessing Louis XIV sign a defensive treaty with the Dutch. But he still opposed the financial drain of a war.

The Lord Treasurer, the Earl of Southampton, agreed with Chancellor Clarendon. Sir Henry Bennet, Secretary of State, did not. Bennet had a personal stake in colonial commercial enterprise through his shareholding in the Royal African Company, and a financial stake in a successful war once he was appointed, at £1,000 a year, Comptroller of the Commission of Prizes which administered the proceeds of merchantmen and warships captured from the Dutch.[49]

It would be naive to say these interests did not move him, but unrealistic to contend that the considerations completely clouded his judgement. People entered politics at that time not entirely for "what they could get out of it" but aware that the service of the State granted them substantial pickings on which they could base their fortune. Honor was still important. Clarendon refused a £10,000 bribe from the French[50] though he favored their policy. He made his money in the more conventional manner by selling places.

Bennet keenly desired the advancement of British commerce and believed that a war against the Dutch would be short and successful—being greatly deceived in this matter by the misjudgement of the English ambassador at The Hague, Sir George Downing (who gave his name to Downing Street) when he reported that the pacific Dutch would make the valuable concessions desired by the English commercial interests if war were merely threatened.[51]

Bennet was also influenced, against any deep judgement of the situation, because the anti-Clarendon party which he had promised the King to form within the House of Commons for domestic policies was also in favor of war. This party was led by Sir Thomas Clifford and Sir William Coventry, the secretary to the Duke of York. York himself was no titular royal puppet. He was a professional soldier and, applying the narrow tactics of the time, learned to make himself a competent seaman. As Lord High Admiral he administered and fought the navy. He had a direct interest in hostilities against the Dutch when in March, 1664, he was granted the Dutch territory on both sides of the Hudson River, called New Netherlands, which he was requested to conquer in order to ease the harassment of the English inhabitants of Long Island by Dutch aggression. He involved Charles Berkeley, Lord Fitzharding, in the operation by giving him a share of the land between the Hudson and the Delaware.*

*The Duke of York's deputy, Captain Nicholls, took the territory in the autumn of 1664 before any official declaration of war, capturing New Amsterdam in spite of stout resistance by Governor Stuyvesant. Charles II wrote to his sister (Whitehall, October 24, 1664): "You will have heard of our taking of New Amsterdam, which lies just by New England. 'Tis a place of great importance to trade, and a very good town. It did belong to England heretofore, but the Dutch by degrees drove our people out of it and built a very good town, but we have got the better of it, and 'tis now called New York." Among the Duke of York's titles was Duke of Albany in Scotland. When the English captured Fort Nassau in 1664, they named it Albany.

In the Committee of Foreign Affairs the Duke of York and Sir Harry Bennet favored war against the Dutch; the Earls of Clarendon and Southampton opposed it. Over great matters it was still only an advisory committee and the final decision lay with the inclination of the King and, more importantly, with the financial support of Parliament. Parliament was fairly skilfully managed on this issue by Clifford and Coventry. The King was highly susceptible to the suggestions of the re-formed cabal—Bennet, Fitzharding, Ashley, Buckingham and Lauderdale—which was now meeting again at Lady Castlemaine's and was actively in favor of war. Against this tide the French were doing what they could to influence the King and those who could bend his thoughts towards Charles's own fundamental inclination of an alliance with France entailing peace with the Dutch.

Lady Castlemaine was always willing to be courted, if only to see the color of the French money, although until Louis XIV increased his allocation for bribery in England she did not find it impressive. Equally, she had no objection to dispensing lavish hospitality in these diplomatic exchanges so long as the Privy Purse accommodated the expense. She gave a party in King Street "in the most magnificent manner" for the French Ambassador and his wife at which, Cominges reported to Paris, "the King did the honors of the house in a way befitting more a host than a guest."[52] The function was so successful that the fact that the hostess was on the brink of labor went unmentioned. But next day, September 5, 1664, Barbara gave birth to her fourth child, Charlotte.

The advent of yet another "royal charlie," whom the King plainly acknowledged, aroused the wrath of certain courtiers. Cominges gave a return supper party for the King and

Court at which Barbara was not present. But when she did stir abroad she was abused. She had visited the Duchess of York at night, and was walking home across St. James's Park escorted only by a maid and a page. Three men accosted her. They wore the rich clothes of courtiers but were disguised by masks, which were then coming into fashion at court entertainments and at the theatre. These men called Barbara a plain whore and every wounding variation of the word that could be expressed. They reminded her that Jane Shore, the mistress of Edward IV, had died on a dunghill, alone and hated.

Lady Castlemaine ran across the park to the Palace, pursued by the shouting men until she came within call of a sentry. She stumbled to her room and fainted. Word of her condition was sent to the King and he came running to her bedside. He had the park gates shut and ordered the arrest of all the people still inside this much-frequented haunt of assignment. But after being questioned they were released.[53]

It was not an isolated act of resentment against the Miss of State. In the lockup of the Westminister Gatehouse there were imprisoned five debtors to Lady Castlemaine—Barbara had so many creditors in relation to her debtors that there must have been a perverse satisfaction in incarcerating anybody. These five ganged up against a sixth, the daughter of Colonel Alured, one of the regicides, and ingratiated themselves by informing that she had said that "Mistress Palmer", as she still called the lady, was the King's whore and she could prove it.[54] Even in the King's chapel in Whitehall a seventy-year-old doctor of divinity referred unambiguously to Jane Shore and another royal mistress before the Monarch and his court. "He told the King and the ladies, plainly speaking of death and of the skulls and bones of dead men and women, how there is no difference; that nobody could tell that of the great Marius or Alexander from a pioneer; nor, for all the pains the ladies take with their faces, he that should look in a charnel-house could not distinguish which was Cleopatra's, or fair Rosamund's,* or Jane Shore's."[55]

In November, 1664, the Duke of York hoisted his flag at Portsmouth as Lord High Admiral with orders from the King to "fight, burn, smoke and destroy" all warships of the Dutch United Provinces and to seize all Dutch merchantmen.

At the same time the King was negotiating through Berkeley in Paris for a commercial treaty with France to be followed by a formal alliance. Since Louis had only a defensive treaty with the Dutch, merely binding him to assist the United Provinces if they were attacked, Charles devoted much effort to denigrating the Dutch by demonstrating, in terms with a familiar modern ring, "that they are the aggressors and the breakers of the peace and not we ... I do not doubt but Van Beuninghen [the Dutch Ambassador to King Louis] will use all sorts of arts to make us seem the aggressors."[56]

Berkeley came back conveying compliments rather than promises, but the Duke of York, home from the sea for Christmas, pressed it as a personal favor on the King that their mutual favorite should be made an English earl. Clarendon, who was alone with the royal brothers when the

---

*Henry II's mistress, whose father changed his name to Clifford from the formidable Norman surname of Fitzponce. She was kept in a secret room at Woodstock and, on her death in 1176, she was buried in Godstow nunnery.

request was made, could advance no cogent reasons to reject it: "and so," he noted jealously, "he was created Earl of Falmouth before he had one foot of land in the world."[57] He was, in fact, given land bringing in £3,000 a year to sustain the title.[58] It was the last significant gift made to Charles Berkeley, for he had not long to live.

With the advent of war Clarendon showed himself the sage statesman which his own rather piddling apologiae and the interplay of contemporary intrigue tend to obscure. He was a very unpopular man. He had never shaken off the public odium he had incurred for his supposed responsibility for the sale of Dunkirk, from the price of which he was supposed to have taken his share. He had begun the erection of the first home of his own he had ever had in England, but even the early works on Clarendon House in Piccadilly revealed that it was to be one of the most ambitious palaces in London, and it was promptly nicknamed "New Dunkirk."*

He had opposed the policy of war with the Dutch from the beginning, but now he saw that hostilities were inevitable. Clarendon and Southampton therefore proposed in the "cabinet" Council that Parliament should be asked to vote the then unprecedented sum of £2½ millions for the prosecution of the war—alarming Bennet and the war party, who thought it was a cunning stratagem to propose a sum that would never be granted. But Clarendon, by superb management, persuaded three rich Norfolk landowners to move and support the motion in the Commons. He wanted

*Clarendon meant to spend the grant given with his 1661 barony, £20,000, on his house, but being an impractical man he was duped by his architect, Roger Pratt, who finally constructed an edifice costing £50,000. Clarendon paid £500 a year rent for Worcester House in the Strand.

none of the King's party to speak for it—a court politician, in fact, proposed an amending motion naming a much smaller sum[59]—and he would not have the vote moved by poor gentlemen who would be comparatively unhurt by the heavy taxes which the supply vote would entail. Consequently, the King, to his great surprise, was granted this vast sum solely for the pursuit of the naval war.

Writing to his sister to explain that the money, once voted, was now being collected,* Charles illustrated the easy atmosphere in which war at the top was conducted in his day. The nation could hardly be said to be stripped for action. Court life was divided "between business and the little masquerades we have had."

Charles had found £2,000 at the bottom of his purse to give to Win Wells, but might get half of it back: courtiers believed she would lay it out as a dowry, since "Ralph Sheldon is so well sweetened that he would marry Mistress Win Wells provided the King would make him an Irish viscount, which I suppose will not be denied, for (according to my Lady Castlemaine's estimation) that honour is not valued at above £1,000."[60]

There were the usual pregnancies, private and dynastic. Barbara Castlemaine was in the middle of a six-months fallow period and was consequently one of the blazing stars dominating the Queen's great Candlemas masquerade, who "in vizards, but most rich and antique dresses, did dance admirably and most gloriously."[61]

---

*Before the commissioners had gone into the counties to prise the money from the taxpayers, Clarendon and Southampton had gone to the Common Council of the City of London, which the King had asked the Lord Mayor to summon, and came back with £200,000 lent on the credit of the House of Commons vote.

Charles wished Minette well in her own pregnancy and, describing the lying-in of the Duchess of York, echoed the current contempt for girl-children, though the baby he wrote of was the future Queen Anne:

"I am very glad to hear that your indisposition of health is turned into a great belly. I hope you will have better luck with it than the Duchess here had, who was brought to bed Monday last of a girl. One part I shall wish you to have, which is that you may have as easy a labour, for she dispatched her business in little more than an hour. I am afraid your shape is not so advantageously made for that convenience as hers is;* however a boy will recompense two grunts more."[62]

The Duchess of Orleans passed on to her brother-in-law, Louis XIV, the political messages which Charles constantly entrusted to her. The French King decided that he must make one supreme effort to preserve the status quo between England and Holland. He had no objection to a running sore of belligerency existing between them, which would give France an opportunity to build up her navy and her maritime commerce. But he neither wanted the English to gain decisive supremacy—which would mean he would have to honor his treaty and fight for the Dutch—nor the Dutch to be conclusive victors, for he intended to occupy the Spanish Netherlands that year, which the Dutch would certainly oppose. Louis therefore ostentatiously reinforced his ambassador in London with two more high-ranking envoys in a triple *célèbre ambassade extraordinaire* which descended on England amid the greatest pomp with the avowed object of stopping the war with Holland.

*For the pelvic girth of the Duchess of York, see page 39. Minette's child was stillborn.

The *ambassade* made a beeline for Lady Castlemaine as a well-tried means of gaining the ear of the King. But also—since their sources of court intelligence were alert and accurate—they separately courted Frances Stuart: "She is the rising sun and, to tell the truth, she is incomparably more beautiful than the other."[63]

Unfortunately for the French, they were still deprived by their monarch of any liquid money considerable enough to divert the interest of Lady Castlemaine. Still more unluckily, a Spanish delegation had arrived very well supplied with the means of bribery. The Spanish envoy was empowered to conclude Harry Bennet's old dream of a full alliance with England. From Bennet's point of view it would directly gain some of the commercial advantages for which the Dutch war was being fought, and it would give England a substantial ally if France honored the Dutch treaty and declared war on England.

The Spanish Ambassador, the Conde de Molina, followed established protocol and speedily addressed himself to Lady Castlemaine, who received him and his presents with far more rapture than she had accorded to his rivals.

The French were left with Frances Stuart and, lacking money, could only make her gifts of incense.[64] The unambitious Frances received this offering gratefully. But whether or not she was the rising sun in the King's estimation, she was, unlike Castlemaine, an entirely unpolitical creature. She could not urge on the King policies which her mind could not grasp, and her only practical use to the French was to provide an entry into *soirées* with King Charles.

At Lady Castlemaine's salon, on the other hand, the cabal was now breathing the strong fire of direct war talk against

France. Lauderdale was back in it, to Barbara's personal profit as well as the enhancement of her prestige. For, either through his meanness or his poverty, it was said that Lauderdale could not generally "support himself by presents to her, so he could not be admitted into the cabal which was held in her lodgings."[65] By whatever means, the violent, warty Scot was back in the clique and, the ambassadors informed Louis, had delivered a most aggressive speech against France there one evening, on which it was not even necessary to employ spies to report, "for the gist of his speech is on the lips of every Englishman. You have only to go to the Exchange to hear it repeated any morning."[66]

But the English fleet had yet to be blooded in a full scale naval action against the Dutch. Alive to the prospect of sea warfare, in which he had recently had some experience, Roger Palmer, Earl of Castlemaine came bustling back from Europe. Alive to the usefulness of significant gossip, the French Ambassador reported the fact to Paris, not denying himself an ironical reference to the Earl's consternation at finding his family enlarged from two to four after three years' absence abroad.[67]

Roger Castlemaine, although he had condemned himself to exile, had not degenerated into shiftlessness. He had developed as a controversial writer. His interests were the Catholic religion and naval affairs. During his absence from England he had served for some time with Andrea Cornaro, Admiral of the Venetian fleet engaged in war with Turkey. King Charles and Lord Castlemaine did not despise each other to the extent that they could not correspond on practical subjects, and Roger had written for the King an account of this war which was later published.\* The King was later to grant Roger other commissions in the Levant. For the moment Castlemaine reported to the Duke of York, who took him on his staff with Baptist May and Henry Brouncker, and went down to the sea.

As Roger bought his last-minute necessities before embarking, his separated wife "lay impudently upon her back in her coach asleep with her mouth open"[69] in Hyde Park, only waking to exchange greetings with an old friend and bedmate, the Lady Anne Hamilton, recently transformed by marriage into Lady Carnegie,[70] and beginning a court career in which she was to pass through the hands of several gentlemen before reaching the arms of the Duke of York.[71]

On that day all the gay ladies were riding in the park, and the gallants were priming their pistols. The brave thunder of the distant drums had reached Whitehall, and gentlemen made haste to be accepted as volunteers in what could rightly be regarded as the greatest fleet England had ever assembled, ninety-eight men-of-war with fireships. The fleet put to sea, cruising off the Texel to tempt the Dutchmen out. Three weeks passed, and the Hollanders stayed within their harbors. To the volunteers sea service seemed less entrancing. They wrote courtly ballads mocking their sea-

---

\*"An Account of the Present War between the Venetians and the Turks, with the State of Candie, in a Letter to the King," London, 1666. Candie was the island of Crete, where the union of Pasiphäe and a bull produced the Minotaur, and it was therefore, according to Marvell,

> That isle
> Where Pilgrim Palmer travell'd in exile
> With the bull's horn to measure his own head
> And on Pasiphae's tomb to drop a bead.[68]

sick, lovesick state, which must mean they would lose to
the Dutch:

> For what resistance can they find
> From men who've left their hearts behind?[72]

Then, on Sunday May 28, 1665, the Dutch fleet stood out to
sea. The Republic had collected 110 warships with
accompanying fireships, outnumbering and outgunning the
English.

On June 2 the King and his friends were having supper in
Lady Castlemaine's Whitehall apartments when an excited
man was led in with an express despatch from the east coast.
The King recognized Samuel Pepys and told him to read
the message aloud. It announced that the English fleet had
sighted the Dutch, had sailed to meet them and must now
be in action. All next day the guns were heard in London,*
then they faded as the Duke of York chased the Dutch to
their home ports. At midnight, after the Duke had gone to
bed, there occurred the most costly act of poltroonery in
English naval history. Henry Brouncker, a court rake who
was Gentleman of the Bedchamber to the Duke of York,
decided that he had had enough fighting, and of his own
initiative went to the acting captain of the flagship *Royal
Charles* with false orders to shorten sail purporting to come
from the Duke. The speed of the pursuing fleet was therefore reduced. When the Lord High Admiral awoke at dawn
he saw, too far away, the surviving Dutch ships passing over
their home shallows into the Texel. Had the English fleet
maintained its full pursuit and been able to get in among

---

*An incredible fact, since the battle was off Lowestoft, 120 miles
away to the northeast, and being fought in a south-southwest gale; yet
Pepys and Dryden describe this phenomenon confidently.[73]

the forty-three Dutch warships bunched in flight, Clarendon's £2½ million would have achieved its purpose and the King, the navy and the people would have been spared the humiliations of the rest of the war.

On June 8 Baptist May rode into London with the full despatches from the Duke, understandably doubling in the immediate confusion the estimated enemy losses, which at a true total of twelve ships, four admirals and five thousand officers and men were grave enough. York himself had lost eight hundred men, including many volunteers. But to Charles the victory had lost its savor, for the first casualty he had to be told of was the death in action of the Earl of Falmouth. Dear Charles Berkeley, whom no one save the royal brothers saw any great reason to love, had been aboard the *Royal Charles*, acting as aide to the Admiral when a roundshot sent his brains flying in the Duke's face. "I have had as great a loss as 'tis possible in a good friend," said the King.[74] But in cruder terms Marvell pronounced a commoner verdict:

> Such as his rise such was his fall, unprais'd:
> A chance shot sooner took than chance him rais'd.
> His shatter'd head the fearless Duke distains
> And gave the last-first proof that he had brains.[75]

As he waited for the final news of the Battle of Lowestoft, Samuel Pepys noted: "The hottest day that ever I felt in my life. This day, much against my will, I did in Drury Lane see two or three houses marked with a red cross upon the doors, and 'Lord have mercy upon us!' writ there; which was a sad sight to me, being the first of the kind that, to my remembrance, I ever saw. It put me into an ill conception of myself and my smell . . ."[76]

The Plague had come to London. Six hundred people died that month, including a number in aristocratic King Street,[77] although bubonic plague was supposed to be a disease of the poor. By the beginning of August it was claiming three thousand Londoners a week, and in the month of September it took thirty thousand.

At first fashionable life went on, regardless. Lady Castlemaine had a slight indisposition which was immediately interpreted in Court circles by the theory that she was "slipping her filly." She was able to confound the scandalmongers by promptly accompanying the King, soignée and polished, hale and hearty, to the theatre.

Also in the audience, and adding spice to the reporting of the gossips, was a fifteen-year-old Cockney gamine actress, Mistress Nell Gwyn, who was already so remarkably successful in her first season at the King's Playhouse that she was a byword with the cognoscenti as "pretty, witty Nell."[78]

Lady Castlemaine generously gave Nell Gwyn her patronage,[79] with even more disastrous results than her previous misjudged encouragement of the fifteen-year-old Frances Stuart.

In other matters the Court continued its sparkling routine. The French and Spanish ambassadors fought each other with the steel of smiles and only the merest hint of poison in their intercourse. The Conde de Molina entertained Lady Castlemaine and her friends so royally at a celebration for the Battle of Lowestoft that his servants made the visitors' coachmen, footmen and postilions drunk, Barbara and her set refused to be driven home by them and accepted an offer of the services of the Spanish staff, the drunken English drivers reacted to such an insult by staging a swingeing riot, and an avid French observer enthusiastically reported to Paris "the greatest, most delightful shambles imaginable."[80]

In early July the Plague forced the Court to retreat to Hampton. The theaters closed, and Nell Gwyn, cut off even in the blossoms of her fame, rested by becoming the mistress of Charles Hart, leading actor at the King's Playhouse and the grandnephew of William Shakespeare.

Charles Stuart was suffering an intensification of his passion for Frances Stuart, and Barbara Castlemaine, in annoyance, refused to stay at Hampton Court Palace on the pretext that her lodgings were not suitable.[81] Charles unconcernedly arranged to take his suppers with Frances, and Sir Harry Bennet—now created Baron Arlington—* obligingly took over the temporary exercise of Berkeley's duties as court pimp and was the official host at these parties.

The French thought Lady Castlemaine was taking excessive risks by her extravagant umbrage, "and if she continues in her rage she may well lose the best rose in her hat."[82]

But they underappreciated Barbara's tactical skill. Soon she had manoeuvred the one court appointment which was to secure her future prosperity—the nomination to Berkeley's old post as Keeper of the Privy Purse. Princess Henriette Anne had made a special plea to Charles that the office should go to James Hamilton,[83] the former lover of both Lady Castlemaine and Lady Chesterfield. (Lady Ches-

---

*He took the title from his childhood home, Harlington, in Middlesex. There is no satisfactory explanation why the College of Heralds dropped the initial H.

terfield, long banished by her husband to Derbyshire, was dying in Wellingborough: the gossips said she had been poisoned by her husband,* and her husband said she was a victim of the Plague.)

But Charles appointed Baptist May—always referred to as Bab May. He was a particular crony of Barbara Castlemaine's and became the instrument and even trustee of her wealth. His own reward was £1,000 a year from the King with £4,000 estimated perquisites, and what he could make at tennis—no inconsiderable sum, for he was one of the best players in the country and one courtier lost £5,000 at tennis within three months.

The Earl of Clarendon watched moodily as money was channeled to Lady Castlemaine from sources over which he had no control. "Her principal business," he wrote, "was to get an estate for herself and her children." She "procured round sums of money out of the Privy Purse (where she had placed Mr May)."

In addition she got other grants inconspicuously made to her in other names, principally to her uncles, the Earl of Suffolk and Viscount Grandison, who were to pass the proceeds on to her. Knowing that Chancellor Clarendon and Treasurer Southampton would obstruct grants of land in England, "all the suits she made of that kind were with reference to Ireland, where they had no title to obstruct, nor natural opportunity to know, what was granted; and in that Kingdom she procured the grant of several great quantities of land, like to prove of great benefit and value to her or her children."

*The story was that the jealous Earl insisted that she should take the Sacrament as a pledge of her innocence with regard to the Duke of York, and the sacramental wine was poisoned. Chesterfield's daughter-in-law, Lady Gertrude Stanhope, never dined with him afterwards without bringing her own cup, wine and water.[84]

Yet she was only at the beginning of her depredations. At this stage, Clarendon alleged, her procurements "amounted to little more than to pay her debts, which she had in few years contracted to an unimaginable greatness, and to defray her constant expenses, which were very excessive in coaches and horses, clothes and jewels."[85]

In August the Court tried to avoid the approaching Plague by moving farther afield to Salisbury.

Within a month a man had fallen stiff and dead of the disease almost outside the King's residence there, and when these deaths in the street became, in the eyes of the French ambassadors, "too much of a bad habit"[86] the great train of coaches and wagons was reloaded and turned north for Oxford.

The King's young sons by Barbara, Charles and Henry, only three and two years old, were lodged opposite Merton College gate in the house of Antony Wood, the university historian. Barbara herself had rooms in Merton as one of the Queen's ladies, who complained bitterly that they deserved much better accommodation and that Clarendon, Chancellor of the University, could arrange this.[87]

Though the Queen stayed at Merton, the King took over the dean's lodgings at Christ Church, and the Duke and Duchess of York were also quartered in the House. It was a surprising public claim that the Duke and Duchess, unlike the King and Queen, were a united couple. The Duke had just begun his long liaison with Arabella Churchill, sister of the future Duke of Marlborough, and the Duchess, indulging in her first and only infatuation outside marriage, was extremely sentimental over her Master of Horse, handsome Harry Sidney. Both husband and wife were the worst of dissemblers. Everyone knew in which waters the Duke was currently angling, and when the Duchess now suddenly fell in love even the Duke noticed it, and banished Sidney from his household.[88]

The five-months descent of the factious, frivolous and surprisingly dirty court was a disaster for the academicians of Oxford, though the tradesmen ran to curry favor and enter debits. Antony Wood said, "The greater sort of the courtiers were high, proud, insolent and looked upon scholars no more than pedants or pedagogical persons ... Though they were neat and gay in their apparel, yet were they very nasty and beastly, leaving at their departure their excrements in every corner, in chimneys, studies, coalhouses, cellars. Rude, rough, whoremongers; vain, empty, careless."[89]

Barbara Castlemaine made herself widely unpopular. Her natural shrewishness was intensified by bad temper stemming from the poor quality of her lodgings and the necessity to pass the last months of her pregnancy in such uncomfortable surroundings.

The King's constant visits to her left the scholars in no doubt as to their relationship. And after Barbara had given birth to her fifth child, George, in Merton College on December 28, 1665, the men of the gown posted a notice on her door explaining at large that it was only the privilege of her special position that kept this scold and strumpet from the ducking stool which Oxford retained for such unruly women. The notice was written in elegant Latin and explicit English:

> *Hanc Caesare pressam a fluctu defendit onus*
> (The reason why she is not duck'd?
> Because by Caesar she is fuck'd.)

A thousand pounds reward was offered for information on the author of this verse. But Oxford pursed its twitching lips and kept quiet.[90]

The French ambassadors, who had found and recorded many instances of uncorrected *lèse-majesté* in the uncouth northern island, missed the opportunity to report to their Most Christian King this characteristic comment on the affairs and performance of His Britannic Majesty. For they had left their lodgings in Magdalen for the journey home, and at the time of the birth of young George they were enduring long quarantine in frosty sheds at the sandy mouth of the Somme until King Louis was satisfied that they and their servants were not importing the Plague into France.[91]
They had failed to negotiate a peace and had therefore been obliged to warn of a state of war between France and England. Lord Arlington would have liked to finish the war with the Dutch before taking on the French. But he had already negotiated a commercial treaty with the Spanish and had high hopes that a firm alliance with Spain would follow. While he waited, unrealistically, for this consummation he was prepared to drag his feet, and the English at large were not unwilling.
The Parliament held at Oxford had voted a further £1 million for the navy, but the cost of the war was proving far heavier than had been expected. When Pepys went over the navy accounts with Lord Treasurer Southampton he knew before the campaign had started that the navy was £800,000 short of its minimum requirement, which meant that the sailors and contractors would not be paid.[92] It was little wonder that when King Charles made his formal tit-for-tat declaration of war against the French it contained "such

mild invitations of both them and the Dutch to come over hither with promise of their protection, that everybody wonders at it."[93]

Under the drain and demoralization of almost a year of plague there was certainly not in England the national enthusiasm for fighting that had made the stirrup-cup bumpers of the previous summer so *pétillant*. Typically of many, Roger Castlemaine was not volunteering. He applied for, and received, the King's permission to leave the country while the fleets were manoeuvring for the big four days naval battle of the campaign.[94] But it is probable that he did not use his pass immediately. He wanted a final settlement of his position *vis-à-vis* Barbara, and because of the extraordinary circumstances of the year this took long to conclude. His pamphlet, generally called "The Catholic's Apology,"[95] was being prepared for the press: it was received as a reasoned and unbigoted statement of the Roman Catholic case for toleration in England,[96] though it was immediately seized by the House of Commons and suppressed.

The King came south in January but he left the Queen and her entourage at Oxford, since "our women are afraid of the name of Plague, so that they must have a little time to fancy all clear."[97] Consequently, it was in Charles's absence that Queen Catherine, in Merton College, Oxford on February 4, 1666, miscarried a son. There was, at last, undoubted medical evidence that Catherine could conceive, if not achieve her full term,[98] and the King was at first happily convinced of this. But Clarendon tells an ugly story that the women around the Queen persuaded Charles that it had been only a false conception, "insomuch that His Majesty, who had been so confident upon a former occasion as to declare to the Queen his Mother and to others that upon his knowledge Her Majesty had miscarried of a son, suffered himself now to be so totally convinced by these ladies and other women that he did as positively believe that she never had, never could be, with child."[99]

And from that time he withdrew more markedly from the Queen and handed himself over more completely to Lady Castlemaine and his other favorites.

Barbara Castlemaine exuberantly celebrated her return from Oxford by a mighty tug on the purse strings of the King. She had second improvements made to the now permanent apartments which she held at Hampton Court Palace.[100] She bought, on credit, an £850 ring from the City jeweler, John LeRoy, and ordered from Edward Bakewell, the City of London goldsmith who acted as the King's banker, two diamond rings costing £1,100 and £900 for which—since she neglected to pay—the King later allocated £2,000 of his Customs receipts.[101] Since Lady Castlemaine, besides being fond of jewels, was devoted to gambling for high stakes—she was credibly reported to have lost £25,000 in a night[102] and the King was her only ultimate security—there was *prima facie* justification for the anguished taunt against the King's cabal, that they "sit at cards and dispose of the revenue of the Kingdom."[103]

At the time of the King's birthday, when Restoration bonfires burned less numerously east of Temple Bar because of the coolness towards the King of the City of London, and when the fleets led by Prince Rupert and the Duke of Albemarle put out at either end of the English Channel to try and prevent the joining of the French and Dutch forces, a major domestic battle flared in the Court of Whitehall.

It was notable for the fact that the King publicly

reprimanded Lady Castlemaine for insolence before the Queen, and it was clear, also, that the "hectoring" Barbara—an adjective that was increasingly used to describe this aggressive mistress—had taken the opportunity to comment acidly on the King's attachment to Frances Stuart. The Queen was possibly stung beyond her normal mildness by knowledge of the slander leveled against her miscarriage by this incubus of a lady-in-waiting who had so long been imposed on her. She was sitting with her ladies in her drawing room when she said to Lady Castlemaine, "The King has caught cold, and I fear it is by staying so late at your house."

"He does not stay late at my house," Barbara retorted sharply, "for he always leaves early."

"At three in the morning," commented one waiting woman quietly to another.

"It must be," the lady continued, "that he is staying somewhere else." At this point the King came into the room, having overheard the exchange. He took Lady Castlemaine aside. "You are a bold, impertinent woman," he told her. "Leave the Court, and do not come back until I send for you." Barbara did not obey immediately, but savagely turned on the King. "I will be even with you," she shouted. "I shall print the letters you have written to me." She hurried to her apartment, called her women, and left Whitehall for lodgings in Pall Mall.

Immediately she began an intrigue to gain the favor of the Duke of York. The Duke was restless with idleness, since the King had ordered him not to go to sea as Lord High Admiral. Both Charles Berkeley and Lord Muskerry had been killed by his side at Lowestoft, and it was thought that the succession to the throne should not be put in peril by unnecessarily exposing the Duke. Consequently, once he had despatched his fleets and maintained the minor supervision that then was only possible, he had only his amours to fall back on.

He had just concluded a clandestine affair with Mistress Goditha Price, one of his wife's maids of honor. The Duchess was in the last month of another pregnancy, and the Duke's eyes had lit on Margaret Brooke, Lady Denham, the twenty-year-old bride of the King's surveying architect, Sir John Denham. Lady Denham accepted the Duke's advances, but with remarkable coolness told him that the position would have to be acknowledged as by royal appointment. "I will not be your mistress like Miss Price," she said, "to go up and down the Privy Stairs. But I will be owned publicly."[104]

Lady Castlemaine, who suspected that the King wished to capture Lady Denham first,[105]* joined with Henry Brouncker in getting this arrangement accepted. The Duke of York was an assiduous lover, and to Brouncker the task was only a refinement of his normal role.** His treachery to the Duke of York at the Battle of Lowestoft had not yet been publicly

*So did the ballad-singing public. A song of 1666 went:

*As I went by St. James's I heard a bird sing*
*That Denham's fair wife was a miss of the King,*
*But the King goes without her, as I have been told,*
*And the Duke does enjoy her, though Nan pout and scold.*

Nan was Anne Hyde, Duchess of York.

**Gramont suavely sums him up: "He was not young; his face was disagreeable; however he had a great deal of wit and an immoderate passion for women ... He kept, four or five miles outside London, a little country house which was always stocked with several working girls. Otherwise he was a very worthy fellow and the first chess player in the Kingdom."[106] Brouncker temporarily joined the Castlemaine faction later after his dismissal by the Duke of York.

exposed and he was still on his confidential staff, where he was said to be only one of a number of the Duke's pimps who brought him women "through the Matted Gallery at Whitehall into his closet; nay [the Duke] hath come out of his wife's bed and gone to others laid in bed for him."[107]

It was, however, a novel extension of Lady Castlemaine's court activities to become an open bawd and extend the hierarchy of *maîtresses en titre* to include the women of the Heir Apparent. But in retrospect it seems that the Court was now abandoning any vestige of gallantry, wit or even good manners in the pursuit of illicit love and entering a trough of degradation.

Lady Denham was publicly acknowledged the mistress of the Duke of York and he called on her at Scotland Yard in some state attended by his waiting gentlemen. The shock drove her husband, thirty years older than she, undoubtedly mad for a time. Lady Denham fell ill and openly said that her husband had poisoned her. Within seven months of the start of the affair Lady Denham was dead. The Duke of York said he would never have a public mistress again,[108] but instead he continued an intrigue he had already started during Margaret Denham's illness—with Lady Carnegie, the former Lady Anne Hamilton with whom young Barbara Palmer had lain "abed together a-contriving how to have the company of Lord Chesterfield."

The Duke of York's new liaison was by no means as secret as the couple intended. Lord Carnegie heard of it and joyfully allowed himself to be credited with devising a fearful revenge: deliberately to contract a venereal disease and pass it on to his wife, hoping to infect the Duke of York. (Carnegie was delighted to have this story that he had "bought a twenty-guinea clap" publicly believed, but later denied its truth.)[109] It was all a savagely ironic commentary on the dying plea made to his wife by William Duke Hamilton, mortally wounded for King Charles II at the Battle of Worcester in 1651, who sealed up with his will this note to Anne's mother: "Dear Heart, . . . Forget and hate the empty pleasures of a licentious Court, or of London . . . I recommend to you the care and the education of our children: for the Lord's sake study to get them acquainted with God in their young years, and to imprint his fear in their tender hearts; keep all light and idle company from them . . ."[110]

A few days after her quarrel with the King Lady Castlemaine sent a message to him asking if she could remove her belongings from her rooms. Charles replied that she should first come and view them, "and so she came, and the King went to her, and all friends again.[111]

But the notoriety of corruption at the Court continued. Harry Killigrew, a witty debauchee who was son of the King's Master of the Revels, was banished for "saying that my Lady Castlemaine was a little wanton when she was young."[112] Harry Killigrew was always being banished, but he was of the Duke's household and the incident made bad blood between Lady Castlemaine (who had demanded the sentence) and the Duke of York. Bab May went jauntily down to Winchilsea to be, as he imagined, subserviently elected a member of Parliament on the royal recommendation; but he was rejected in favor of a private candidate after the electors had "cried out they would have no Court pimp to be their burgess."[113]

National good will for the monarchy was sinking. A petition was presented to the King "from a subject who is but a woman and can only pray for His Majesty" mourning that "people say Give the King the Countess of Castlemaine and he cares not what the nation suffers."[114]

The great four days sea battle had cost the English fleet twenty ships and eight thousand men.* The four days of the Great Fire of London had destroyed £10 million in property and done incalculable damage to commerce, to public revenue, and to the war effort. Parliament debated a further vote of £1,800,000 for the navy but ominously suggested that they ought first to inspect the King's accounts. Still the Court maintained its frivolity. Six weeks after the fire, Charles put the whole of his court into a new black and white uniform of calf-length vest with a white underskirt, shorter surcoat, and "the legs ruffled with black ribbon like a pigeon's leg."[115] In derision King Louis XIV dressed all his servants in this magpie costume in the astonishing interval—considering the delays in tailoring and intelligence harassing a country at war—of only five weeks.[116] Meanwhile, the Queen of England gave a birthday ball at which the dress motif was black and silver. It was "a glorious sight to see Mistress Stewart in black and white lace, and her head and shoulders dressed with diamonds ... and the King in his rich vest of some rich silk and silver trimming." Fifteen ladies danced the bransle, "all most excellently dressed in rich petticoats and gowns, diamonds and pearls." The uncrowned monarch of the assembly was present but not active, being thought to be pregnant. Her constant admirer from the gallery noted: "My Lady Castlemaine, without whom all is nothing, being there, very rich, but not dancing."[117]

---

*Fought on the first to the fourth of June, 1666. The lesser celebrated St. James's Fight of July 25, 1666, cost the Dutch about the same losses, and on August 8, 1666, an English raiding force destroyed over one hundred Dutch merchantmen and £1 million worth of stores.

Barbara Castlemaine could afford to be in a richly complacent mood. She had reached a favorable final settlement with Roger, "parted for ever, upon good terms, never to trouble one another more."[118] And she had money. Unhappy and insubordinate seamen clustered outside holding worthless vouchers instead of pay, and the exchequer was so bankrupt that the fleet could not be sent to sea for the next campaign. But the King had paid £30,000 to clear Lady Castlemaine's debts, and the jewels she had ordered in his name were hers. Moreover, she reflected—as she noticed the King's glance held by Mistress Frances Stuart in her lace and diamonds—this could well be the last court ball that La Belle Stuart was to attend for some time.

Barbara Castlemaine had formed an alliance with Will Chiffinch, the King's new pander. He was an old man, corrupt and further corruptible, but in most things loyal to the King. He was aged fifty-eight when, with the Restoration, he took the aptly named post of Page of the Back Stairs, and on his elder brother's death from the Plague he had now been promoted to Keeper of the King's Closet, otherwise His Majesty's spy, eavesdropper, "confidential agent, procurer-general and pawnbroker-in-chief."[119]

Chiffinch, who "above all predecessors carried the abuse of backstairs influence to scientific perfection,"[120] had discovered that the Duke of Richmond\* was paying serious court

---

\*Not the son, but the second cousin by marriage of Mary Villiers, sister of the Duke of Buckingham and dowager Duchess of Richmond when she called Barbara Castlemaine a Jane Shore (see page 51). Charles Stuart, born 1640, was grandson of Esme, Duke of Lennox, who was the cousin of Darnley, husband of Mary Queen of Scots and father of James VI and I. In 1660 he succeeded his cousin Henry as sixth Duke of Lennox and fourth Duke of Richmond, also bearing the title of Earl of Lichfield, and Great Chamberlain and Hereditary Lord High Admiral of Scotland. His second wife died in January, 1667. He was nearer in kin to the King than their "cousin," Frances Stuart.

to Frances Stuart. When the Duke's wife died his devotion flamed into love. Frances, still only eighteen, found this twenty-six-year-old widower the best prospective husband of a poor selection. According to John Evelyn, who knew her well and confided in Pepys, "When the Duke of Richmond did make love to her . . . she was come to that pass as to have married any gentleman of £1500 a year that would have her in honour; for it was come to that pass that she could no longer continue at Court without prostituting herself to the King, whom she had so long kept off, though he had liberty more than any other had, or he ought to have, as to dalliance . . . She had reflected upon the occasion she had given the world to think her a bad woman, and that she had no way but to marry and leave the Court . . . that the world might see she sought not anything but her honour."[121]

But as yet the King knew nothing of a serious attachment between Frances and any other man except the indulgence she gave her sovereign. All he was aware of was that at this time even the indulgence was not extended. Frances was noticeably prim towards him. He wondered why. Barbara Castlemaine resolved to enlighten him. She went by the backstairs to the King's Closet, to which Chiffinch readily admitted her. Charles had come back from Frances Stuart's apartment at her request, because she said she had a headache. He was in a bad mood, and the hectoring and proprietary Castlemaine made it worse. She told him bluntly that she knew he had been sent away by Mistress Stuart on a feeble excuse, and that he ought to know that the Duke of Richmond would soon be taking his place in her room. "Come and see," she insisted, pulling him by the hand out of his room and into the gallery which had its private access to the favorites' apartments, just as Bab May came up to give her the nod that the stage was duly set.

Chiffinch, who might normally have gone scouting ahead
to warn the maidservants and conduct a routine reconnais-
sance, was under the influence of Barbara and made no
effort to tell Frances of the King's approach. Bab May followed Charles to the corridor outside Frances's room. "It
was near midnight," said the Court's favorite raconteur.[122]
"The King encountered his mistress' women who respect-
fully put themselves in his way, informing him in a whisper
that Miss Stuart had been very poorly since he left but had
now gone to bed and, thank God for it, was getting some
sleep. 'That remains to be seen,' he observed, thrusting aside
a maid who obstructed his passage. And indeed he did find
the Stuart in bed, but she was not sleeping; and the Duke of
Richmond, who sat at her bed's head, seemed, according to
the evidence, even less asleep. The stupefaction on one side,
the rage evinced upon the other, were such, as in a similar
surprisal, may easily be imagined."

The Duke, a younger man than the King, bowed deeply
and retired. Frances, protesting that she had been on the
point of receiving the first honest proposal of her life, dis-
dainfully required the King to do the same. He was deeply
hurt, as much from a genuine protective love for Frances as
from possessive jealousy—and it was true that young Richmond was, although a conscientious courtier, dim, bibulous
and broke.

Frances was aware of the King's mortification and threw
herself on the mercy of the Queen, who made what intercess-
sion she could. It was a difficult role to arbitrate between a
husband who desired her maid of honor and the maid who
wished to preserve her honor: especially when the Queen
knew that there had been plots in the past and would be
more in the future to annul or invalidate her own marriage

to Charles in favor of his union with a fertile partner—and no other name was mentioned but Frances Stuart.

Faced with the pleading of the Queen, the King ostensibly agreed to a marriage between Frances Stuart and the Duke of Richmond, provided the Duke's shaky financial affairs could be put in order so that a favorable marriage settlement could be agreed upon.

The King instructed Chancellor Clarendon to examine the Duke's accounts. He confidently expected that Clarendon would report that the Duke was so insolvent that no marriage could be recommended. Instead, the Chancellor's conclusion was that although Richmond was financially in a perilous position, yet, "a family so nearly related to the King could never be left in distress, and such a match would not come Mistress Stuart's way every day; so she had best consider well before she rejected it."[123]

This report infuriated the King, who interpreted it as an indication that Clarendon was encouraging the match by any means in order to remove Frances Stuart from the possibility of eventually marrying the King. Clarendon was thus supposedly quashing any danger to the present probability that a grandchild of the Chancellor's (a child of the Duchess of York) would be a future sovereign of England.*

In his impetuous desire to stop the match at any cost Charles now offered to make Frances a duchess in her own right and with her own estate if she would stay unmarried. It was a tempting choice, but Frances knew what the price would be. She was a simple girl and she realized that the King was in love with her, after his fashion. But she had the more rewarding and romantic conviction that the penniless

*In the event two of Clarendon's grandchildren reigned: Mary II and Anne.

Duke of Richmond was passionately in love with her, even though she had no title, estate or dowry. When the Duke, who was nervous of facing the King after their last encounter, asked her to elope with him she consented.

She stole away from under the very nose of the King and met her lover by assignment at the Bear Tavern in Southwark. There his coach was waiting, and they raced to his family seat at Cobham Hall in Kent to be married before the King could forbid it. Charles had been suspicious of what might be planned, and went to Frances Stuart's apartments in Whitehall Palace, arriving just a little too late. He found the room deserted and in the disorder of a feverish flight.

As he came out of the door, black with fury, he met Lord Cornbury, who was coming to Frances's room on a perfectly innocent errand.[124] Lord Cornbury was a member of the Queen's household—but he was also the son of the Earl of Clarendon. The King assumed that both father and son were in the plot and, in a rare abandon of self-control, "spake to him as one in a rage, that forgot all decency, and for some time would not let Lord Cornbury speak in his own defence."

Barbara Castlemaine was triumphant at the course of events, which had left her supreme. The King was shaken in his confidence, and surprisingly vindictive. The Duke and his new Duchess attempted to come to court to make their peace, but were rejected and drove back to Kent. Many months later, Charles's sister Minette urged him to forgive the girl who had once been her own maid of honor, sent across to Charles's court at the Princess's own suggestion.

The King replied:

"I do assure you that I am very much troubled that I

cannot in everything give you that satisfaction I could wish, especially in this business of the Duchess of Richmond, wherein you may think me ill natured. But if you consider how hard a thing 'tis to swallow an injury done by a person I had so much I . . ." (Charles was writing in English and he stopped and crossed out the word "love" which he had begun to form), ". . . a person I had so much tenderness for, you will in some degree excuse the resentment I use towards her. You know my good nature enough to believe that I could not be so severe if I had not great provocation, and I assure you her carriage towards me has been as bad as breach of friendship and faith can make it. Therefore I hope you will pardon me if I cannot so soon forget an injury which went so near my heart. . . ."[125]

He never wrote with such tender anguish about Barbara.

Lady Castlemaine was less concerned with lover's anguish than with status and security. If she surveyed her prospects after the departure of Frances Stuart in the spring of 1667—and it would be unrealistic to suppose that such a shrewd woman did not—she saw no great rival threatening her personal dominance of the Court. Win Wells, it was true, was still about, not having secured the husband or the Irish viscounty she was cogitating. She was an occasional concubine of the King's, and was indeed to continue so for years,[126] but she was neither possessive nor predatory, and the King could confidently be allowed to return to her as a diversion. The Queen must be preserved as the bulwark of Lady Castlemaine's own position.

The one man who potentially threatened both the Queen and Lady Castlemaine was Barbara's cousin George, Duke of

Buckingham. He had attempted in the past to gain influence with the King by installing a puppet mistress or working to contrive a divorce. On the other hand he had the great value of being the strongest opponent of Clarendon, and the man most likely to bring the Chancellor down.

But for the moment he could be discounted in either purpose. George Buckingham was on the run, with the King's warrants out for his arrest and imprisonment in the Tower. The exquisite Arlington was enthusiastically, if inefficiently, supervising the hunt for him, and George's future could be temporarily left to flash Harry. This emphasized a breach in Lady Castlemaine's cabal, but the volatile Buckingham had long retreated from his former prominence in the party favoring the war against the Dutch, and the war party itself was singing *pianissimo*, paying regard to the dismal condition to which that war had now reduced the country. Arlington's facile diplomacy had failed. Louis XIV had skilfully used the minimum of pressure to neutralize Spain, and England was now unsupported by any ally, but at war with the Dutch, with France, with Sweden and with Brandenburg. "We must have a peace," said the Duke of York, "for we cannot set out a fleet."[127]

The two hitherto constant remaining risks to Lady Castlemaine's personal and financial security were her old enemies, Clarendon and Southampton. The first was already doomed and the second was dying.

The Earl of Southampton, Lord High Treasurer, had been suffering severely from stone of the kidney and had resolved to be cut for it in one of the few operations of the contemporary savage surgery which promised a fair chance of survival; but he took a quack medicine which made him too weak to endure the ordeal. He died on May 16, 1667, maintaining to the last his financial squeeze on the wayward generosity of the King: among the exploits celebrated in his obituary was the fact that he had delayed a grant of £4,000 worth of plate to Lady Byron, "the King's seventeenth mistress abroad," until the lady herself had died,[128] and the gift was ineffective.

Within days of Southampton's death Barbara Castlemaine secured her first fixed pension. A ninety-nine-year grant of £1,000 a year out of the profits of the post office was passed to her nominees—her uncles, Viscount Grandison and Edward Villiers, and her toady, Baptist May.[129] Using her new freedom of the Privy Purse like a modern debutante making hay with a credit card, Barbara went to a city goldsmith to inspect his plate, chose what she wanted, and, "Wilson," said she to her waiting woman, "make a note for this and for that to the Privy Purse."[130] Other plate she borrowed from the King's Jewel House in the Tower, as was then customary for ambassadors and court officials, and the moment the Chancellor's guard was dropped she wheedled the loan into a gift.*

On June 13, 1667, Lady Castlemaine believed she had lost her entire fortune. There was a panic run on the bankers, who said they would pay nothing for twenty days—and in twenty days, it was seriously thought, London would be in the hands of the enemy. For although the English had not been able to afford to equip a fleet, the Dutch sent sixty ships into the Thames to attack the heart of England. Covered by the main force, seventeen of these warships,

*See page 156.

with twenty-four fireships and smaller craft, sailed into the River Medway bound for the great naval base of Chatham. Here were the hulks of the English main fleet, laid up with skeleton crews and, in some cases, even stripped of their guns.

The Dutch men-of-war, manned in part by captured English seamen who were paid in rare ready money and who knew the channels, broke through a chain boom and used their artillery against a completely ineffective defense to cover the fireships they sent into the dock. They burned fourteen ships of the line and retired with the 80-gun flagship *Royal Charles*—from which the King had landed at Dover for his Happy Return—canted to one side to reduce her draft and towed ignominiously by six men in a boat. "We did heretofore fight for tickets, now we fight for dollars," the English mercenaries shouted across the water to their former comrades, asking to be kindly remembered to Tom, Dick and Harry.

And, in Wapping and on Tower Hill, the wives of the sailors called to the navy commissioners, "This comes of your not paying our husbands."[131]

The material loss caused by the Dutch in the Medway was less than they had incurred from the great English raid on Vlieland and Schelling the previous year. But the blow to English morale through the disgrace of their navy was vital. The public reaction was riotous. It was mainly and illogically concentrated on Chancellor Clarendon, the man least responsible for the undertaking of the war. He was openly insulted in Westminster Hall and the mob streamed to his still unfinished palace, "Dunkirk House," as they

called it, where they broke his windows, cut down the trees
he had planted, and set up a gibbet outside his gate with
additional insults on a placard:

*Three sights to be seen;*
*Dunkirk, Tangier, and a barren Queen.*

But from the moment the Dutch were known to be in the
Thames the capital had collapsed and the courtiers feared
for their lives. Lady Castlemaine screamed that she would
be the first to be torn in pieces.[132]

It was Barbara's most turbulent summer. The fact that
she still emerged from it successfully cajoling the King and
feathering her own nest must be ascribed to luck as well as
masterly management, but above all to the extraordinary
witchery she exercised over Charles. For, misjudging her
own security, she had had two extramural and varyingly
sordid love affairs, from which she was pregnant; and she
had botched a dabbling entry into personal politics so dis-
astrously that she directly defied the King on his own ground
as the fount of honor and mercy, and found herself the
champion of her most unscrupulous enemy.

The enemy was her resourceful and unpredictable cousin,
George Villiers. She had used him in her cabal—or he had
used her—while his opposition to Clarendon was serviceable.
But in the main his court intrigues had been against her. It
was Buckingham who had tried to make Frances Stuart
supreme; and from the time of her conversion to
Catholicism their disagreement had been more intense.

As a witty and social soul Buckingham was a delight to
Charles. His throne-room mimicry of Arlington was a del-

icately observed pastiche, but when he acted Clarendon before the Court the effect was of uproarious buffoonery—he
hung bellows from the belt of his puffed-out paunch for the
Chancellor's purse and had a courtier walk before him with
a fire shovel over his shoulder as the beadle with his
mace.[133] His irreverence, intelligence and familiarity—for
the King and the Duke were brought up together from the
time of Charles's birth—had laid down a solid fund of
affection in the King's heart, on which, in extremity, he
could usually draw.

But Buckingham, "everything by starts and nothing long,"
had passed an insubordinate *annus mirabilis*. In his arbitrary
mischief he had been active for the last year in taking the
lead in parliamentary opposition to Charles's administration,
plying a sharp goad in the Lords and inciting his gang in the
Commons to make trouble over alleged softness towards the
Papists, maladministration in Ireland, and incompetence
among the King's English ministers in the conduct of the
war.[134]

The last charge, by far the easiest to justify, drove
Arlington, in particular, to work for Buckingham's downfall,
and as head of the secret service he was in the best position
to do it. He made the Duke's vociferous insistence that the
seamen must be paid (though Buckingham did not specify
where the money was to come from except the Privy Purse)
the ground of an accusation of inciting mutiny.[135]

But he went deeper than that. He set his agents to work
and produced evidence of Buckingham's leniency to religious
nonconformists (*ipso facto* to political levelers) in his lord-
lieutenancy of the West Riding of Yorkshire.[136] Then the
spies scored a coup by unearthing an astrologer at Tower
Hill with whom the Duke had had apparently intimate deal-

ings. When the seer was arrested and interrogated by Arlington in the Tower, papers were found showing that he had told Buckingham's fortune and hinted that he might eventually be king. Meanwhile the astrologer was addressing him (in letters that had been impounded) as Prince, and the darling of the people, whose stars still promised great things.

Most damaging of all, a confession was obtained substantiating certain written evidence that Buckingham had instructed the astrologer to cast the horoscope of the King. This could be—and promptly was—construed as "compassing or imagining the King's death."[137] Charles dabbled with astrology himself, though he may not have believed this accusation of treachery. But he found it convenient to act upon it. He dismissed Buckingham from his court post of Gentleman of the Bedchamber, his "cabinet" office as a Privy Councilor, and his active administrative duties as Lord Lieutenant of the West Riding. He then had him publicly proclaimed a traitor to be arrested and sent to the Tower.

Buckingham, who rather enjoyed the experience and was in no real fear for his life, simply disguised himself and lived quietly for three months in and around the City of London—being taken up by the watch on two or three occasions for haunting the streets too late at night for a workingman, but not identified. Though it had been his wife, Mary Fairfax, who decoyed and deceived the King's sergeant while Buckingham first made good his escape, characteristically, he abandoned her. He used part of his vacation cultivating a historic adultery which he had already begun with the Countess of Shrewsbury. She was the young Anna Maria Brudenell, of the erratic family of the Earl of Cardigan. She had already defied her husband to indulge in a dangerous liaison with the libertine, Harry Killigrew. But Killigrew had been renounced, injured by the self-inflicted wound of strongly recommending her to George Buck-ingham.

A fortnight after the Dutch raid on the Medway the Duke became bored with seclusion and dined ostentatiously at the Sun Tavern in the Strand. He found, as he expected, that public opinion was strongly behind him as a consistent, self-appointed scourge of the administration. Accordingly, he wrote to the King saying that he intended to give himself up, and at dinner at the Sun next day sent a message to the lieutenant of the Tower that he would report in as soon as he had dined satisfactorily.

He could not have come out at a better time. Politically he had the country behind him, as he wittily and caustically acknowledged in the face of the King: Arlington was conducting his prosecution before the King in Council, and mentioned as one of the charges that Buckingham had conspired to obtain the favor of the people in a manner unbecoming to a privy councilor. "A person has only to be committed to prison by my Lord Chancellor or my Lord Arlington," the Duke retorted, "and there is little doubt of his becoming popular."[138]

Buckingham's great strength—which he skillfully revealed but did not overplay in his defense—was that the flow of protest which he had energetically started pumping a year ago was now flooding where he had not wilfully directed it, at the steps of the throne. Popular anger was beating not only against the King's administration but also against the persons of the Monarch himself and of his favorites.

Already the gossip was being retailed—there is no real evidence that it is more than a canard—that following the news of the Medway disaster the King "was very cheerful that night at supper with his mistress,"[139] or, even more circumstantially, "the King did sup with my Lady Castlemaine at the Duchess of Monmouth's, and there were all mad of hunting a poor moth."[140]

Frequently the calamity was compared to the destruction of Rome by burning while Nero fiddled, or otherwise passed the time:

> As Nero once with harp in hand survey'd
> His flaming Rome and as that burn'd he played,
> So our great Prince, when the Dutch fleet arriv'd,
> Saw his ships burn'd, and as they burn'd he swiv'd.
> So kind he was in our extremest need,
> He would those flames extinguish with his seed.[141]

It was while the capital was in such a mood of revolt that Lady Castlemaine chose to come out strongly, tactlessly and blatantly on behalf of Buckingham, and therefore in opposition to Arlington and by implication in condemnation of her own set.

In private she urged Charles to release the Duke and restore him to his offices. In public she hectored him to the same end. It was the one approach that was certain to provoke the King's anger. "Jade" he called her, "meddling with things you have nothing to do with at all." And "Fool!" Lady Castlemaine called the King. "If you were not a fool," she added, furiously tossing petards among all her eavesdroppers, "you would not suffer your business to be carried on by fools that do not understand it, and have your best subjects and most able servants imprisoned."[142]

The quarrel had its usual sequel in a sulking withdrawal

from the Court by Lady Castlemaine. Yet, though she had pierced Charles in his most delicate susceptibility—that he was dominated by a woman—she won her argument. Within days Buckingham was free. Within weeks he had regained all his official positions. This last was a restoration which no practical intriguer of the day believed so soon possible. It was only brought about by a triple alliance between Castlemaine, Buckingham and Arlington, temporarily sinking all their differences in order to destroy the man who had obstructed them for so many years: Lord High Chancellor Clarendon.

But, so disordered were Barbara's affairs at this time, she could not concentrate single-mindedly on this great, culminating aim. Her personal life was in wild disarray, and she was driven to the most termagant behavior towards the King in respect of her own dishonorable pregnancy, while at the same time she urged on him extreme antiparliamentary and dictatorial political doctrines, and still battered at her main theme of the dismissal of Clarendon.

She had succeeded in a liaison with Harry Jermyn. The sexual attraction of this courtier was legendary but arcane. The features normally visible in his big-headed, short-legged physique were singularly unprepossessing but, according to retiring-room gossip, they were more than compensated by his private stature. It was said that Jermyn had contrived to let Castlemaine glimpse these charms by allowing himself to be discovered, apparently asleep, somewhat negligently draped after a bath.[143] (It was also reported that, as is sometimes the case, this noble prospect was a whited sepulchre.) However, the intrigue was consummated. But it did not wholly inhibit the affairs which both partners were conducting on the side.

Lady Castlemaine had a fancy for one of her running foot-men, a jogging lackey who padded and sweated alongside her coach, rippling brawny thighs that were a piquant contrast to Jermyn's.* In addition she had to allow the King the exercise of his normal *droit de seigneur*, though on one occasion the incautious Jermyn had to dive for an ignomin-ious vigil under her bed when Charles decided on an unheralded *divertissement*.[144]

Harry Jermyn, on his side, was more delicately infatuated with Mary Bagot, Countess of Falmouth, Charles Berkeley's young widow who—to complete the full court dossier on her past—had, in the days of her innocence, been pursued by the predatory Miss Hobart, a maid of honor with lesbian tend-encies: but Mary, who "blushed at everything but never did anything to raise a blush herself,"[145] was rescued by Charles Berkeley and he secretly married her. Later she became less grudging and loyally surrendered to the King.

By July, 1667, the Court knew two things for certain: Harry Jermyn wanted to marry Mary Falmouth, and Barbara Castlemaine was pregnant. Barbara deeply resented Jer-myn's wish to marry, but could not act too openly because she wanted the King to acknowledge her unborn child. The King, who had his usual excellent sources of information, uneasily tolerated the recognition of Barbara's first five chil-dren but was more than hesitant over accepting the sixth. These paternity decisions were always difficult for, as a sat-irist made the King say:

> Alas! I never got one brat alone,
> My bitches are by ev'ry fop well known,
> And I still willing all their whelps to own.[146]

*For the blunt public discussion of this coupling, see page 172.

But on this occasion Charles was unwilling to own the whelp. Barbara went into action to hector the King on this issue. "God damn me, but you shall own it," she told him.[147] "I will have it christened in the Chapel at Whitehall and owned as yours, as other Kings have done. Either that or I will bring it into Whitehall Gallery and dash its brains out before your face."[148] "I did not get this child," said the King. "Whoever did get it, you shall own it," she told him,[149] and swept out of the palace to the house of a new confidant, Anne Montagu, wife of Sir Daniel Harvey.

Charles froze, alone in his humiliation. And the town sifted the news, parceled it neatly and distributed it with malice: "The King is mad at her entertaining Jermyn, and she is mad at Jermyn's going to marry from her; so they are all mad, and thus the nation is governed."[150]

After some days Lady Castlemaine sent to the King and told him that if he wanted to see her he must come to Sir Daniel Harvey's house. Obsequiously, Charles attended her. The Court believed—and repeated—that at this reconciliation, "she made him ask her forgiveness upon his knees, and promise to offend her no more so; and that indeed, she did threaten to bring all his bastards to his closet-door, and hath nearly hectored him out of his wits."[151] Certainly she continued at Harvey's house for some time and the King dutifully visited her, staying regularly twice a week.

This quarrel occurred at the height of a political crisis which might have been expected to claim all the King's attention. Instead, he had not only to address himself to his personal difficulties parallel with his constitutional problems, but he realized that his political insecurity was exacerbated by his lady love. The teeming Lady Castlemaine found time and energy to give tongue on the internal situation and to be heard doing so. "How imperious this woman is!" sighed Pepys, "and hectors the King to whatever she will."[152]

"You must rule by an army or all will be lost," she told the King[153] when the revelation of deep popular support for Buckingham convinced him that he must recall Parliament and risk all the accompanying petitions, "complaining of the wrongs they have received from the Court and courtiers."[154] This advice was the most explosive counsel that could be audibly offered at a time when the nation's supreme fear was a standing army making the King independent of Parliament: on the one day allowed it in summer session the Commons raised, on the adjournment, the grievance of "the new-raised standing army."[155]

When the town repeated that Lady Castlemaine had pronounced for rule through an army no one paused to reflect whether she had any weight as a counselor: the public concern was that she was saying these things. Her advice was reiterated by Bab May, the rejected member of Parliament. He told the King to crush the English gentlemen, for those who lived at court were the men who needed the revenue. "£500 a year is enough for a country gentleman to drink ale, eat beef, and to stink with," he said gaily:[156] words wryly received when they were reported to the country gentlemen who had left their shires to attend the House of Commons, had been summarily dismissed, and had stayed in London to compare their disaffection. But what could be discounted as mere wild talk when it came from Baptist May and Lady Castlemaine had much more serious implications when the news sped round that Clarendon was also for an army: "Nothing is more sure than that the King, and the Duke of York, and the Chancellor are desirous of labouring all they can to get an army, whatever the King says to Parliament; they are at last resolved to stand and fall all three together."[157]

It was certainly not true of the Chancellor. But the Commons believed it, and also believed that it was Clarendon who had advised the King to dismiss them as soon as they met in July. There was plain talk of a plan to impeach him when Parliament met in October.

Charles saw that the swiftest way to deflate the tumescent situation was to dismiss Clarendon and have him ready trussed up to be thrown to the wolves of the Commons before Parliament reassembled. And this plan was a convenience to many people. The King, the mistress, the minister and the mimic were all of one mind. Charles, therefore, asked the Duke of York to request his father-in-law to surrender the Great Seal of his office.

Clarendon had been prepared for this since the death of Southampton, which he saw as "a fatal breach into the Chancellor's fortune, with a gap wide enough to let in all that ruin which soon after was poured upon him."[158] But he would not immediately resign, and requested an interview with the King. He had lately moved from Berkshire House—St James's, which he had rented after the Fire of London—to take tardy possession of Clarendon House in Piccadilly, and he pleaded his gout to suggest that the King should visit him there. But Charles said he was going to take the Seal from him, it would be compromising to prise it out at this controversial new palazzo, and he would see Clarendon in the Chancellor's Whitehall office.

At this meeting Clarendon still argued doggedly. After

two hours he tactlessly referred to Lady Castlemaine's part in this cashiering "with some reflections and cautions which he might more advisedly have omitted."[159] The King was offended and left the room, and the Chancellor had to go home. As he passed Lady Castlemaine's lodgings he saw her, with Lord Arlington and Bab May, "looking together out of her open window with great gaiety and triumph, which all people observed."[160] The Lady was, in fact, in her smock, for though it was noon when the Chancellor left she had been in bed, and the men had called her out to enjoy the sight of the old man's departure.[161]

Lady Castlemaine's first practical and acquisitive move was to get Arlington to inform the Master of the Jewel House that the 5,600 ounces of silver that the King had lent her was now to be registered as an outright gift.[162]

Four days after the final interview the King officially sent for the Great Seal. When it was brought to Charles in his Closet, Bab May knelt to kiss the Monarch's hand. "Sir, you are now King," he said, "which you have never been before."[163] It was true enough. Charles had cut out from the machinery of state the operation of a heavy flywheel, sacrificing the administrative smoothness given by its forward momentum in order to overcome the inertia with which it resisted delicate personal adjustment. Henceforth, the cogs of government were to bite deeply and directly. The antagonism between Crown and Parliament, Court and People, arbitrary rule (however shrewd and tolerant the governor) and committee decision (however selfish and corrupt the members) was posed much more plainly.

For three months after his dismissal Clarendon endured a daily diminution of his hopes. By his own self-analysis, he was guilty of being "too proud of a good conscience. He knew his own innocence and had no kind of apprehension of being publicly charged with any crime."[164] He looked forward to the reassembly of Parliament so that he could energetically defend himself. But, even though he was out of office, the rancor of the Commons was increasingly manipulated against him, and he was finally impeached for high treason on seventeen charges. The first was that Clarendon had advised the King to dissolve Parliament and govern by a standing army, a charge which the King had plainly denied, and broadcast his denial, a few days previously. Clarendon concluded that amid the current outcry for the atoning blood of sacrifice he would be condemned, if not to death at least to long imprisonment, which he could not bear. He realized that the King wanted no more of him.

He had a curious insistence that his downfall was caused by his crossing the King's woman, Lady Castlemaine, and by supposedly crossing the King over his not-impossible-she, Frances Stuart. He had been told that the King believed "that the Chancellor had a principal hand in the marriage of the Duke of Richmond, with which His Majesty was offended in the highest degree."[165] He wrote one appealing letter to the King, mainly a pathetically abject declaration that he had nothing to do with that affair. The King burned it in the flame of the candle on his desk.

Clarendon prepared to fly the country. Crippled by his gout, he was pushed out in a wheelchair to take one last look at the vista of Clarendon House, which he had loved though he had occupied it so shortly, and which had ostentatiously corrupted his reputation from its foundation.*

*Clarendon told his son when he left England that, if his friends would excuse the vanity and folly of the great house, he would answer for any other charges that could be leveled against him. Clarendon House was eventually sold to the young Duke of Albemarle for £25,000, half its cost price.[166]

He sat in the garden amid the replacements for the trees which the mob had heaved out from the avenues of "Dunkirk House" a few months before, and watched his men set up the gates of the grounds facing to the north—and Tyburn.[167] Then he made a furtive journey to Erith and escaped by ship to France. Parliament promptly outlawed him and he died in exile.

As Clarendon wrote again and again, he believed his dismissal was effected by "The Lady and her party."[168] Historians have depreciated Lady Castlemaine's influence in the affair. The extinction of Clarendon was primarily what the King blindly desired. It suited Arlington, who could fob off his many diplomatic, administrative and military failures of the Dutch war and the peace which had now concluded it. It gratified Buckingham, whose personal and political ambition was recharged by the gift of all his old offices of state and by his overwhelming popularity in the Parliament. It pleased the Cavaliers in the Commons who had a justifiable class resentment against the moderation and comparative impartiality of Clarendon's constructive resettlement, and it delighted the mob who were tossed a scapegoat they had always wanted.

A statesman of Clarendon's stature must have seen the width of the interest in his defeat, and, if he was convinced, ought to have acknowledged it in the history he wrote as his own memorial. Why did he insist so exclusively on giving the preeminence to "the power of the Great Lady with the conjunction of his known enemies"? He was there. He knew. Perhaps the positive thrust of Barbara Castlemaine was greater than modern analysts consider.

Certainly the deposition fulfilled personal and emotional desires which had long been her principal prayers. From the moment she came to court the Chancellor had forbidden his wife to call on her—and the Countess had died only a few weeks before her husband's dismissal. He had stood in her path since the time of the bedchamber crisis, blocking, impeding, refusing to recognize the orders which concerned her. "I hope to see his head on a stake among the regicides on Westminster Hall," she shouted in the Queen's Chamber when she learned he had stopped a particular grant,[169] and if Clarendon had not fled she might well have had that satisfaction. Just before the end he stopped a grant of £2,000 a year payable to her nominee, Viscount Grandison. When the King gave Barbara the grant of a place in the ministry, which had its money value to her, Clarendon stopped it, saying, "This woman will sell everything shortly." But she bypassed his stop and told him, "I have disposed of that place, and do not doubt in a little time to dispose of yours."[170] That threat she had fulfilled.

Was the power of the "Great Lady" greater than has been later estimated? Did it approach the value given it by the clearly resentful but—if only because his histories display so many other resentments—evidently not pathologically obsessed ex-Chancellor, who at the balanced age of fifty-eight began to compose his exhaustive autobiography? Clarendon was not alone in ascribing the conclusive *push* (not the whole impetus) to Lady Castlemaine as the leader of a coalition of his enemies. Pepys reported as the current belief: "This business of my Lord Chancellor's was certainly designed in my Lady Castlemaine's chamber."[171] And the Archbishop of Canterbury, as soon as the King informed him in his political capacity of the decision to remove Clarendon, made a rejoinder whose significance has been underappreciated. Instead of making any comment relevant to the future administration of the country, he kept silent. When the King pressed him for an opinion the Archbishop only said: "Sir, I wish you would put away this woman that you keep."[172]* It was an astonishing tribute to the influence of Lady Castlemaine.

Whatever her power, the moulders of the nation's policies decided it must end. The combination in one person of restless political intrigue and unconcealed amorality was offensive.

Parliament felt no obligation to her for the removal of Clarendon. Buckingham stayed on good terms with her for a short time while she used her influence to extract him from his worst disgrace yet, then ungratefully deserted her and renewed an enmity which was to be outstanding in its virulence against her. The King, sardonically asked by his own licensed jester whether he approved of being henpecked by his mistress,[175] resolved to pay her off and have the board cleared of both Clarendon and Castlemaine before Parliament reassembled—if only he could get her to agree to the terms of her pension.[176]

But Lady Castlemaine fought back. Within a fortnight of the talk of a pension she was said to be "as high as ever she was" with Charles, even though "the King is as weary of her as is possible, and would give anything to remove her, but he is so weak in his passion that he dare not do it."[177]

*It is unconvincing to suggest that this was an irrepressible moral judgment: in the first place because of the political ambience of the confrontation—the Archbishop was concerned with political and judicial appointments and was at that time a member of the King's cabal or cabinet;[173] in the second place because the Archbishop (he was Gilbert Sheldon who endowed the Sheldonian Theatre at Oxford) was reputed to be "as very a wencher as can be" and was at that time the subject of court gossip which the King could be presumed to be well aware of that he was quarreling with Sir Charles Sedley for stealing and seducing one of his wenches away from him. He might, of course, have been attacking the King as the best form of defense.[174]

The unborn child over whom part of the passion had raged was, either before or after birth, extinguished from history and no further mention of it occurs in any annals.

For many years yet the King was to be saddled and fascinated with her dominant personality. The nation was to continue to observe its sovereign "only governed by his lust, and women, and rogues about him."[178] A foreign king was to bribe her for what she could whisper in the closet; and another chief minister was to fall through her intrigue.

It was not all plain sailing, for she had to plot a devious course as the winds of royal favor filled and dropped. There were rivals in the King's bed, some of them shrewdly scheming but others blessedly unconcerned with politics—and these the nation warmed to.

Most of his subjects were prepared to indulge King Charles II in his conviction that "he was no atheist but he could not think God would make a man miserable for taking a little pleasure out of the way."[179] All that they required was that the providers of his pleasure did not try to mix it with business. When Nell Gwyn was the King's delight, a ballad-cobbler knocked up a rough and tumbling rhyme:

*Hard by Pall Mall lives a wench call'd Nell.*
  *King Charles the Second he kept her.*
*She hath got a trick to handle his prick*
  *But never lays hands on his sceptre.*
*All matters of state from her soul she does hate,*
  *And leave to the politic bitches.*
*The whore's in the right, for 'tis her delight*
  *To be scratching just where it itches.*[180]

As far as the nation was concerned, pretty Nell had a trick which they longed for the politic Barbara to learn.

## 5 ⊅ *Venereal pleasures, accompanied with looseness, debauchery and prophaneness, are not such heinous crimes and crying sins, but rather they do mortify the flesh*

At the appropriate time after the Restoration of Charles II, the Monarch and the nation endured their seven years itch. For three years, following the autumn of 1667, a condition of turbulence overwhelmed Whitehall, both as the center of the political direction of the country and as the world's unsurpassed court of love. It was not a state of chaos. There was an undisputed governor of the situation, and he was the King.

It was no coincidence that the period began with the fall of Clarendon and the deliberate decision by Charles to attempt the control of this recalcitrant kingdom on his own. Nor was it fortuitous that in the absence of Clarendon the Court progressed into its wildest excesses of experimental morality. His gout, his principles and his singular lack of levity all barred the Chancellor from the role of "mere court butterfly, that flutters in the pageant of a monarch." But he had been in the strictest sense a courtier, who merely by his presence and his friends affected the tone of the palace as long as he was in power.

Politically, Charles moved forward with tentative and pragmatic gait as he grappled with the complex new problems of the man-management of privately prosperous men running a bankrupt* administration: but the direction *was* forward. He was moving towards a well-considered objective: an alliance with Louis XIV of France—an understanding between men, blood cousins, members of the rare fraternity of kings—which was motivated (whatever cousin Louis' ambitions) solely by Charles's considerations of the imperial commercial prosperity of an England governed as arbitrarily as possible by shrewd Charles Stuart.

In personal affairs Charles was far less resolute because, like many men with the seven years itch, he knew what he was trying to escape from but was not clear on what he wanted in replacement.

An amorist in search of peace, he had now been thrust into a state of acute disturbance by the behavior of Barbara Castlemaine. The longing to cut bowstrings and finish with her was intense. Yet she maintained over him an extraordinary fascination—intermittently phallic, much more steadily emotional.

If ever a man was hagridden it was he. Five years previously he had declared: "I have undone this lady and ruined her reputation, and I am obliged in conscience and

---

*For the first half of the reign of Charles II the normal peacetime cost of the administration of England was £1,200,000 a year, and Parliament kept the King about £400,000 a year short of this sum. During the second half of his reign the country's increasing prosperity raised the King's undisputed revenue from Customs and Excise and other sources to a level where he had no financial dependence on Parliament.

honour to repair her to the utmost of my power." It could be maintained that, in the years between, Lady Castlemaine's conduct had absolved him from this obligation. But during that time she had developed an outstanding rapacity which continually presumed upon his conscience and honor.

Moreover, Charles had acknowledged five of Barbara's children as of his begetting.* He was not only fond of them but extremely considerate their station in life. Like many a discarded wife (the relationship between Charles and Barbara is much more characteristic of the marital state than the connection between Charles and Catherine), Lady Castlemaine continually used these children as a powerful lever to extract financial benefits from the King.

While Frances Stuart had been in the Court Charles had had a fixed star by which to orientate himself. The emotions she had inspired constituted more of frustration than idealism, but the yearning had been there: she had been a not-impossible future queen, and if Catherine had died Frances would have been the first woman since Lady Anne Boleyn and the last consort before Prince Philip Mountbatten whom a sovereign of England married out of unprompted

---

*Strictly, he had then owned only four. As in other royal houses, acknowledgement of the King's bastards was at first informal, by private acquiescence in the mother's claim of his paternity, and later formal, by the grant of noble rank. Charles II hesitated longest over the acknowledgement of Henry Palmer, later Henry Fitzroy, Barbara's second son, born on September 20, 1663, who during his infancy was speculatively assigned to Charles Berkeley, Earl of Falmouth. But Charles II finally acknowledged him, created him Earl of Euston and later Duke of Grafton, and rejoiced in his achievement as the youngster showed himself the most accomplished and best loved of all his sons, including the Duke of Monmouth. See pages 217 and 222. In general Barbara's children by Charles were of low intelligence and were popularly referred to as "the blockheads."

love: as it was, the gap of unfulfilled ardor stretched across four centuries.*

But Frances Stuart had accepted the Duke of Richmond as the best of the gentlemen who would have her in honor, in order to escape the compulsion of the King. The impact of this rejection was cataclysmic on Charles's emotions.

He began a series of socially outrageous liaisons, intermittently spiced with irresistible returns to the superior erotic expertise of Lady Castlemaine—and every regression was used by the lady to reforge broken links in the chain of obligation which bound him. Consequently there was no swift separation, and for a number of years he conducted these disordered amours in the turbulence of his slow disengagement from Barbara.

Eventually, free at last from emotional subservience to her, though never from the material demands she made on him, Charles was ready to devote himself to a new woman whom he elevated to the position of *maîtresse en titre*—the Duchess of Portsmouth, baby-faced as Frances Stuart had been baby-minded.

It was characteristic of this period of political opacity and emotional turmoil that, while Arlington toiled assiduously but ineffectively as secretary of state, the "chief minister," the only man allowed even to approach the overriding position once held by Clarendon, was that *opéra bouffe* figure, the Duke of Buckingham. That this ambassador peculiar and plenipotentiary extraordinary could be put up, even as a dupe, to represent the intentions of the Crown of England is a measure both of Charles's dearth of "statesmen" and his contempt for them.

*Catherine's natural death was the only solution. Charles said he could more easily poison her than divorce her. See page 196.

George Villiers had capitalized on, and even anticipated, his reinstatement in the King's favor with a cynical disregard of caution. A week after his release from the Tower he publicized his liaison with the Countess of Shrewsbury in a notable fracas inside a London theatre.

He had originally seduced the Countess on the earnest recommendation of his then crony, Harry Killigrew, who was already her lover and was in the habit of expatiating on her charms in the utmost detail over dinner. When Anna Maria Shrewsbury accepted Buckingham into her bed she expelled Killigrew from it, which surprised and offended him because he had intended that George Villiers should only share her favors with him.

Accordingly, Killigrew, whose coarseness of speech shocked even his contemporaries, began a repeated public recital of the erotic eccentricities of his former mistress, no longer praising them but obscenely condemning them.

Seeing Buckingham at the Duke's Playhouse almost immediately after his release from imprisonment, he taunted him openly from the next box, and in the pauses, when he allowed the actors to speak, indulged himself in pulling vulgar faces at him.

Buckingham told Killigrew to pull himself together. Killigrew lurched out of his box to ask a friend to carry an immediate challenge to the Duke—a decision he may have thought safe enough since Buckingham had a certain reputation for "mistaking" the venue of the duels he accepted and turning up on the wrong side of the river.[1]

But Killigrew's friend refused to risk the King's displeasure by delivering a challenge in a theatre. Killigrew returned to his box and hit Buckingham twice over the head with his sword, still sheathed in the scabbard, and then hooked off the Duke's periwig.

Buckingham drew his sword and leapt out of his box and, wigless and slashing wildly with his weapon, chased Killigrew through the ring of boxes and down over the benches. Thoroughly frightened, Killigrew fell down and begged for mercy, gasping, "Good Your Grace, spare my life!" Buckingham contented himself with kicking Killigrew hard, returned to his box, put on his wig, and graciously allowed the actors to get on with the play.

The King committed Killigrew to the Tower for this degrading brawl, but the courtier sent in a medical certificate claiming that he was badly injured in the head, and obtained leave to serve his confinement in his own lodgings.[2]

Soon, harassed by creditors, he borrowed £30 and fled to France, where he obtained a post at the court of Henrietta Maria, Charles's mother, who had always favored him.[*]

Within a short time he was charged with having drugged a mother and daughter and raped the daughter, and was saved from the Paris gallows only by the intervention of the Queen Mother and the Duchess of Orleans.

Buckingham was reinstated in his offices. He so blatantly continued his association with Anna Maria that the Earl of Shrewsbury himself challenged him. The duel was fought at Barn Elms with three men a side. All the combatants were injured. One of Buckingham's seconds was killed outright. The Earl of Shrewsbury, run through the body, lingered for seven weeks and died.

Lady Shrewsbury was said to have witnessed the affray, disguised as a page and holding her lover's horse, and after-

---

[*]A somewhat apprehensive Charles wrote to his sister regarding Killigrew: "I am glad the poor wretch has got a means of subsistence; but I have one caution of him, that you believe not one word he says of us here, for he is a most notorious liar and does not want wit to set forth his stories pleasantly enough.[3]

wards Buckingham took her to bed wearing his bloody shirt as a trophy.[4]

The killing in such circumstances of the hereditary premier earl of England by the King's intimate companion was a scandal of some magnitude even by the standards of the period.

Pepys reflected: "This will make the world think the King hath good councillors about him when the Duke of Buckingham, the greatest man about him, is a fellow of no more sobriety than to fight about a mistress."[5]

But by a rare conjunction, Lady Castlemaine was then both highly influential with the King and still well-disposed towards her cousin George, and she successfully suppressed any official condemnation of the ugly affair.[6]

Buckingham, quite unperturbed by any backlash from the public, carried off the Countess he had widowed to his own home.

His wife protested that she could not live with the Countess under the same roof. "So I thought, Madam," said the Duke of Buckingham icily, "and have therefore ordered your coach to convey you to your father's."

Buckingham promptly got his chaplain to "marry" him to his mistress. When Killigrew came back from France and again boasted openly of having beaten Buckingham in the race to debauch her it was Anna Maria who this time took the initiative. She set her own servants to ambush Killigrew's coach, while she watched the attack from her own carriage.

Killigrew took nine sword thrusts in his body yet still lived—prudently abandoning his campaign against Lady

Shrewsbury but graduating to another banishment for insulting Nell Gwyn.

Although the King knew who had instigated the attack, he took no action against the Countess of Shrewsbury, who lived flagrantly with Buckingham in his love nest at Cliveden and contemptuously referred to his wife as the "Dowager Duchess."

Anna bore George Villiers a son—he had no child by his wife—for whom he persuaded King Charles to stand as godfather, and illegally passed over to the boy his subsidiary title. The child died in infancy, but Buckingham manipulated such influence that the baby was buried among the kings in Westminster Abbey in the style of Earl of Coventry.[7]

A man with such astonishing capacity as Buckingham's to ride roughshod over public conceptions of morality might be thought to have little need of the intervention of Barbara Castlemaine to assure his favor with the King. If Buckingham seriously relied on his cousin to ease his position at the Court and in the Council* he was exercising an effrontery which must have given keen secret delight to the King as well as himself.

For George was determined to oust Barbara from all hold on Charles, and had already begun intrigues to replace her. He had not wholly abandoned his plan to install Frances Stuart as her substitute, and had hopes soon after the fall of

*The King's Privy Council could be more easily managed than Parliament, which, with all its privileged membership, still represented some aspects of public opinion. The Duke was summoned to the bar of the House of Lords for scandalously living with the Countess of Shrewsbury, having killed her husband and expelled his own wife. They eventually separated and the Countess married again in 1676.

Clarendon that she might return to the Court and receive Charles's forgiveness for her marriage.

The mere prospect of this so upset Barbara that she took to her bed, "ill more in mind than body."[8] The situation was temporarily saved for her when Frances caught smallpox and, Lady Castlemaine was delighted to hear, was so scarred in her face that she was likely to lose all her beauty.[9]

In the meantime Buckingham had entered his second string in the contest for the King's affection. These were the actresses Moll Davis and Nell Gwyn and an otherwise obscure sexual athlete named Jane Roberts.[10] Moll Davis, reputed to be the illegitimate daughter of one of the family of the Howards, Earls of Berkshire, was not a great dramatic actress: she danced a pleasing jig and sang with some pathos. Nell Gwyn—whose father died in Oxford prison and whose mother floated away drowned drunk in a ditch at Westminster[11]—was then eighteen and had been a protégée of Lady Castlemaine before becoming the mistress of the actor, Charles Hart, and the poet-rake, Sir Charles Sedley: when she came to the King she consequently called him her ·Charles the Third. Jane Roberts was a clergyman's daughter whose early training instilled in her a masochistic terror of .the hellfire awaiting her on account of the behavior she could not repress: a contemporary said of her, "It was hard to find one with limbs more brawny, conscience more supple, or principles more loose; all these extreme qualifications for a lady of pleasure."[12]

These three concubines were deliberately pandered to the King by Buckingham in order to supplant Barbara Castlemaine. The fact that, for the first time since his Restoration, Charles stepped outside the social circle from which he had previously drawn his mistresses, and yet unconcernedly introduced them to the Court, is an indication of the psychological revolution he was experiencing.

They were not generally welcomed. Moll Davis, naively showing off her £700 ring that the King had given her, and talking of the house in Suffolk Street which Charles had taken and furnished for her, was immediately summed up as an impertinent slut,[13] and Queen Catherine, normally so tolerant of her husband's "pretty little fools," stalked out of the theatre in the Palace when Moll came on to dance her jig.[14]

Barbara Castlemaine, though unguardedly permitting herself to be seen "melancholy and out of humour" when the brassy Miss Davis first came to Court, used the King's new exploration as a license to cover her own fascination for coarser lovers.

She indulged a fancy for Charles Hart, the leading actor of the King's Playhouse, a grandnephew of Shakespeare,* and the man who had originally debauched Nell Gwyn—"and by this means she is even with the King's love for Mistress Davis."[15]

Such a lover was a financial liability, but Lady Castlemaine willingly pressed gifts and an allowance on him. She was used to paying for her pleasures. Diminutive Harry Jermyn was a gentleman and a courtier, but his upkeep had been costly enough, prompted by the overpowering passion she had felt for him, which "bound her to the chariot wheels of one of the most ridiculous conquerors that ever was."[16]

It would be ingenuous to maintain that Lady Castlemaine began the liaison with Hart out of pique. An actor was then

*He was the eldest son of William Hart, eldest son of Shakespeare's sister Joan.

a person of a low social order, but her tastes had already strayed literally into the gutter: so much so that she compelled the man of her choice, the running footman to her coach, to share a bath with her—one of the very rare references to this phenomenon, (taken either alone or in company), among Restoration chronicles.

The satirist who recorded and no doubt embellished this episode cruelly exaggerated her age, which was only twenty-seven:

> Paint Castlemaine in colors that will hold
> (*Her*, not her picture, for she now grows old):
> She through her lackey's drawers, as he ran,
> Discern'd love's cause and a new flame began.
> Her wonted joys thenceforth and Court she shuns,
> And still within her mind the footman runs:
> His brazen calves, his brawny thighs (the face
> She slights), his feet shap'd for a smoother race.
> Poring within her glass she readjusts
> Her looks and oft-tri'd beauty now distrusts;
> Fears lest he scorn a woman once assay'd,
> And now first wish'd she e'er had been a maid.
> Great Love, how dost thou triumph and how reign,
> That to a groom could'st humble her disdain!
> Stripp'd to her skin, see how she stooping stands,
> Nor scorns to rub him down with those fair hands,
> And washing (lest the scent her crime disclose)
> His sweaty hooves, tickles him 'twixt the toes.
> But envious Fame, too soon, began to note
> More gold in's fob, more lace upon his coat,
> And he, unwary and of tongue too fleet,
> No longer could conceal his fortune sweet.
> Justly the rogue was whipp'd in porter's den,
> And Jermyn straight has leave to come again.[17]

If the muscular lackey was alternating in Lady Castlemaine's infatuation with the puny Jermyn he may well have sired the child whom Barbara demanded that the King should christen in Whitehall Chapel, with her "God damn me but you shall own it. Whoever did get it, you shall own it."

And knowing this, as Charles eventually knew most scandal, the King may have had more force than was immediately apparent in a suggestion he was said to have made to Barbara when he quarreled with her over Jermyn.[18] "Lie with Jacob Hall and get your money's worth back," he told her, "rather than squander your wealth on Harry Jermyn, and all for nothing. Better pass as the mistress of the first than the abject bond-slave of the second."

Jacob Hall was a rope dancer— then performing in a booth at Bartholomew Fair—of considerably lower social position even than Charles Hart. By a whim of the King's he had recently received such royal encouragement that he described himself as "sworn servant to His Majesty." Besides dancing and vaulting on the ropes his performance included— according to his showbill—a stage act with "variety of rare feats of activity and agility of body . . . as doing of somersets and flipflaps, flying over thirty rapiers and over several men's heads, and also flying through several hoops."[19]

Pepys got into conversation with him in a tavern and learned that he had fallen many times but never broken a limb. "He seems a mighty strong man," Pepys noted.[20]

The same thought had occurred to Lady Castlemaine. "His nimbleness and his strength greatly delighting his audience in public, it prompted a desire to see what he was like in private. He appeared to have quite a different physique and certainly very different legs from those of the favoured Jermyn. This acrobat by no means disappointed conjectures which had been ventured on this subject by

Lady Castlemaine—at least if one may believe the burden of innumerable street ballads, which did the dancer more honour than the Countess."[21]

In this wild year the "sworn servant" of the King and lover of the King's mistress capitalized on his prestige to build a booth at Charing Cross, not 200 yards from the palace, for the demonstration of his more recondite flip-flops.

An official ordered him to demolish it, and committed him to prison when he refused. But Lady Castlemaine had him released with a permit to complete the booth, and extended her patronage to his performance.[22]

For her it was a trifle. Her influence was felt in higher spheres than the fairground. She had her mother's uncle, Dr. Henry Glemham, "a drunken swearing rascal and a scandal to the Church,"[23] consecrated Bishop of St. Asaph.[24] For more involved family reasons she had already marked out Dr. Thomas Wood, the Dean of Lichfield and Coventry, for promotion to a bishopric, in which he was later disgraced.[25]

With another motive of what can only be hazarded as morbid or necrophiliac superstition she also had a remarkable encounter with the body of the dead Bishop Braybrooke.

This divine, Bishop of London from 1381 until his death in 1404, had been buried in St. Paul's Cathedral. After the Great Fire of London it was discovered that his mummified body, "all tough and dry like a spongified leather," had fallen out of its tomb into the chapel of St. Faith's in the crypt. For a time it became one of the sights of London. "A great man in his time and Lord Chancellor," philosophised Pepys.[26] "And now exposed to be handled and derided by some, though admired for its duration by others. Many people flocking to see it."

When the *réclame* had died down, Lady Castlemaine came to see the body for herself. It was unmarked except for two pickaxe wounds unintentionally inflicted by a laborer clearing the site after the fire. "Yet it later received a greater maim than these beforementioned," the antiquary Henry, Lord Coleraine, wrote with somewhat facetious severity, "by a female's defrauding (shall I say?) or deroding of the virile instrument, as I was told by Thomas Boys, Keeper of the Chapter House, then present."

According to Lord Coleraine's account, Lady Castlemaine was accompanied to the ruined cathedral by a gentleman and two or three gentlewomen, but she told the keeper that she wished to be left alone with the body. He therefore retired with her attendants, noticing as he went, "Her Ladyship addressing herself towards the carcass with many crossings and great tokens of superstition."

Later she rejoined her gentlewomen "with much satisfaction," gave the keeper a gratuity and left. Thomas Boys "returned to shut up the carcass but unexpectedly found it served like a Turkish eunuch and dismembered of as much of the privity as the lady could get into her mouth to bite (for want of a circumcising penknife to cut.)"

Lord Coleraine could not deny himself a topical pleasantry. "Though some ladies of late have got Bishopricks for others," he commented, "yet I have not heard of any but this that got one for herself."[27]

Coleraine still called Barbara a lady. There were some chroniclers, including Antony à Wood, whose minds exploded and whose pens shook so virulently when they wrote her name that they had afterwards to cross out their descriptions of her.

The diarist John Evelyn, unable to record his thoughts, left a blank. At a great celebration at court on Shrove Tuesday, 1668, he saw Lady Castlemaine appear in Corneille's *Horace* acted in translation by amateurs, with a sumptuous masque danced between each act. "The excessive gallantry [display of jewels] of the ladies was infinite," he wrote. "Those especially on that . . . . Castlemaine esteemed at 40,000 pounds and more and far outshining the Queen."[28] Forty thousand pounds was no more than Lady Castlemaine could then expect to win from three lucky nights at cards,[29] but the jewels she wore on that occasion were estimated by another onlooker at worth £200,000.[30] A courtier took a mental note of the occasion and soon was able to air his resentment publicly.

On the Monday and Tuesday after Easter the London apprentices, combining their holiday mood with some useful moral fervor, sacked a number of brothels. This was a fairly regular caper, usually performed on Shrove Tuesday to aid Lenten penance. But it created unusual apprehension in the Court this year—possibly because the apprentices immediately said they had been too easily contented with pulling down the little brothels: "Why did we not go and pull down the great one in Whitehall?"[31]

The King's Guards were beaten out by drum and trumpet to put down the disturbance "and all to their colours, and to horse, as if the French were coming into the Town."[32] A court wit seized the opportunity to write and have printed and distributed by the hundred a mock petition from the oppressed prostitutes of London appealing for protection to the nation's principal punk, Lady Castlemaine.

It was headed, "The Poor Whores' Petition," and it was addressed: "To the most splendid, illustrious, serene and eminent Lady of Pleasure, the Countess of Castlemaine: the Humble Petition of the undone company of poor distressed whores, bawds, pimps and pandars humbly showeth:

"That Your Petitioners having been for a long time connived at and countenanced in the practice of our venereal pleasures (a trade wherein Your Ladyship hath great experience, and for your diligence therein have arrived to high and eminent advancement for these late years). But now we, through the rage and malice of a company of London apprentices and other malicious and very bad persons, being mechanic, rude and ill-bred boys, have sustained the loss of our habitations, trades and employments; And many of us that have had foul play in the Court and sports of Venus, being full of ulcers but were in a hopeful way of recovery, have our cures retarded through this barbarous and un-Venus-like usage, and all of us exposed to very hard shifts, being made uncapable of giving that entertainment as the honour and dignity of such persons as frequented our houses doth call for, as Your Ladyship by your own practice hath experimented the knowledge of . . ."

The petition went on, calling Lady Castlemaine a whore by implication in every other line, and pleading for her protection in return for a self-imposed tax agreed to by the prostitutes for their patroness. It was purportedly signed by "Us, Madam Cresswell and Damaris Page,* in the behalf of our sisters and fellow-sufferers (in this day of our calamity)

---

*Madam Cresswell was a famous brothelkeeper who on the twenty-second of November, 1681, was "convicted after above thirty years practice of bawdry, some of her does most unkindly testifying against her."[33] Damaris Page was the great bawd of the seamen, and the Duke of York flippantly complained that by the sacking of her brothels he had lost two tenants who paid him £15 a year for their wine licenses.[34]

in Dog & Bitch Yard, Lukeners Lane, Saffron Hill, Moor-fields, Chiswell Street, Rosemary Lane, Nightingale Lane, Ratcliffe Highway, Well Close, Church Lane, East Smith-field etc. this present 25th day of March 1668."[35]

Lady Castlemaine was reported by Pepys "horribly vexed" at the libel which was "not very witty but devilish severe against her and the King; and I wonder how it durst be printed and spread abroad, which shows that the times are loose, and come to a great disregard of the King or Court or Government."[36]

But the lampoonery did not stop there. A few weeks later a mock reply from Barbara Castlemaine to the poor whores was circulating throughout London.

It was a large broadsheet entitled, "The Gracious Answer of the most illustrious Lady of Pleasure, the Countess of Castlem ... to the Poor Whore's Petition," and it was dated, "Given at our Closet in King Street Westminster, Die Veneris April 24, 1668."

It greeted and thanked the "Right trusty and well-beloved Madam Cresswell and Damaris Page, with the rest of the suffering sisterhood" and acknowledged the titles of honor granted her in the original petition, "which are but our due, for on Shrove Tuesday last splendidly did we appear upon the theatre at W. H. [Whitehall] being to amazement won-derfully decked with jewels and diamonds which the (abhorred and to be undone) subjects of this Kingdom have paid for.

"We have been also serene and illustrious ever since the day that Mars was so instrumental to restore our goddess Venus to her temple and worship; where by special grant we quickly became a famous lady: and as a reward of our devo-tion soon created Right Honourable the Countess of Cas-

tlemaine. And as a further addition to our illustrious seren-
ity, according to the ancient rules and laudable customs of
our Order, we have *cum privilegio* always (without our husband) satisfied ourself with the delights of Venus; and in
our husband's absence have had a numerous offspring (who
are bountifully and nobly provided for). Which practice
hath episcopal allowance also, according to the principles of
Seer Sheldon*: 'If women have not children by their own
husbands they are bound (to prevent their damnation) to
try by using the means with other men' . . . ."

The Countess was then made to explain that she had left
the Church of England for the Church of Rome, where
"Venereal pleasures, accompanied with looseness, debauchery and prophaneness, are not such heinous crimes and crying sins, but rather they do mortify the flesh."[37]

"The Poor Whores' Petition" and "The Gracious
Answer" were shocking and decisive to King Charles II, for
they were a permanent record of malignant opposition cen-
tered in the Court and dangerously near the Throne.

For the first five years of his reign he had endured no
published personal criticism at all. Later, the calamities,
beginning with the Dutch War, brought keen enough controversy but never direct censure of the King. Even Marvell
ended *The Last Instructions to a Painter* with a direct
address to the King disclaiming malice. As inventive men
built the telescope and trained it on the sun, the poet said,
they discovered unsuspected spots; and there were similar
blemishes—the courtiers—visible when one intently examined the Throne.

*The Archbishop of Canterbury, "as very a wencher as ever was," see
page 160.

*And you, great Sir, that with him empire share,*
*Sun of our world, as he the Charles is there,*
*Blame not the Muse that brought these spots to sight,*
*Which, in your splendor hid, corrode your light:*
*Kings in the country oft have gone astray*
*Nor of a peasant scorn'd to learn the way.*[38]

But now there was no excuse or disclaimer or apology. The broadsheets attacked the King's mistress, his children by her "bountifully and nobly provided for," and the King's advancement of his concubine to titles of honor.

Public restraint had broken, and the libels of the next two decades were in fact to be far graver. They could be endured if they attacked a cause or person to whom the King was passionately devoted, but after eight years of Barbara Castlemaine he could no longer reliably or consistently say this of her. There had been talk in the past of pensioning her off, and now the King made a serious effort to stabilize her position so that she could exist independently of him.

He began by buying her a house. It was both a generous and a utilitarian gesture. It endowed her with property and it removed her from lodgings in Whitehall Palace.

Four days after the publication of "The Gracious Answer" the King borrowed £11,500 from his City banker, the goldsmith-alderman Bakewell, on the security of two customs tallies. He lent £3,500 to Lord Arlington and spent the rest on Berkshire House, which he bought from the Earl of Berkshire and gave to Lady Castlemaine.[39]

Berkshire House was a fine, old mansion near St. James's Palace, the home of the Duke and Duchess of York, with broad grounds extending over what is now the Green Park as far as Piccadilly. Clarendon had briefly occupied it in the interval between the Great Fire and his occupation of his own new palace.

Barbara thus had the triple pleasure, well within a year of the death of Treasurer Southampton and the fall of Chancellor Clarendon, of getting past the Privy Council a large sum which Southampton would formerly have stopped; taking possession of the house which Clarendon had occupied, and spitting in the eye of Moll Davis for whose reputed family the house was their London seat.

She installed herself there immediately and, with characteristic good nature, Charles began visiting her every day—a gesture of which Lady Castlemaine took full advantage.

"She is busying herself," the French Ambassador noted, "getting her gift valued and having the house furnished."[40] The King's good will had to be used speedily.

There was no question of Roger Castlemaine having any claim on the title to Berkshire House, but in any case Charles sent him to the Levant. He knew the area well. The Levant trade was important to English commerce and there was a major diplomatic crisis pending over possible Turkish reprisals against English merchants because of the intervention of a Scots mercenary regiment in the Venetian-Turkish war. Charles sent Sir Daniel Harvey as his ambassador to the Porte and asked Roger to accompany him.

It was at the home of Sir Daniel and Lady Harvey that Barbara Castlemaine had taken up her station during her quarrel with the King the previous summer, and it was on the Harveys' floor that Charles had had to kneel for his mistress's forgiveness.

Lady Harvey was a woman of a very active mind and reputed lesbian tendencies.[41] She certainly got on badly with her husband, and Charles slyly asked for her approval for sending him away to Turkey. Her reply illustrates the extraordinary freedom with which some privileged people addressed the Monarch but also the persistence of the idea that Queen Catherine, who had lately had another miscarriage, should be divorced or otherwise removed in favor of a successor who could bear an heir to the throne.

"I hope, Lady Harvey," said the King, "that I have pleased you by sending your husband far enough from you."

"I acknowledge your goodness," replied the lady, "and only wish it were in my power to return it by sending the Queen as far from Your Majesty."

"Oddsfish," cried the King, retreating swiftly, "I had better have let my compliments alone."[42]

As Barbara was moved somewhat out of Charles's orbit, Frances Stuart was brought into it. "If you were as well acquainted with a little fantastical gentleman called Cupid as I am," the King had written to his sister when he had to deny a reconciliation with Frances, "you would neither wonder nor take ill any sudden changes which do happen in the affairs of his conducting."[43]

Now, amid the sympathy engendered by Frances's smallpox, the fantastical gentleman was given his head. When the King learned that she was recovering he began to visit her, noting certain blemishes in her face but hoping all would he well. In the fervor of reunion he raised eyebrows at court with antics certainly indicating that "he is mighty hot upon the Duchess of Richmond."[44]

On the very day he had helped Lady Castlemaine to decide the furnishing of Berkshire House "he did on a sudden take a pair of oars, or sculler, and all alone, or but one with him, go to Somerset House, and there, the garden door not being open, himself clambered over the wall to make a visit to her, which is a horrid shame!"

The Duke of Richmond, an amiable but not markedly bright young man, was repeatedly requesting foreign service from the King, a favor with which Charles, with the best motive in the world and the example of Roger Castlemaine before him, could not immediately honor him. Instead, the two men occasionally drank together. At one of these carousals the King was unable to resist scoring a final, mean triumph. He told the Duke of Richmond that, however firmly Frances had rejected him before her marriage, the case was altered now.[45]

The relations between Barbara Castlemaine and the rivals whom Buckingham was still mischievously sponsoring were not cordial. When Lady Castlemaine and the Duchess of Richmond passed each other in their carriages in the park, they were distant.[46] When Lady Castlemaine went to the theatre with the King, and saw Moll Davis catch Charles's eye from another box, she "looked like fire."[47]

But Nell Gwyn showed her natural irreverence for all. Nell was earthy, which is a simpler designation than being dirty. Pepys summed up one aspect of her with the finest economy of art when he wrote one May Day morning:

To Westminster: in the way meeting many milkmaids with their garlands upon their pails, dancing with a fiddler before them; and saw pretty Nelly standing at her lodgings door in Drury Lane in her smock sleeves and bodice, looking upon one; she seemed a mighty pretty creature.[48]

Nelly looked on one, straight. Her charm was immediate and her revenge was direct. When she knew that the King was to visit Moll Davis, she asked Moll first to supper, mixed a highly purgative jalap in her sweet pudding, and incapacitated the plaintive mistress for the night's planned activities.[49]

She disposed of Barbara Castlemaine by having the King's silversmith fashion her a silver bedspread adorned with cupids and crowns—and a rope dancer. And whenever the King was inclined to honor her she could look over his shoulder at the *memento mori* figure of Jacob Hall performing his most breath-taking trick.[50]

But Barbara was not beaten. She had not only time on her side—for she long outlived them all—she also had money. When Nell Gwyn was first offered accommodation by the King, her charge was a simple £500 a year. Barbara Castlemaine, with the realism of experience, wanted £5,000 as a solid base from which to move to higher things and more speculative profits.

She gained this in her first assault on Treasury pensions, when in January, 1669, she grabbed £4,700 a year of the £5,382 10s. previously granted to the Duke of York from the profits of the post office. For form's sake the grant was made, not to Lady Castlemaine but to her uncles, Lord Grandison and Edward Villiers, "and their heirs."[51]

The Duke and Duchess of York, who had been cool to Lady Castlemaine since they had been aware of her part in the movement leading to the dismissal of the Duchess's father, Clarendon, not only had to endure this financial and physical encroachment of their new neighbor in Berkshire House; but they apparently welcomed it. There was a genuine *rapprochement* between them.[52]

The reason for this was primarily political, but based on religious affinity at a time when religion and politics were virtually inseparable. Lady Castlemaine was a Catholic: not, perhaps, one of whom the Church boasted, but a woman who had had the courage, at a time when public conversion demanded courage, to acknowledge a faith towards which the Duke and the Duchess were still making a storm-tossed passage. If she combined her religion with the advocacy of certain sympathetic policies, that was only another reason to accept her as an ally.

For, in addition to time and money, Lady Castlemaine had political power. This is a factor which has been strongly denied since her lifetime, and it would have been contradicted most vociferously by Charles himself.

The fact remains that the Duke of York depended on Lady Castlemaine in 1669 as the reliable voice then reaching the King's ear and opposing the policies of Buckingham and Arlington;[53] that contemporary political opinion considered that she was "instrumental" in a great diplomatic turnabout,[54] and that Louis XIV "set great store on the counsel of this lady" whom his ambassador in London assured him "can put more pressure on the King to effect this end than any other person."[55] All these judges may have misplaced their emphasis, and there is no doubt that the brilliantly devious Charles II overpowered them all in practical negotiating skill.

The truth was that Barbara Castlemaine had no stamina for the exercise of political power, and she would drop any abstract campaign which did not lead quickly and identifiably to her own aggrandizement by wealth or position.

The political movement in which these aspects of the pursuit and neglect of power were shown was the complex negotiation of a close treaty of alliance between England and France. This had been a preoccupation with Charles II for many years, and he always knew that it would be an extremely difficult alliance to be accepted by the English Parliament and English public opinion outside it.

Was this alliance intended to introduce Roman Catholicism as the state religion of England, Scotland and Wales? Charles said so at one time* in a famous secret conference with the Duke of York, Lord Arlington, Lord Arundell of Wardour, and Sir Thomas Clifford on January 25, 1669, the feast of the Conversion of St. Paul. His brother said that he then spoke with tears of earnestness in his eyes. There is no convincing indication that this possibly temporary sincerity of feeling was ever translated into sincerity of intent.

Charles wanted freedom to govern based on financial independence of Parliament which, *faute de mieux*, Louis might provide. He wanted religious tolerance because it made government easier; personally, no doubt, he would have welcomed tolerance of his own inclination to Catholicism and to the authoritarianism that then went with it, but politically there is no evidence that he would willingly have established a confessional Catholic Church in Great Britain on the exclusive and intolerant lines by which it was then understood in Europe.

---

*As the Duke of York reported it: "When they were met, according to the King's appointment, he declar'd his mind to them in the matter of religion and repeated what he had newly said to the Duke, how uneasy it was to him not to profess the faith he beleev'd, and that he had call'd them together to have their advice about the ways and methods fittest to be taken for the settling of the Catholick religion in his kingdoms and to consider of the time most proper to declare himself, telling them withall that no time ought to be lost."[56]

The main purpose, in Charles's eyes, of an alliance with France was its potential guarantee for English and Scottish commercial prosperity. Internationally, it was a fluid period. Charles had diplomatic understandings with the rulers of Holland and France. An alliance with France might lead (as it did) to a war with Holland which would not necessarily aggrandize France, because she did not need to fight the Dutch to gain territorial aims. A contrary alliance might mean a war against France, a great land power which, in Europe, did not threaten British prosperity, whereas every month brought news of the minor prickling of bellicose Anglo-Dutch commercial opposition in many parts of the profit-yielding world.

On balance a war with the Dutch would be more easily accepted and might even be hailed with an uncomplicated welcome as the quickest way to secure maritime supremacy and long-term imperial advantage.

Louis XIV was left in no doubt about Charles's material aim, though he may have underrated its emphasis and been far more idealistically dazzled than Charles at the prospect of the eventual *"Catholicité"* of Great Britain.

Five days before the St. Paul's Day conference Charles wrote to his sister, who throughout was the intermediary between the two kings:

"You will see, by the letter I have written to the King my brother, the desire I have to enter into a personal friendship with him, and to unite our interests so for the future as there may never be any jealousies between us. The only thing which can give any impediment to what we both desire is the matter of the sea, which is so essential a point to us here as an union upon any other security can never be lasting.

Nor can I be answerable to my kingdoms if I should enter into an alliance wherein their present and future security were not fully provided for. I am now thinking of the way how to proceed in this whole matter, which must be carried on with all secrecy imaginable till the particulars are farther agreed upon. . . ."[57]

Did this secrecy exclude Lady Castlemaine? Hindsight historians maintain this, saying that Charles would have been a fool to trust a person so temperamentally unreliable as Barbara Castlemaine. But—apart from the ultra-secret clause in the eventual treaty stating that Charles would publicly declare his reconciliation with (not the State Church's acceptance of) the Roman Catholic religion, and would receive money "to aid him in this declaration"—nothing, including the prospect of war against the Dutch, was finally agreed upon that had not been forecast in sophisticated public opinion fourteen months[58] before the (still secret) Treaty of Dover was ratified, and twenty months before the open, simulated treaty was signed.

During the five months of intense preparation of the treaty, from January to May, 1669, when the King of France was employing every pressure and subterfuge to gain Charles's agreement in principle, Lady Castlemaine was assiduously courted by King Louis XIV and by his ambassador in England, the Marquis Charles Colbert de Croissy.

Colbert arrived in England in the autumn of 1668 with a list of instructions to report minutely on every English particularity from the fashions of men and women and the wines ordinarily drunk by the gentry to the state of the Royal Navy. Naturally, he devoted considerable attention to activities within the Court at Whitehall, to the leading lady members of which he gave expensive presents.

"I have heard read with great pleasure," King Louis informed him, "the curious details you have despatched about the intrigues of the English Court and the highly involved imbroglios of the principal ladies there."[59]

Colbert found it difficult to continue his work at court as he wished because, as had happened a few years before, his King was not keeping him sufficiently remunerated to maintain the flow of presents which the English ladies seemed to demand. Certainly he could not keep up with Lady Castlemaine's appetite, and yet his French master seemed to think it essential that she should be bribed in this way.

"I have given away everything I brought from France not excepting my wife's skirts," he complained, "and I have not enough money to continue this outlay. Nor do I see the use of going to great expense to satisfy the greed for costly keepsakes that I meet in the women here. The King often says that the only woman who has a real hold on him is his sister, the Duchess of Orleans.[60] As for Lady Castlemaine, if we lavish handsome gifts on her King Charles will understand that we believe she rules him in spite of his denials. We ought to dispense no more than ribbons, dressing gowns and other little fineries."[61]

From Paris Colbert was sent trinkets and bagatelles for Lady Castlemaine "which your wife can give her as woman to woman,"[62] although Louis XIV was contemplating a far grander present. In the meantime, neglecting no opportunity to influence King Charles, he sent an astrologer over to Whitehall.

The seer was an Italian monk called the Abbé Pregnani. He cast horoscopes and told fortunes—which was not uninteresting to Charles—and he also had a skill in chemistry, which the King found more promising.

When Charles agreed, on the enthusiastic recommendation of the Duke of Monmouth, that the Abbé should come, merely as a transient celebrity, Louis XIV primed the seer with strict instructions that he should discover enough astrological omens to convince the superstitious English Court that it would be highly dangerous to neglect any opportunity of a firm French alliance.

Unfortunately for Louis, Charles decided to test this prophet first on the Newmarket racecourse, with results that obliterated his influence: "L'Abbé Pregnani was there [Newmarket] most part of the time," Charles wrote to his sister, "and I believe will give you some account of it, but not that he lost his money upon confidence that the stars could tell which horse would win, for he had the ill luck to foretell three times wrong together, and James [Duke of Monmouth] believed him so much as he lost his money upon the same score."[63]

While the King was being exposed to Pregnani, Colbert was concentrating on Lady Castlemaine, and he made no ambiguity of what he was discussing: an open alliance between England and France. The results delighted Louis XIV, and his reaction gives convincing evidence of the political importance he ascribed to her.

"The King highly appreciates the confidence you have cultivated with Lady Castlemaine," the Ambassador was told by the French Foreign Minister, "and is most impressed with the unreserved frankness with which she revealed to you that the King of England was well aware that Lord Arlington had no wish for a French alliance, but that the King was resolved to reach it in spite of any obstacle which this minister might put in the way. His Majesty sets great store on the counsel of this lady, and since you add that she seemed to you very well disposed to such an alliance, and you believe she can put more pressure on King Charles to effect this end than any other person, His Majesty wishes you to cultivate this good beginning with her. He agrees that you should assure her, if you think fit, that having reported your conversation to King Louis he charges you to make her a very handsome requital for her kindness. In this regard he has ordered your brother [Jean Baptiste Colbert, the French Finance Minister] to send you a gift of jewels from France which you may present to her in your own name—and jewels always go down well with ladies, whatever their mood."[64]

Armed with the promise of this imminent present, Colbert was instructed next to get Lady Castlemaine to discourage King Charles from extending general religious indulgence "by putting it into his head that the Presbyterians and Nonconformists are ill-affected towards the Monarchy,"[65] and further—though the superfluity of this advice to Charles raises doubts about the grasp on English affairs possessed by the French Foreign Ministry—that Lady Castlemaine should discourage the King from reconvening Parliament.

"I am entertaining Lady Castlemaine to supper tonight," Colbert replied, "and I think it will not be difficult to persuade her of this."[66]

Lady Castlemaine's gift—it was valued at £1,000 and Charles admired it as in the best possible taste[*67]—was duly presented and resulted in even greater intimacy between the Countess and the French Ambassador and his wife.

King Louis wrote personally to Colbert: "I have paid great

---

*Clearly therefore Louis did not care if Charles "understands that we believe she rules him in spite of his denials." (See page 189).

attention to the remarks which Lady Castlemaine made to l'Ambassadrice, and in my opinion it has given me more illumination than I have ever had before on the secret aims of the different people with whom you are engaged in your negotiations for a close alliance, and their real feelings based on the individual character of each."[68]

Colbert replied to his sovereign: "I can assure Your Majesty that she [Lady Castlemaine] will do everything possible to carry the King towards the speedy conclusion of a favourable alliance with Your Majesty, because she thinks it is very advantageous to the King and consequently to herself."[69]

These judgements by the most active political intelligence on the French side* counter any theory that Lady Castlemaine was a cipher during the political negotiations preceding the French Alliance, and the early speculations of the English bear this out, mistaken though they were in attributing some of the influence to the exiled Clarendon.

"I find," said Pepys over a year before the secret Treaty of Dover "that it is brought almost to effect (through the late endeavours of the Duke of York and Duchess, the Queen Mother and My Lord St Albans, together with some of the contrary faction, as My Lord Arlington) that for a sum of money we shall enter into a league with the King of France wherein ... My Lord Chancellor [Clarendon] is also concerned; ... and that this sum of money will so help the King as that he will not need the Parliament ... But hereby we must leave the Dutch, and that I doubt will undo us ... My Lady Castlemaine is instrumental in this matter and [my

*Charles II thought Colbert of second-rate competence—he referred to his "insufficiency"[70] and insisted that both he and Ralph Montagu, Charles's ambassador in France, should not be told prematurely of the solid progress being made between the Kings towards an alliance. Louis XIV thought highly of Colbert, and Louis' judgement of Lady Castlemaine, though based on Colbert's reports, was objective and cross-checked.

informant says] never more great with the King than she is
now. But this is a thing that will make the Parliament and
Kingdom mad, and will turn to our ruin; for with this
money the King shall wanton away his time in pleasures, and
think nothing of the main till it be too late."[71]

"My Lady Castlemaine is instrumental in this matter and
never more great with the King than she is now." Yet
Barbara, busy as usual with personal wars on multiple fronts,
was badgering the King with private vendettas, pleas for pensions, and passionate denunciations of his infidelity in spite
of her own outrageous amours, at the same time as her
promotion of this major political cause.

At what one would have supposed a crucial and delicate
time when her post office pension of £4,700 was being negotiated, Lady Castlemaine divided the Court into furious partisan warfare on an entirely frivolous issue.

She had quarreled with Lady Harvey, her former hostess
in time of trouble (and the sister of Ralph Montagu,
Charles's ambassador to Louis, who was to loom large in
Lady Castlemaine's life later). Lady Harvey had been
offended at the manner in which an actress, Mistress Corey,
had imitated and caricatured her when playing the part of
Sempronia in the tragedy of *Cataline*. (Sempronia, wife of
the Roman consul Decius Junius Brutus, was a woman of
great personal attractions and literary accomplishments but
of a profligate character, which, on the face of it, is a fair
description of Anne Montagu, Lady Harvey.)

Since Lady Harvey's cousin, Edward Montagu, Earl of
Manchester, was the Lord Chamberlain it was easy for her
to get him to consign Mistress Corey to prison for her impudence; and he did so.

Barbara Castlemaine had greatly enjoyed the actress's

impersonation, and told the King to overrule the Lord Chamberlain and release the actress; and he did so. She then told the King to order the play to be presented again, and she sat with Charles in the royal box to enjoy it. Mistress Corey, taking natural advantage of the furor over her characterization, caricatured Lady Harvey more outrageously than ever, to the manifest appreciation of Lady Castlemaine.

But Lady Harvey had paid people to hiss the actress and throw oranges at her. Consequently, the performance ended in a riot. What ought to have been dismissed as a joke pushed too far was exaggerated into a major court crisis in which normally dignified persons divided into factions, bringing Whitehall into disrepute, "making the King cheap and ridiculous," and exciting a public scorn "expressed mighty freely of the folly of the King in this woman's business."[72]

No sooner was this uproar over than Lady Castlemaine caught the King seducing her maid. This was not the first time such a thing had happened. The previous year there had been a very handsome girl called Wilson whom Pepys had had his eye on, and managed to sit next to in the theatre, but he confined himself to polite conversation when he heard she was with child by the King.[73]

Now, in February, 1669, when Charles on his side was carrying out the first negotiations arising from his St. Paul's Day conference, and the French Ambassador on his was speculating on the price of Lady Castlemaine's persuasion, Colbert's attention was drawn to a remarkable mood of despondency which had overcome the King. What could it portend? What unsuspected crisis might be threatening international accord?

Busily the Ambassador set his spies to work, and at last he reported to Paris:

"The gloom which was evident in the King's face left no doubt that its cause was serious. I made every enquiry to seek an explanation. I have discovered that his misery has been induced by a new amour.

"The new beauty was a maid of Lady Castlemaine's. The grace with which she served His Majesty when he came to see her mistress had plucked at the heart of the King, who is fond of change. As for the girl, she thought it her duty not to oppose his will too long. As for the mistress, she became so enraged that she threw the maid into the street at midnight."

Colbert added a note of political reassurance. "This new amour does not stop Lady Castlemaine from being as powerful as ever."[74]

Only a month earlier, during discussion of the Lady Harvey affair, Pepys had made a blunter statement of the situation: "My Lady Castlemaine is now in a higher command over the King than ever, not as a mistress, for she scorns him, but as a tyrant, to command him."[75]

Altogether it was a dreary private outlook for a monarch whose great desire was to show himself what Bab May had assured him he was—now, for the first time, King of England. The provision of a fine house and a high pension for his mistress had not yet eased him from her dominance.

Yet, in state affairs there was a surer touch in the course towards arbitrary rule. He replaced his high-principled lord lieutenant in Ireland with successors more likely to be subservient in a political crisis. He got Lauderdale to persuade the Scots Parliament to permit a strong militia to serve south of the border. He newly fortified his ports and posted to them reliable commanders to ensure "the keeping of them in such hands as I am sure will be faithful to me upon all occasions."[76]

When Buckingham, Ashley and Lauderdale once more urged him to divorce Catherine he was strong enough in his prerogative, his loyalty and possibly his religious principles to reject the proposal out of hand. "If my conscience would permit me to divorce her," he said, "it would consent that I should despatch her out of this world."

And all the time, in pursuit of his "Grand Design" of the alliance with France that would bring his kingdoms certain benefit without ensuring any reciprocal advantage for Louis, he played men and women against each other, revealed portions of his plan a little to one minister, another little to another, used Arlington, fooled Ashley, bored Castlemaine, and kept Buckingham so busy that the Duke thought he alone was pioneering a new foreign policy.

The alliance took two years to shape, and Lady Castlemaine deserted the enterprise before she could claim any credit in it. She was extremely busy arranging her material affairs. She sold the mansion and grounds of Berkshire House for building land, reserving for herself only the south-west corner, where she built herself a new red brick residence, when finished called Cleveland House, opposite St. James's Palace.

The unjust recall of the Duke of Ormonde from the lord-lieutenancy of Ireland prompted her to resume a long-standing legal squabble regarding the ownership of the house and grounds of Phoenix Park, Dublin: the King had long ago given it to her, but Ormonde had refused to pass the warrant and had instead converted the house into a viceregal lodge.

When Lady Castlemaine met the Duke of Ormonde in the galleries of the Court after his dismissal, she turned on him erupting with the magma of long-pent fury wishing him several sorts of disfigurement and dismemberment and finishing with the hope that she would see the disgraced man hanged.

The Duke gazed at her calmly and said: "I am not in so much haste to put an end to your days, Madam, for all I wish is that I may live to see you old."[77]*

Phoenix Park was not her only interest in Ireland. Lady Castlemaine had estates in the West and pocketed useful rents. By various other resources, including the sale of offices and occasionally of her body,† she was making some further £15,000 a year.

In the novelty of attention to her property in St James's and Dublin she cadged and consulted in all directions, even as far as Bretby.

The Earl of Chesterfield ordered for her fountain in the grounds of her new house the sculpture of a kneeling Cupid shooting a stream of water into the sky. "This may be interpreted by some," he wrote with all his old gallantry, "that tears are the best arms with which that place [Heaven] is to be assaulted; but my meaning in it is that Your Ladyship, not being content with the conquest of one world, doth now by your devotions attack the other."[78]

"Devotions" were not greatly in evidence in Barbara's behavior. For a short time she had as a lover John Ellis, a

---

*Ormonde served two further terms as lord lieutenant of Ireland. Barbara was forty-eight when he died.

†See page 230.

young civil servant formerly at Westminster School and student of Christ Church, and characterized as an "epitome of lewdness."[79]

Ellis's fate, as set in verse by Pope—who probably got the information from Barbara's lover, Wycherley—was that he boasted so blatantly of having succeeded the King in his connection with "the imperial whore" that a resentful Lady Castlemaine took drastic action, à la Lady Shrewsbury. She hired some bullies to attack Ellis and had him castrated:

> *What push'd poor Ellis on th' imperial whore?*
> *'Twas but to be where Charles had been before.*
> *The fatal steel unjustly was applied,*
> *When not his lust offended, but his pride:*
> *Too hard a penance for defeated sin,*
> *Himself shut out, and Jacob Hall let in.*[80]

The deprived Ellis managed to live a busy life as an undersecretary of state and died, unmarried, in 1738, at the advanced age of ninety-five.

In May, 1670, while he prepared to meet at last his loved sister, Minette, for the signature of the secret Treaty of Dover, the King dismissed Ormonde's short-lived successor in the lord-lieutenancy of Ireland and looked around for a replacement. He appointed Lord Berkeley of Stratton, and the nomination cost his lordship £10,000 down and £10,000 to come,[81] paid to the Countess of Castlemaine. The down payment was among the last remittances ever made to her under that title, for she had contrived to grab a greater one.

Minette came to Dover, the treaty was signed, Barbara was unconcerned. Minette returned to France and immedi-

ately died. Barbara was concerned to the extent that the
King's grief delayed her advancement.

A fortnight after the funeral of Princess Henriette Anne,
Duchess of Orleans, King Charles made a public announce-
ment in the Queen's drawing room to the assembled court.
He declared that he had created the Lady Castlemaine
Duchess of Cleveland, Countess of Southampton and Baron-
ess Nonsuch of Nonsuch Park in Surrey "in consideration of
her noble descent, her father's death in the service of the
Crown, and by reason of her own personal virtues."[82]

Graciously recognizing some of the fruits of her personal
virtues, the King simultaneously scattered such an assort-
ment of titles on two of his sons by her—thereby promoting
them to the House of Lords when they came of age—that a
cynic pretended to see in the King's virility a bright solution
to England's legislative and administrative manpower difficulties: Charles could be used to stock the Lords, and leave
the Commons and the Commission of the Peace to the
workhorse country gentlemen: "If Lords should persist in
enfeebling their bodies so as not to be able to get heir males,
yet England in a few years may be so happy as to see a
House of Peers truly noble when they are all extracted out of
royal blood, and there will be no need of calling away country gentlemen from the service of their country either at
their own houses or that of the Commons."[83]

The wit was speaking more truth than he suspected.
Altogether, Charles was to create six dukedoms and one
earldom for his illegitimate sons and ensure that four of his
daughters became countesses. Already another mistress was
in sight, to be created a duchess after serving a much shorter

probation than Barbara—and she was to squeeze Charles even more inexorably than the Duchess of Cleveland, as the Monarch was made ruefully to say:

> "This making of bastards great
>  And duchessing every whore,
>  The surplus and Treasury cheat,
>  Hath made me damnably poor,"
>      Quoth Old Rowley the King
>      Quoth Old Rowley the King*
>      At Council Board
>      Where every lord
>  Is led like a dog in a string.[84]

The rival duchess-to-be was Louise de Kéroualle. Princess Henriette Anne had brought her to Dover as one of her maids of honor.

She was a plump Breton beauty, and Charles had been so impressed that when brother and sister discussed what parting presents they should give each other Charles said boldly, "I will take Louise." Soon Louis XIV found the opportunity to bestow the beauty on him almost as a bequest from dead Minette.

As Frances Stuart had been, the French newcomer was coy and slow. It was clear that she would take a certain time to seduce. The new Duchess of Cleveland looked keenly around her broadening horizon—to the new estates, to Ireland and to France. The indication was for a swift and last-

---

*Old Rowley was the name of an old goat which used to roam about the privy garden, "a rank lecherous devil that everybody knew and used to stroke because he was so good-humored and familiar; and so they applied this name to King Charles."[85] But whether the King was called after the goat or the goat after the King (from the middle syllable of Caro*lus* Rex) has never been very clear.

ing feathering of nests. If only she could restrain one per-
verted passion, she might come prosperously out of the next
few years. But, Lord, she could never contain the liberality
of her bounty when a ripe young buck captured her. And
the younger she found them the more penniless they were,
and the more it cost her to renew her own youth. The sap
was rising again. There were many exciting lovers ahead.
And the Duchess sealed a fond note to that most raptur-
ously attractive and indigent soldier, John Churchill, stamp-
ing the duchess's crest which the King had newly granted
her. The motto read: *Et decus et pretium recti*: decency
and the price of virtue.

"**I** love my love with an A," said Anne Hyde, Duchess of York, and, never having had a lover herself, she looked across at her husband and thought of Arabella Churchill who was bearing him children almost as regularly as Barbara had once borne them to King Charles. "I love my love with an A, because he is so ... arabesque...." she hazarded, and she laughed as high as her ladies when the reference was quickly seized.

The Duke looked glum, not in offense but in apprehension,* and the game passed across the floor: the Duke of York and all the great ladies in his faction were sitting on a drawing room carpet because there were no chairs, having had a merry meal in the Treasurer's partly furnished house.

*Another mistress of James (both as Duke of York and King James II), Catherine Sedley, Countess of Dorchester, said, puzzling over why she attracted him: "It cannot be for my beauty, for he must see I have none; and it cannot be for my wit, for he has not enough to know that I have any."

"I hate my love with a C," said Barbara Villiers, and she ruffled disparagingly through charming/changeable Charles, cherishing/cherry-bummed Chesterfield, and with only the slightest hesitation said, "because he is so . . . churlish." "I should have thought he was *chirpy*," said one lady. "Certainly not too *churchy*," said a second. "Not *another* Churchill!" came a disingenuous exclamation.

"I don't know who you mean," said Barbara, and permitted herself the delight of a swift surreptitious thought of Ensign John Churchill, like a virgin darting into her bedroom to reread a secret entry in her diary.

"D," said the Duchess of York. "And nobody is to love the Duke." She settled herself on her broad buttocks and shared her high spirits like a sacrament. For the severest criticism of this lady was that she affected stateliness and was inclined to be pompous—but she could not be pompous from the floor.

The Duchess of York was dying of cancer, and for three years tried not to surrender her resolution. Her agonizing regret was that she had not the final courage to defy fabricated reasons of state and acknowledge the Catholic faith which the *haut monde* knew she accepted. Barbara, Duchess of Cleveland, could do so; but until he was put to the final parliamentary test her husband, James, could not, and she would not precede him. Her two little girls, the only survivors of the many babies James had given her, were being brought up in strict Anglicanism, as became future Queens.

And so when, at the age of thirty-four, the time came for her to die she went out alone and uncomforted. With the genius always hovering over the prose of the time, her end was simply told in an ordinary letter with words that challenge the account of the death of Falstaff. She had dined heartily at Burlington House and retired to pray, when she collapsed.

"The Duke sent for the Bishop of Oxford out of the chapel, who came, but her senses were first gone. In the meantime the Duke called Dame, do you know me? twice or thrice. Then with much stirring she said Aye. After a little respite she took a little courage and, with what vehemency and tenderness she could, she said Duke, Duke, death is terrible. Death is very terrible. Which were her last words. I am well assured she was never without three or four of her women, so that it was impossible a priest could come to her."[1]

The Duchess of Cleveland was a realist, and concerned herself with thoughts of the living rather than the dead. The Duke would certainly remarry soon, and his choice of a wife, who might well be a rich widow, could affect her own choice of an heiress as bride for one of her young sons. They were now aged eight, seven and five and there was the beginning of a scramble for relationship with the King by marriage among rich fathers wanting nobility for their daughters, and noble fathers wanting royal dowries for their sons.

"I shall come into mighty favour," the Baron Howard of Castle Rising* confided to John Evelyn, "by my marrying my eldest son to one of the King's daughters by the Duchess of Cleveland."[2]

Meanwhile, the extrovert Duchess had eight horses harnessed to her coach and drove with some ostentation

---

*Later Earl of Norwich and confirmed as hereditary Earl Marshal of England; later Duke of Norfolk. He came "into mighty favour," though, without resorting to the expedients he had mentioned to Evelyn as his intentions: to abandon Roman Catholicism as his religion and to achieve a marriage with one of Barbara's daughters.

through the park, assuring acquaintances who commented admiringly on her equipage that the next time she appeared it would be behind *twelve* horses.[3] For it was necessary to make something of an *éclat* to show that she was quite unconcerned by any attention paid to Mademoiselle Louise de Kéroualle. Barbara had already lodged a declaration of status *vis-à-vis* this newcomer nine years her junior by gaining from the King the grant of all the royal plate taken by the Court to Dover for the profuse entertainment offered when Charles had first met Louise with Minette—less to scotch any sentimental value it might have for Charles than to capitalize on the material value it held for her.[4] And in a straight contest with the much fancied Bretonne she had emerged as the outstanding belle of the Queen's ball where even the nobility queued for six hours to see the Duchess, "very fine in a rich petticoat and half-shirt, and a short man's coat very richly laced, a periwig, cravat, and a hat and mask."[5]

Louise was content to rise slowly. Her strength was that she knew King Charles wanted her, as he had made abundantly clear when he had first asked for her at Dover. Charles had given his sister a most imposing present of jewelry to express all the starved affection he had generated for her over the years. Minette, taken aback, had sent for her jewel casket. She was never allowed to handle much money, and it was impossible for her to match Charles's gift, but she wanted to give him a keepsake from her own collection. The casket had been brought to her by Louise de Kéroualle. Charles had taken Louise by the hand and said she was the only jewel he wanted, if Minette would bestow her.

But the Duchess of Orleans, having plainly said that she

would restore the girl safely to her parents, had done so, and died.

When the Duke of Buckingham went to France to represent Charles at his sister's funeral and (unsuspectingly) to try to negotiate a French alliance which had in reality already been signed, he thought he had persuaded Louis XIV to send Louise to the English Court in order to cultivate better relations between the two kings. His only mistake was that Louis had thought of it first, but preferred that Buckingham should believe that it was his own idea.

From the French point of view Louise de Kéroualle was intended, and meticulously instructed, to pipe to Charles's pillow a consistently soothing version of the advantages of French policy, and once she reached the pillow she did it well.

From Buckingham's point of view she was intended, with not much consideration of the project, as another means to oust his cousin Barbara.[6] But, possibly dazzled by the false image in his own mind of Buckingham the Diplomat, and additionally bemused by Louis XIV's gift through him of 10,000 livres (£750) advance on a regular pension for his mistress Lady Shrewsbury,[7] Buckingham blundered.

He dispatched Louise, like a parcel, to await him at Dieppe and then forgot all about her and finally returned to England by way of Calais. Ralph Montagu, Charles's ambassador in France, fortunately heard of Louise's plight and sent a yacht to bring her to England. She had no further regard for Buckingham, and Lord Arlington promptly took over the sponsorship of the lady.

Buckingham reverted to the use of Nell Gwyn in her most

natural capacity, as sheer mischievous and anarchic distraction and diversion for the King, ridiculing all politicians and all political mistresses.

Arlington began his "promotion" of Mademoiselle de Kéroualle, intending her to be a kind of opium, sedating Charles and keeping him good-humored while his ministers got on with the government.

As Colbert reported it:[8] "My Lord Arlington told me recently that he was very glad to see the King his master attached to her, for although His Majesty is not disposed to communicate his affairs to women, nevertheless as they can on occasion injure those whom they hate and in that way ruin much business, it was better for all good servants of the King that his attraction is to her, whose humour is not mischievous and who is a lady, rather than to comediennes and the like on whom no honest man could rely, by whose means the Duke of Buckingham was always trying to entice the King in order to draw him away from all his Court and monopolise him... The advice that should be strongly urged on the young lady [Louise] should be that she should skilfully handle the regard the King has for her, not discuss business with him, not ridicule or show dislike for those who are near him, but to let him find his pleasure exclusively in her company."

And really, he concluded, the only way for her to achieve this end was for her to consent to be the King's mistress.

Colbert listened to this expression of intent without betraying his own purposes, for he needed Arlington as the principal pander in the final deflowering of the cautious Louise. It was then a year since she had come to England, and Louis XIV had already been thinking he had picked the wrong woman when he was suddenly cheered by a report from Colbert that she had had an attack of nausea while dining with him.[9]

The news electrified the French Foreign Ministry, and a special messenger sweated from Paris to London to inform Colbert: "The King was greatly surprised at the news of the attack of nausea which you gave me. Her conduct while she was here and since she has been in England gave no grounds for belief that such good fortune would befall her so soon. His Majesty is anxious to be informed of the outcome and of the terms on which you believe the King stands with her."[10]

The attack of nausea was a false alarm, but within a month Colbert knew he had no need to rely on such indirect indications of pregnancy. He played the bawd in person.

He took Louise down to Arlington's country seat at Euston in Suffolk for the October race meeting at Newmarket which the King and all the Court attended. But on this occasion the King largely ignored the evening delights of the gay race town, possibly being influenced by Nell Gwyn's inaccessibility, for she was seven months pregnant. Until he got what he wanted Charles came over from Newmarket to sleep for as many nights as possible at Euston, where Louise lay.

It was a house party of rare magnificence. "Came all the great men from Newmarket and other parts both of Suffolk and Norfolk to make their court," reported John Evelyn who was there as a fascinated but disapproving (and, in the climax, disappointed) *voyeur*. "The whole house filled from one end to the other with lords, ladies and gallants, and such a furnished table had I seldom seen, nor anything more splendid and free. So, as for fifteen days, there were entertained at the least two hundred people and half as many horses, besides servants, guards, at infinite expense. In the mornings we went a-hunting and hawking. In the afternoon till almost morning to cards and dice etc., yet I must say without noise [uproar], swearing, quarrel or confusion of any sort. I, who was no gamester, had often discourse with the French Ambassador Colbert, and went sometimes abroad on horseback with the ladies to take the air, and now and then to hunting; thus idly passing the time, but not without more often recess to my pretty apartment, where I was quite out of all this hurry, and had leisure, when I would, to converse with books."[11]

It was at this house party, while Evelyn was conversing with books, that Louise finally yielded to Charles in a great mock marriage which was public for the more sophisticated courtiers.

Not having been present, Evelyn quirkily denied that it had happened: "Came His Majesty almost every second day with the Duke, who commonly returned again to Newmarket, but the King lay often here, during which time I had twice the honour to sit at dinner with him with all freedom. It was universally reported that the fair Lady——was bedded one of these nights, and the stocking flung* after the manner of a married bride. I acknowledge she was for the most part in her undress all day, and that there was fondness and toying with that young wanton. Nay, 'twas said I was at the former ceremony, but 'tis utterly false. I neither saw nor heard of any such thing whilst I was there, though I had been in her chamber and all over that apartment late enough, and was myself observing all passages with curiosity

*On the wedding night one of the bride's stockings was thrown into the circle of guests, and the person it hit was said to be the next to be married.

enough. However, 'twas with confidence believed that she was first made a miss, as they call these unhappy creatures, with solemnity at this time."[12]

With the loyal punctuality which Barbara had once shown, Louise confirmed this confident belief by bearing the King a child nine months later. In an air of Roman triumph Charles carried his consummated capture in the royal coach and six off to Newmarket, with "jolly blades, racing, dancing, feasting and revelling more resembling a luxurious and abandoned rout than a Christian Court," and even the rollicking presence of the Duke of Buckingham, "now in mighty favour, and had with him that impudent woman the Countess of Shrewsbury with his band of fiddlers."

While the outcome of the promotion of Louise de Kéroualle was in doubt, Colbert had not compromised himself with the Duchess of Cleveland. "I think it safer, while undermining that lady, to keep her on our side by appearing to be with her," he told King Louis.[13]

When hopes were rising later with Louise's nausea, he mentioned the "furious tantrums of the Duchess of Cleveland"[14] with other signs of her "waning influence." Furious tantrums could be expected of the Duchess at almost any provocation, but it is difficult to prove waning personal influence apart from any faint, political consequences of her dislodgment from the royal couch.

In the nine-months interval between her "undermining" and her "furious tantrums" the Duchess of Cleveland had gained £10,000 a year from the customs receipts to bring her income up to a minimum of £24,000 a year; she had trapped a seven-year-old heiress into marriage with her son, which brought her an additional guaranteed minimum of £4,000 a year plus £20,000 cash; she had appointed another bishop;

she had chased and won a prestigious new lover and was presenting a child to an old one; and this was only the beginning of a spectacular campaign of glory.

The most complicated maneuvers concerned the marriage of her eldest son Charles, now, as her heir, styled the Earl of Southampton. Possibly overhasty in selecting a fortune for him, Barbara had decided that the money should come from Sir Henry Wood.

Sir Henry Wood was an old palace servant, an accountant. He had been Clerk to the Spicery under Charles I, Treasurer to the Queen Mother, and, finally, Comptroller of the Board of Green Cloth under Charles II. He was a public miser.

When Charles II was starving in exile and got his first meager pension from King Louis in 1652, Wood got hold of it first and annexed it to the Queen Mother to pay for what Charles had already eaten at her table.[15] Even at the delirious time of the Happy Return, Ormonde had to report to the King of Wood's activities among the gentlemen gathered to bring him back: "He is universally cursed, and as universally curses the volunteer eaters."[16] His parsimony even spread to the Holy Communion. In the chapels royal he was notorious for "damning the parsons for so much spending the wine at the Sacrament."[17]

His appearance was as odd* as his manner of life. At the age of sixty-seven he engendered his first child, a daughter, Mary, for whom he asked Clarendon to stand as godfather.

---

*"Still his hook-shoulder seems the blow to dread,
And under's armpit he defends his head.
The posture strange men laugh'd at, of his poll
Hid with his elbow like the spice he stole.
Headless St. Dennis so his head does bear,
And both of them alike French martyrs were."[18]

As an accountant, he had been as frugal in his private life as in public affairs. He had amassed a large personal fortune with extensive landed estates in Suffolk: once Bayning country from which Barbara's family had been ejected during Cromwell's financial reprisals against royalists during the interregnum.

The Duchess of Cleveland noted not only the fortune but the facts that there was a sole, minor, direct heiress and that Sir Henry Wood seemed unlikely to live much longer. She therefore suggested to the King that young Mary Wood would make a suitable match for their son, and got the King to propose it to the Comptroller.

The King sent for young Charles Southampton to meet Sir Henry Wood. The boy was eight years old and not the best living advocate for royal polygamy. He was of simple intelligence. Lady Cowper spoke of him as "a natural fool"[19] and this was confirmed by Humphrey Prideaux, his tutor at Oxford: "He will for ever be very simple, and scarce, I believe, ever attain to the reputation of not being thought a fool."[20]*

John Aubrey thought him very good-looking, while admitting his simplicity, for which he gave a reason, though it was more a characteristic Aubrey old wives tale: "The Duke of Southampton [he was advanced to this dignity in 1675] who was a most lovely youth, had two foreteeth that grew out, very unhandsome. His cruel mother caused him to be bound fast in a chair and had them drawn out; which has caused the want of his understanding."[21]

Without accepting Aubrey's psychophysiology, it is notable that Queen Catherine also had "two foreteeth that grew out, very unhandsome," and this may have been an incite-

*For his son, "an even greater fool," see page 259.

ment to Barbara Villiers to have them drawn and delete any resemblance.

In 1671 this boy of eight confronted the old man of seventy-four before the King. Sir Henry Wood said—or was said by the Southampton lawyers much later to have said[22]:

"As I got my estate under Your Majesty and the Queen Mother, I do desire and think it just to dispose it according to Your Majesty's pleasure, which I am ready to do when Your Majesty pleases, and I am sorry it is no more for this young Lord's sake."

The King, accordingly, consented to the marriage and thankfully turned the matter over to the Duchess of Cleveland's lawyers and his treasurer.

The attorneys drew up a marriage settlement of some intricacy.

A marriage between the seven-year-old Mary Wood and the eight-year-old Earl of Southampton was agreed, but it was not to take place until the girl was sixteen, when she was to be given the opportunity to refuse the match.

If the Earl of Southampton had died by then, his rights in the marriage settlement were to be taken over by his brother George, then aged five.

If Mary accepted Charles Southampton or his successor George, the King would give her a dowry of estates worth £2,000 a year, and all Sir Henry Wood's estates, then producing £4,000 a year but ultimately worth far more, would be entailed on Mary and her husband and her heirs.

If, however, Mary at the age of sixteen refused to marry either Charles or George, £20,000 compensation would be paid out of her estate to the disappointed suitor and the estate would pass to others in the Wood family, primarily

Sir Henry's brother, Dr. Thomas Wood, Dean of Lichfield and Coventry.

Though it was not, and could not, be put as part of the marriage settlement, it was understood that the Duchess of Cleveland would use her influence to get Dr. Wood a speedy bishopric; and this indeed she did within a few weeks of the settlement when he was "elected" to the vacant see of Lichfield and Coventry.

As soon as the settlement was signed, old Sir Henry Wood made his will, and within days he died—on May 25, 1671. Mary was sent, under the terms of his will, to his sister, Lady Chester, widow of Sir Henry Chester, Knight of the Bath. She was to be paid £450 a year to bring up the girl "firmly instructed in the true Protestant religion."

But the Duchess of Cleveland took arbitrary action almost immediately. Within a fortnight of Sir Henry's death she demanded of Lady Chester that Mary should be given over into her custody. When this was refused, she kidnapped Mary from her aunt's home and took her to Berkshire House. Lady Chester sent to the Duchess requiring that the girl should be returned under the terms of Sir Henry's will. She was scornfully rejected.

"I have her and I will keep her," said the Duchess of Cleveland. "I wonder that so inconsiderable a Person as you will contend with a Lady of my Quality." And, after demonstrating that possession is nine points of the law, she took the tenth point by having the two children married there and then, when Charles was just celebrating his ninth birthday. This effectively stopped any counter-bodysnatching by the puny Chester/Wood faction with the object of marrying Mary to a lad of their choice and forfeiting the £20,000. The Duchess then claimed the whole of Sir Henry Wood's estate for her son on the ground that it was willed to Mary, if single at the age of twenty-one, but to Mary and her husband on the day of her marriage: and that day had dawned. Moreover, since there was no guardianship of Mary now being exercised by Lady Chester, she prudently stopped the £450 allowance.

Law suits were immediately begun by the Wood family, but they were bogged down on a number of points exploiting the individuality of the two documents: the marriage settlement and the will. Principally, it was found that it was difficult to touch the Duchess of Cleveland because of her close connection with the King (who never remembered to pay Mary her dowry of £2,000 a year) and because she held a duke's title in her own right, which gave her immunity from being sued in the normal courts. As an abortive petition to the House of Commons put it:

"And all these things transacted by the Duchess of Cleveland against whom no relief is like to be had in an ordinary course, as well in respect of her greatness as for that she is

(1) A person privileged as a Peer, and so cannot be sued,

(2) A Feme Covert whose husband is beyond sea and so no satisfaction to be got against her on him if privilege were out of the case."

The lawsuits in this cause went on for a full generation, long after the death of the pathetic bride, and were delayed, in his turn, by Dr. Thomas Wood, pleading his privilege as a bishop once he had got an advantage: (though, characteristically of Barbara's nominees, he was suspended from office by the Archbishop of Canterbury for gross neglect of duties, yet hung on to his see, and his seat in the Lords, for a further eight years until he died, when the chancery suit was resumed).

But in 1671, as Barbara, Duchess of Cleveland, surveyed her family and reviewed her proposals for their advancement and prosperity, this was their disposition:

Anne, born May 25, 1661, was making her second stay in Paris. Barbara had boarded her at the Queen Mother's monastery* of Chaillot for a year when she was eight, and now sent her to the Abbey of Pontoise. It is very likely that Roger Castlemaine managed to see her in France during his wanderings in Europe.[23] He was attached to Anne even until his death.

Charles, born mid-June, 1662, and, after a struggle with Roger, rebaptised on June 18 with the King as godfather, was a married boy in whose name Barbara administered extensive estates and manipulated an enviable personal fortune. From birth he had borne Roger's second title of Lord Limerick, and from 1670 his mother's second title, Earl of Southampton.

Henry, born on September 20, 1663, in gossip-promoting circumstances of obscurity while the Court was at Tunbridge Wells, was not yet acknowledged by the King as his son owing to an exacerbation of his complaint, "Alas, I never got one brat alone." Clearly, in Barbara's eyes this situation needed to be rectified.

Charlotte, born on September 5, 1664, was with Henry and George and sister-in-law Mary in Berkshire House in the care of a governess who had a touch of the bawd about her herself, at least with regard to the interests of John Churchill, the future Duke of Marlborough.

George, born on December 28, 1665, in Merton College,

---

*Since Anne, in her various youthful escapades, was in and out of "monasteries" it should be made clear that the word was then a normal description of a convent of nuns.

Oxford, whose alumni did not immediately in their placards magnify his mother for the honor, was a tall boy, already at the age of five physically much more like his father than any of the other children.

Henry's was the cause to be advanced first. He had been passed over by the King in the patent creating Barbara Duchess of Cleveland.[24] This had pointedly restricted the succession to the dukedom to "Charles Palmer, her eldest son, and the heirs male of his body, and for want of such then to George Palmer her *second**\** son and the heirs male ..."

In the same way, the reversion of the poor, bartered body of Mary Wood, if Charles Southampton had died, would have been to baby George.

Henry was ignored and passed over. This was righted when, in a sudden succession of warrants, Arlington was given his reward for discretion over the Treaty of Dover, a recompense which had been agreed and promised to Minette in her lifetime, but delayed until a less significant moment. He was made first an earl, then Knight of the Garter, and the King agreed that his only child Isabella, aged five, should marry Henry Palmer, now recognized as "our dear natural son Henry Fitzroy"—and speedily advanced to the titles of Earl of Euston, Viscount Norwich and Baron of Sudbury— territorial labels all based on Arlington's own Suffolk estates, to which little Isabella was sole heir.†

This child marriage took place almost immediately, after a short delay while Henry's mother was delivered of a baby

---

*Author's emphasis.
†She was full heir, also, to her father's title, and became, on his death, Countess of Arlington in her own right.

whom not even Barbara could browbeat the King into acknowledging.

If the Duchess of Cleveland could ever have altered the timing of one of her pregnancies this would have been the occasion. For, although the marriage of Henry and Isabella had been a possibility for some time, she was always alert for better matches.

On July 13, 1672,[25] Buckingham—possibly for motives of sheer mischief, to spite Arlington even if it favored Barbara—proposed to Charles II that he could bring off what was undoubtedly the match of the decade: the marriage of young Henry, now nominated Earl of Euston, with Lady Betty Percy, daughter of the late Earl of Northumberland, the richest girl in England with the additional advantage of having a father already dead. Like Isabella, she was just five years old.

Charles told the Duke that it was too late to advance this project, but, had Barbara been active there is little doubt that it would have been pushed much more strongly.

However, Barbara was within three days of childbirth. She earmarked Lady Betty for George and produced a daughter.

A fortnight later, at Arlington House,* the Archbishop of Canterbury married eight-year-old Henry to five-year-old Isabella in the presence of the King and all the grandees.

Next year, when the boy was still only nine, he was given the office of Receiver General and Comptroller of the Seals of the King's Bench and Common Pleas as a hereditary perquisite. Shortly afterwards he went with his elder brother to

*Strictly still called Goring House until it was burned down and rebuilt by Arlington in 1674. It stood on what is the site of Buckingham Palace.

Paris to expand his education, as his mother regarded education. This caused a serious quarrel with Arlington, who wished to control the training of the boy who was to inherit all his estates.

The Duchess of Cleveland peremptorily refused to let Henry go from her control. "I care for no education other than what nature and I myself can give him," she said, "which will be sufficient accomplishment for a married man."[26] And no doubt, by her own standards and tutorial capacity, she had made an incontrovertible point.

Anne had come back from Paris in 1672, and in the following year was formally recognized as his daughter by the King when, with Charlotte, she was granted royal arms, crest and supporters: she displayed the arms of England differenced with a bend sinister in ermine, and she echoed her mother's motto, *Et decus et pretium recti*. Next year she was married. She was thirteen years old.

The husband provided for her was a gentleman of the King's bedchamber, Thomas Lennard, fifteenth Lord Dacre, who was promptly created Earl of Sussex and given by Charles a pension of £2,000 a year together with a £20,000 dowry for Anne.

It was a grand wedding, held at Hampton Court Palace where the Duchess of Cleveland still maintained lodgings. The King came over from Windsor, and after a long chat with Barbara led his daughter from her mother's apartments to his own antechamber. The Duke of York escorted the Duchess of Cleveland, and Prince Rupert and the Duke of Monmouth followed with the families of the bride and groom. When the Bishop of Oxford had married the couple, "the King first kissed the bride and by and by the bride-cake was broken over her head, which done the married couple retired till dinner was ready."[27] The King presided at the feast, first leading in the bride and placing her on his right hand at table with her mother on his left.

It was a month of weddings, for almost at the same time Charles married young Charlotte to another Gentleman of his Bedchamber, Sir Edward Henry Lee, Baronet, whom he made Earl of Lichfield. Charlotte's dowry was £18,000 and again a pension of £2,000 a year was provided for the husband. Since the bride was not yet ten years old, the ceremony was formal and Charlotte was given back to her mother before being bedded.

Barbara incurred debts of some £3,000 for the wedding clothes for her daughters: they were unpaid ten years later, and Charles settled some of them just before his death.[28]

Lichfield, as a territorial title, had belonged to the Duke of Richmond, husband of Frances Stuart. He had died at the age of thirty-four in 1672, without an heir, and Barbara had the pleasure not only of taking the title into the family but also of securing the Garter stall he had left vacant in Windsor Chapel, which was granted to her boy Charles. That the simple Earl of Southampton could be installed at the age of ten as a knight-companion of the Most Noble Order of the Garter is a true travesty of chivalry, but the trappings were taken seriously at the time.*

With all these honors falling to her children, Barbara made sure that young George was not disappointed, and simultaneously with the creation of Charlotte's husband as

---

*When the Duke of Monmouth was disgraced on the accession of James II, a solemn order was made to pull down his achievements from his stall in St George's Chapel, and his hatchments were ceremonially kicked into the Castle ditch.[29]

Earl of Lichfield, George, at the age of eight, was made Earl of Northumberland, Viscount Falmouth and Baron Pontefract.

Still restless, Barbara pestered Charles to grant the final honor and to advance his sons from earls to dukes. Unfortunately, he took her too seriously and remembered others of his sons.

Just when Barbara believed she had succeeded, at least with regard to Charles and Henry, she had the mortifying news that Louise de Kéroualle, now Duchess of Portsmouth, had secured the same rank for her three-year-old son, called Charles Stuart and now to be created Duke of Richmond. (Nell Gwyn, untitled herself, did not then press for rank for her two sons.)

A fantastic contest swiftly developed between the two pinchbeck duchesses as to whose offspring should gain the title first and rank as senior duke of this clutch.

Louise had private information that the Lord Treasurer, who had to sign dockets before the patents were sealed, was going to take the waters at Bath. She therefore got her solicitor to go to him at midnight on the day before he left, with the docket for the Treasurer's signature.

The Lord Treasurer, very apprehensive of the wrath of the Duchess of Cleveland if he favored the Duchess of Portsmouth, made the solicitor wait while he sent to ask the King which boy was to be ennobled first. The wary King would not commit himself, but merely wrote a note authorizing the Treasurer to have the documents sealed in the order that they came to him. Louise's solicitor passed his over, and the Lord Treasurer fled to Bath. When Barbara's solicitor came next morning there was no one with authority to sign a docket. The order of seniority of the three dukes, therefore, became: (1) Charles Stuart, Duke of Richmond; (2) Charles Fitzroy, Duke of Southampton; (3) Henry Fitzroy, Duke of Grafton.[30]

This applies to their descendants to this day, and although the dukedom of Southampton is extinct, the present Duke of Richmond outranks the Duke of Grafton by the same narrow margin. But in 1675 it was in a mood of some chagrin that the Duchess of Cleveland sent her son, the Duke of Southampton, to Oxford a month after his patent had been passed, as it was with distinct regret that Christ Church received this "very cockish, idle boy"[31] who, as soon as he reached fourteen—then the age of male consent—was securely locked by his mother into marriage and prosperity by undergoing a second and binding ceremony with little Mary Wood conducted by Dr. Fell, Bishop of Oxford.

Among the plenitude of titles now sparkling in Barbara's family there were a number of sweet reminders of past defeats now compensated.

Her own title of Cleveland had been held by the old Earl of Cleveland whom her family had been suing over property since 1638. Though frail at the Restoration, the old man had survived until 1667. Her subsidiary of Southampton was the title of Wriothesley, the treasurer who so long had thwarted her with his stopped warrants, and for good measure, when Charles was made Duke of Southampton he also took old Wriothesley's second title and became Earl of Chichester. The transfer of Lichfield was a treble smack at three duchesses: Mary, Duchess of Richmond and Countess of Lichfield, whose family had owed Barbara's family £18,000 since the Civil War and who had first called Barbara "a Jane Shore" and hoped she would come to the same end—she was still living, somewhat alcoholically, in France; Frances, Duchess of Richmond and Countess of Lichfield, who would surely relish the daily reminder that she was widowed and supplanted; and Louise, Duchess of Portsmouth, whose son was Duke of Richmond but could not be Earl of Lichfield. Sussex was the title of the lady who had taken the estates of Barbara's stepfather, the Earl of Anglesey, away from her mother. Grafton was an estate once owned by the senior Dowager Duchess of Richmond.

The name of Euston rubbed into Arlington's skin that Barbara's son would succeed to his property. Northumberland, one of the oldest noble names in the country, might yet be used as a lure to trap rich Lady Betty Percy for George, since her dead father had held the title. And even Falmouth was a suitably ill-natured gibe to Mary Bagot, now the Dowager Countess, that Charles Berkeley who had been granted the title was not on unfamiliar terms with the mother of the present holder.

But money was needed to support all this honor. Money was therefore procured. Apart from the huge dowries and pensions allotted to the husbands of Barbara's daughters, the income traceable in the now incomplete records as accruing to the Duchess of Cleveland and her sons between 1670 and 1676 includes:

The Park and Palace of Nonsuch (finally disparked, dismantled and sold). There were many years' yield in rent and extensive timber and the building materials of the palace sold for some £7,000.[32]

£10,000 a year from the farmers of the Customs.[33]

£10,000 a year from the farmers of the County Excise on beer and ale.[33]

£4,700 a year from the Post Office.[34]

Reversions of many offices, with fees received for each new appointment.[33]

Estates in Woking, Chobham, Bagshot and Bisley, Surrey.[35]

Rents from the Duchy of Cornwall.[36]

Estates in Huntingdonshire plus £5,000 outright.[36]

£6,000 a year from the Excise plus £3,000 a year for each son, total £15,000 a year.[37]

£5,500 a year pension from the Wine Licenses.[36]

Fines from the Duchy of Cornwall.[38]

£7,000 from the Excise (not mentioned as an annual amount).[39]

£2,200 from the Duke of York.[39]

Rents from ironworks in the Forest of Dean.[39]

£4,000 a year plus estimated £40,000 from Sir Henry Wood's estate.[40]

The House of Commons was shown an account in November, 1673, of £400,000 "given away since last session of which the Duchesses of Cleveland and Portsmouth had the greatest share."[41] Three centuries later this cannot of course be evidence of fact, but it is still evidence of opinion widely held at the time. The figures quoted here hold only for the time when the Duchess's children were young, the eldest boy being under fifteen. From then on their estates were separate and, since they could less easily be plundered by the Duchess to meet her gaming and loving expenses, they proliferated. Within sixty years Charles Southampton's son, though even more of a fool than his father, had an entailed estate bringing in over £100,000 a year *income*.

There seems no doubt that the steadiest drain on the resources of the Duchess of Cleveland was the support of her lovers. In this she was entirely generous. However much she bled the King, she was, except in one case of emergency, meretricious towards nobody else. The royal whore was a jolly whoremaster in any bed outside the palace, not only willing to pay for her pleasures but wanting to. For she was never a Messalina. However deep the cistern of her lust, it was heart as well as body that seems always to have been touched. As she was to explain to the King in humorous mitigation, "You know as to love one is not mistress of one's self."[42]

There is indeed something admirable in the manner in which Barbara disposed of her money. She was inexorably rapacious in acquiring it from the one great fount of wealth which she had been fortunate enough to tap, and she spent it, not like a lord—on gambling and women—but like a lady—on her family first, and then on gambling and men.

Female rakes are rare, because profligacy, with its exaggeration of the natural masculine taste for risk, adventure and sporting insecurity is a gross aberration from the feminine inclination. When women develop as libertines, and retain their maternal instinct to the extent that they give priority to the protection of their children and their lovers, they enlarge the family which must be maintained before they attend to other pleasures; whereas the male voluptuary diminishes or obliterates his family. The consequence is of great psychological interest to an observer, but entirely devastating to the rake's intended prey. For since the woman needs more, she is that much the more rapacious. When Barbara Cleveland wanted something, or someone, men trembled and obeyed.

She wanted William Wycherley, "manly Wycherley," perhaps the handsomest by modern standards of all the men Sir

Peter Lely painted in that endless succession of "Society" portraits which are for the most part duller today than the work of an Edwardian Bond Street photographer. She passed Wycherley in her carriage in Pall Mall when he was driving towards St. James's. She leaned perilously out of the window in the most unladylike way and shouted after him: "You! Wycherley! You are the son of a whore!" Which done, she collapsed on her seat with laughter.

A man addressed in this manner might well regard it as a normal insult, except that it came from a laughing lady. Wycherley, being rapidly carried away from his encounter in his own chariot, set his wit working even faster.

There were two outstanding themes whose connection he swiftly interpreted: first, he was the author of a play then on in London, which was naturally at the forefront of his thoughts; and second, his interlocutor was the Duchess of Cleveland, whom he knew had already been to his play and who was the comparatively unashamed mother of a number of bastards who were doing very well.

The solution of the ribald allusion was clear. In his play, *Love in a Wood*, Wycherley had written "a new song against marriage" which lauded free, uncomplicated copulation and recommended the offspring of such unions compared with the dull legitimate issue of bonded married couples:

> *When parents are slaves*
> *Their brats cannot be any other;*
> *Great wits and great braves*
> *Have always a punk for their mother.*

Clearly the Duchess of Cleveland, believing, as many mothers fondly do, that her children were both witty and brave, had annexed the song as a compliment to herself as

punk and mother; and in return she was complimenting
Wycherley on his wit by calling him the son of a whore.

Encouraged by this satisfactory explanation, the play-
wright ordered his coachman to turn, and drew level with
the Duchess's carriage.

"Madam," he said, "you have been pleased to bestow a
title on me which generally belongs to the fortunate. Will
Your Ladyship be at the play tonight?"

"Well, what if I am there?" the Duchess temporised.

"Why, then I will be there to wait upon Your Ladyship,
though I disappoint a very fine woman who has made me an
assignation."

"So you are sure to disappoint a woman who has favoured
you for one who has not."

"Yes, if she who has not favoured me is the finer woman
of the two. But he who will be constant to Your Ladyship
till he can find a finer woman is sure to die your captive."

Whereupon, incredibly—but it is Wycherley's account—
the lady blushed, and bade her coachman drive away. But
that night she was in the first row of the King's box in Drury
Lane, and Wycherley "entertained her during the whole
play."[43]

"I cannot but publicly give Your Grace my humble
acknowledgement for the favours I have received from you,"
Wycherley later wrote equivocally in his dedication to her of
the printed version of *Love in a Wood*.

Apart from her physical favors, Barbara introduced Wycherley to the Court, where he was not known before, and certainly assisted his fame, acceptance, fortune such as it was,
and even marriage—to a rich young widow, the Countess of
Drogheda, once a maid of honor at the Court—and rendered
so jealous that she would only permit him to go out to one

tavern, exactly opposite their house in Bow Street, where he had to sit with the windows open so that his wife could see there was no woman in the company.

They met in the spring of 1671, and it was a summer idyll, with Barbara stealing to Wycherley's chambers in the Temple "dressed like a country maid, in a straw hat, with pattens* on, and a basket in her hand."[44]

If posterity owes any debt to Barbara Villiers at all, it is that under the exuberance of her attachment to him Wycherley wrote his last and greatest play, *The Country Wife*, the underrated epitome of early Restoration comedy and all the fragile gallantry of an age when "Women of quality are so civil, you can hardly distinguish love from good breeding."[45]

But the amour had to end with winter, for young John Churchill was coming home from Tangier. Barbara had met this handsome soldier—"beautiful, his manner irresistible by either man or woman"[46]—in the nursery. She employed, as governess to her children, Mrs. Godfrey, the sister of John Churchill's mother.[47] Mrs. Godfrey used to invite her nephew into the kitchen at Cleveland House to give him sweetmeats. "The Duchess came one day unexpectedly down the back stairs to take chair, and found them together. He had slipped away, for fear of anger, but not so speedily but she had a glimpse of his graceful person. She asked who he was, and being answered caused him to be called . . . The governess, knowing the Duchess's amorous star, was transported at the happy introduction of her nephew."[48]

John Churchill's regiment was ordered away to serve in Tangier, but he came back to London every winter, and this

*Overshoes with wooden soles to keep one's shoes out of the mud.

seasonal affair with the Duchess of Cleveland lasted for many years. She was astonishingly generous to him, even to the extent that on his account she had finally to flee from her creditors. And he used her as if he were a ponce. This did not escape Charles's notice.

Once, Buckingham, in sheer mischief, contrived that the King should call on Barbara while she and Churchill were together. He came into her room with his usual lack of ceremony, and the appalled Jack Churchill dived out of the window. The King looked sourly down on him and told him, "I forgive you, for you do it for your bread."[49]

Churchill's bread was from an expensive bakery, for he was of an extortionate nature. On one occasion he demanded a capital sum from his infatuated duchess and she found £5,000 for him. He promptly invested the greater part of it with the Marquis of Halifax for a lifelong annuity of £500 a year.[50] (The current annuity terms were nine years' purchase: in this case £4,500.)

For this generosity, Churchill was monumentally ungrateful. Long after they had parted there was a scene between them which seems to have burned itself into the memory of the onlookers as if it were a passage from a morality play.

He was a rich and successful soldier; she was an aging woman with little but cards to divert her. Her pensions were often in arrears and she had asked him to use his influence for her at a court where she was no longer a power, but he ignored her appeals.

One night they sat at the same gambling table in London. Churchill held the bank. Slowly Barbara lost all her money. When she had nothing in front of her she modestly asked

Churchill for the loan of twenty guineas, "which he absolutely refused, though he had a thousand upon the table before him, and told her coldly the bank never lent any money. Not a person upon the place but blamed him in their hearts. As to the Duchess's part, her resentment burst out into a bleeding at her nose, and breaking of her lace; without which aid, it is believed, her vexation had killed her upon the spot."[51]

The deep irony of this refusal lay in the fact that in order to procure the £5,000 which Churchill had once required, and which was "the foundation of his subsequent fortune,"[52] Barbara had had to resort to the only transaction of plain prostitution which has ever been hinted of her. Once she had decided to enter on this course she pursued it with characteristic wholeheartedness, and made a profit on the deal.

Sir Edward Hungerford, a notoriously spendthrift and dissolute knight, was apparently anxious, like John Ellis, "to be where Charles had been before." The Duchess let it be known that her price was £10,000, and an assignation was made. He was a man in his seventies, and more a vain than a glorious lover. In some hilarious scene in a dark room, which Chaucer might have used as a sequel to "The Reeve's Tale," she fooled him, whether by impersonation or a seedier trick, and later let him know he had been fooled, and offered him another chance to rehabilitate himself—for a further fee.

The details were known at the time, but with unusual reticence were never chronicled. "We shall draw a veil," wrote Abel Boyer, "over . . . in what manner she tricked Sir Edward Hungerford of the sum of ten thousand pounds."[53]

Alexander Pope, in his reference to the affair, aptly coupled the cozening with Churchill's later rejection of Barbara,

*Who of ten thousand gull'd her Knight,*
*Then ask'd ten thousand for another night;*
*The gallant too, to whom she paid it down*
*Liv'd to refuse that mistress half-a-crown.*[54]

But as long as it was the mistress who was seeing to the subsidies Barbara was absorbedly happy in this liaison. It was Churchill's child she was carrying when the wedding of young Henry had to be postponed. (It is perhaps more than coincidence that the child was conceived and born at about the same time as Louise de Kéroualle's child by the King.) The Duchess called her new daughter Barbara, and put her in the nursery with her great-aunt. But she never attempted to gain noble honors for her.

Young Charles Southampton was given his dukedom and sent to Oxford in the autumn of 1675. Barbara welcomed Churchill back for the winter, and he enjoyed her and left her forever. He was then twenty-five and she was ten years older.

"He has pillaged the Duchess of Cleveland," the French Ambassador informed his Minister in Paris. "She has given him the value of more than £100,000. In one way or another he has got so much money out of her that in desperation she is obliged to go to France to live quietly for some time."[55]

The Duchess announced that in Paris she was going to live in a monastery,[56] but few people seriously believed that, unless it was their interpretation that she craved retreat in the sheer despair which her lover's conduct had induced. This affair had beaten all pride out of the normally tempestuous Barbara. "If Churchill goes abroad she will set up house with him again," predicted the French Ambassador, and he vetoed an appointment which the soldier was seeking in Paris.*

Barbara finally left England with her colors flying and a good story to tell in Paris. Louise de Kéroualle was completely constant to Charles II, and, consequently, vixenish when she had clues to his promiscuity. She got both a clue and the damages for it when she found that Charles had given her a clap. Charles recovered fairly swiftly, but in Louise's case the cure was prognosticated as likely to take longer. Barbara rehearsed the phrasing of the end of the anecdote: "She has been consoled for such a troublesome present by another more in her line. The King has given her a pearl necklace valued at 4,000 jacobus [£4,800] and a diamond worth 6,000 jacobus. They have pleased her so much that for this price she is prepared to risk another dose."[58]

A pox on a monastery; there was diversion to be found in Paris. Or perhaps the best features of the two *milieux* could be combined. In Paris, as she heard, there was a very amorous archbishop.

*Churchill's treatment of the Duchess of Cleveland indirectly led to his future honors. At this time (1676), he applied to Louis XIV for the colonelcy of the Régiment Royal-Anglois. If the ambassador in London had not reported adversely on his recent conduct he might well have gained this appointment and made a career in the French Army like his illegitimate nephew James (son of the Duke of York and Churchill's sister Arabella), the future Duke of Berwick, and thus he would not have gone on to become the Duke of Marlborough through his generalship against the French. As it was, his liaison with Barbara prompted his rejection in classic terms: "Monsieur de Churchill is too keenly devoted to his own pleasure to be likely to acquit himself well with such a responsibility. What is wanted is a man who will make the Régiment Royal-Anglois both his vocation and his mistress."[57]

*7 ⊅₹ Madam, all that I ask of you,*
*for your own sake, is Live so for the future*
*as to make the least noise you can,*
*and I care not who you love*

I T was a court pleasantry that when Charles first allowed his discontent with Barbara to be publicly referred to he tolerated, if he did not encourage, the singing in her presence of the ditty, "Poor Aurelia's growing old." It ran in part:

*When Aurelia first I courted*
  *She had youth and beauty too,*
*Killing pleasures when she sported,*
  *And her charms were ever new.*

*Conquering Time doth now deceive her*
  *Which her glories did uphold:*
*All her art can ne'er retrieve her.*
  *Poor Aurelia's growing old.*

This was an unwise offensive, for Charles was ten years older than Barbara, and was vulnerable to the counter-attack which the Duchess of Cleveland predictably commissioned:

When by Charles I first was courted
  He had strength and vigour too,
Killing pleasures could afford me,
  But his love was never true.

Conquering Time hath now beguiled him
  Of those powers he did maintain.
Several beauties have so foiled him:
  My poor Charles is in his Wain.[1]

Charles was, in fact, sensitive about his potency, and the court satirists exploited this susceptibility at least from his fortieth year.[2] John Wilmot, Earl of Rochester, assiduously played on the theme[3] with considerable malice and occasional wit:

This you'd believe, had I but time to tell ye
The pain it costs to poor, laborious Nelly,
Whilst she employs hands, fingers, mouth and thighs,
Ere she can raise the member she enjoys.[4]

The legend ran that Charles sank with some relief into the arms of Louise de Kéroualle, Duchess of Portsmouth, as a mistress who, although an accepted beauty and aged only twenty-two, mildly declined to arouse any scrap of jealousy in him or to make any outrageous demands—beyond a passion for finery and jewels in which she speedily eclipsed the Duchess of Cleveland. But the truth was that, much as Charles welcomed Louise as a haven, he still had the thirst for adventurous enterprise that urged him to sail out and board a passing privateer. And no prize was more enticing than the graciously built Duchess of Mazarin, who appeared on his horizon three years after he had captured Louise.

Hortensia Mancini, Duchess Mazarin, was a twenty-nine-year-old Italianate beauty with a continental reputation for libertinism perhaps exceeding the Duchess of Cleveland's insular fame, and with the entirely rare asset of being said to possess a fortune of over £1,000,000.* Her arrival in England was welcomed by those of the King's ministers, who were looking for a lure to counteract the excessive French influence exercised by Louise. But it was actually engineered for purposes of his own self-aggrandizement by Ralph Montagu, who was intermittently for seventeen years Charles II's ambassador to the Court of Louis XIV. Montagu rode ten miles out of London to meet Hortensia and her escorts.[5] He brought her to the house of his sister, Lady Harvey, and swiftly took the credit of having introduced her to the Court. The King duly moved towards her, and Montagu could not be blamed for imagining that out of all his great portfolio of devious plans none had ever worked more smoothly: his great objective, to be the King's first minister, was at last a probability. But in reality he had merely started a tangle which was to embroil the King, the King's then first minister, Danby, Montagu himself, and, of all unexpected persons, the Duchess of Cleveland, in confusion and disaster. He began, with quite uncharacteristic *gaucherie*, by allowing himself to fall in love with Hortensia.

Ralph Montagu, in 1676, was a plump, dark, coarse-featured man of thirty-eight with intelligence and cunning and a surprisingly strong amatory record, based not on his unprepossessing appearance but on his tenacity and wit. He had shown great discretion after his discovery of the then secret French Alliance from the lips of Charles's dying sister,

*Events did not justify this. Her creditors seized her body against her debts when she died twenty years later.

Minette, and the King had marked his appreciation by maintaining him for many years in the ambassadorship.

But the ambitious Montagu's desires were for a post of high influence at court. He did not lack money—he paid £14,000 for the intermediate influence of the post of the Mastership of the Great Wardrobe—but he could not immediately buy his way to the top more directly.

However, he did the best he could by indirect means, and bought himself an influential wife. In 1673 he married the widowed Countess of Northumberland, the mother of Lady Betty Percy, a little girl, who by her father's death had seen the Earldom lapse but held six baronies in her own right and the greatest fortune in the country. Montagu intended, by his manipulation of a marriage between his six-year-old stepdaughter and one of the King's illegitimate sons, to reach towards the power he craved. His wife, still referred to as Lady Northumberland, was an extremely beautiful woman with £6,000 a year of her own—she had been strongly fancied as the second wife of the Duke of York but James married the Catholic Maria Beatrice d'Este (Mary of Modena).

It was unfortunate that within two months of their marriage Montagu and his wife were quarreling savagely, but, although she wished for a separation, Montagu would not relinquish his hold on her and her daughter. Instead, he reverted to his old commitment with Jane Middleton, whose child he had fathered many years before; and it was the timeless beauty of Jane that he deserted for the allure of Hortensia de Mazarin.

"Near my house is the residence of Madam de Middleton," the omniscient French Ambassador reported to King Louis XIV. "She is the most beautiful woman in

England. . . . Monsieur de Montagu, who had a mind to arrange an affair between the King and Madame Mazarin, has himself fallen into her [Mazarin's] toils, and malicious tongues say that he is being unfaithful to the ravishing Madame de Middleton with whom he has been in love for a long time."[6]

The tension was arbitrarily relieved after a month when Charles II sent the unnaturally distraught lover once more to Paris to bargain with Louis about the price of English neutrality in the French war against the Dutch and their confederates. Montagu and Lady Northumberland traveled to the French capital, where Barbara, Duchess of Cleveland, had now comfortably established herself.

Barbara had left England soon after Hortensia Mazarin's arrival—the Comte de Gramont escorted one duchess over the Channel and another one back. She had no direct emotional interest in the relationship between Hortensia and Charles; nevertheless, she had become deeply involved in the affair through the passionate attraction that had been fortuitously developed between the maturely vicious cosmopolitan courtesan and the fifteen-year-old daughter of the King and Barbara: Anne, Countess of Sussex.

Anne was a favorite of her father's. Charles had spent time and trouble as well as £8,000 in collecting pearls to make a necklace for her.[7] The King was doubly delighted when he perceived that Anne and Hortensia were so close. Anne was pregnant with her first child, and—possibly because of the physical difficulties entailed by her tender age—was confined to her apartments comparatively early in pregnancy. These rooms were the suite which had once been occupied by her mother when she had been Charles's mistress, and were immediately above the King's apartments with entry by a private staircase.

Soon Hortensia took to spending the night with Anne.[8] Charles would run lightly up the private stair in the morning and be delighted to find the Duchess Mazarin there.

The French observer, duly reporting to his sovereign, commented on the intimacy between the English king and his daughter's chaperone: "The King goes nearly every day to visit Madame de Sussex, whom Madame de Mazarin is nursing. I happened to be there the day before yesterday when he came. As soon as he came in Madame Mazarin went and whispered to him with a great air of familiarity, and she kept it up all the time the conversation was general, and never called him Your Majesty once. At the end of a quarter of an hour His Britannic Majesty sat on the end of the bed, and as I was alone I thought it proper to retire. But I remain convinced that it is not without foundation that the most enlightened courtiers believe that the King their master desires to profit by his opportunities."[9]

The King was now treating Louise, Duchess of Portsmouth, like a wife, courteously visiting her during the day and staying out for revelry without her until five in the morning. (Queen Catherine by this time had a separate establishment in Somerset House.) Louise not unnaturally believed and declared that young Anne was wilfully covering an intrigue between her father and her friend. Anne's husband, the Earl of Sussex, had the same conviction. The baby had not survived, and in a serious quarrel he told Anne that he would arrange a formal separation unless she gave up Mazarin and came to live with him in the country.[10] With her mother's fiery spirit, Anne refused. The affair became public and the Court took up their partisan positions.

Anne's mother heard of the scandal and wrote to her daughter from France that she would come over and remove Anne to Paris unless she showed some consideration for her husband by abandoning Mazarin. But Anne defied her mother and the King came out openly for his daughter.[11] He wrote to Barbara in Paris in defense of Anne, and he assured his daughter of his support against her husband. Excessively emboldened by this, Anne and Mazarin slipped into a number of escapades which became too public.

They took up fencing, "and went down into St. James's Park the other day with drawn swords under their night gowns, which they drew out and made several fine passes with, to the admiration of several men that was lookers on in the park."[12] The notoriety of this exhibition offended even the King, and he told Anne that her mother was so insistent on her leading a quieter life that he had had to agree that she should accompany her husband to the country.

Anne went with the Earl of Sussex to his seat at Hurst-monceux Castle and pined so much for the Duchess Mazarin, whose miniature portrait she constantly covered with kisses, that the doctors were sent for. [13]

Apart from Charles Southampton at Oxford and Anne at the Court, the Duchess of Cleveland had her children with her in Paris—three of the King's and the baby by Churchill. The correspondence with Charles about their elder daughter prompted a request from the King for a sight of their other girl, and Charlotte came back to London to be remarried, at the age of twelve, to the Earl of Lichfield,[14] with whom she lived in happiness and tranquillity ever after. The rest of Barbara's brood were not so orderly. When Charlotte went to England the opportunity to bolt was seized by the tutor engaged to coach Henry and George in any education additional to Barbara's conception of "what nature and I myself can give, which will be sufficient accomplishment for a married man."

The tutor was Edward Bernard, a deluded scholar of St John's College, Oxford, and his fate was succinctly summed up by Humphrey Prideaux of Christ Church: "My friend Mr. Bernard, who went into France to attend upon the two bastards of Cleveland, hath been so affronted and abused there by that insolent woman that he hath been forced to quit that employment and return."[15]

From other evidence it seems that even young George, aged twelve, was a handful, for he was precociously aware that he was being played by the English Ambassador, Ralph Montagu, as an important bait in the attempt to gain Charles's favor through marrying him to Lady Betty Percy. There was a rival eleven-year-old in the field, and young George Northumberland was picking fights with him whenever they met in Paris.[16]

Charles II, though without legitimate issue, was having heavy experience of the responsibilities of fatherhood in the spring of 1676. His daughter Anne was becoming unmanageable. He feared that Charlotte might go the same way if she were left any longer with her mother, and so summoned her to England to be remarried. A bride was being dangled before him for one of his sons and he was doubtful where to bestow her. Montagu had first offered Lady Betty Percy for "Don Carlos"—Charles's illegitimate son by Catherine Pegge—now nineteen and lately created Charles Fitzcharles, Earl of Plymouth. The King was being pushed by Barbara Cleveland from Paris to annex Lady Betty for their own son, George Northumberland and, though Charles resented the intensity of Barbara's lobbying, this plan appealed to him more.

Nothing was cut and dried, however, for under the complex terms of the will of Lady Betty's father the fact that her mother had remarried nominally deprived her of custody of Lady Betty, who was now theoretically at the disposal of her grandmother: but Montagu had long been contesting this clause in the courts and ridiculed its validity. The little girl's grandmother, however, planned a marriage with young Lord Ogle, son and heir of the Duke of Newcastle, and Ogle had at least to be named as an entry for the great prize.

From Montagu's point of view his principal embarrassment was that all contestants—the Earl of Plymouth, the Earl of Northumberland and the Earl of Ogle—were in Paris, buzzing around Lady Betty and conducting infighting among themselves.

"All the [Villiers] family do reckon that the King has engaged himself," Montagu wrote to Lord Treasurer Danby, "to My Lady Duchess of Cleveland to do all he can to procure this match for My Lord Northumberland, who himself is already cunning enough to be enquiring of me after My Lady Betty Percy, and has taken such an aversion to My Lord Ogle about the report, that when they meet at my house he is always ready to laugh or make mouths at him, so that the governor now will never scarce let them meet."[17]

A month later Montagu wrote Danby a letter of an entirely different tenor, which was by cumulation to send Danby to the Tower for five years.

Montagu said that at that moment France's foreign policy was so dependent on English good will that the French king would willingly pay for its continuance on the present lines of giving no encouragement to France's enemies. Charles's neutrality could be priced at between nine and twelve million livres [up to £1,000,000] a year, and he should ask for it and use the money to ease himself from any dependence on Parliament.

Montagu put the proposition as sheer economic common sense. The rich towns which Louis's army was then capturing in Flanders were, said the Ambassador, really owed to King Charles, "for there is not one of those towns which you see so easily taken that, if they were encouraged by a declaration of the King for them, would not hold out long enough to ruin the best army in France before they yielded. I am sure there is not a man in France, except those French ministers that know the contrary, that do not conclude that our master for his neutrality has every year subsidies to the value of at least three or four millions; I am sure it is worth three times that to the French King."[18]

Danby suppressed this letter, but the seed had been sown. Meanwhile, Montagu turned to deal with the more obtrusive matter of the Duchess of Cleveland.

Barbara had settled well in Paris and, apart from the worries induced by her precocious children, found diversions to take her mind off Churchill.

Edward Bernard, the frustrated tutor to her boys, was able to report on these activities when he returned to Oxford and the news was relayed from there: "She driveth a cunning trade, and followeth her old employment very hard there, especially with the Archbishop of Paris, who is her principal gallant."[19]

This archbishop, Francois de Harlay de Champvallon, had his morals impugned by more than one reliable commentator. But there were successors to the prelate circling in the offing, and among them was the English Ambassador himself.

Barbara's preoccupation with the capture of Lady Betty Percy for her son had led to a new intimacy with the Montagus. It was novel because, although she had long been acquainted with Ralph through his sister Lady Harvey, Barbara had always been on bad terms with his wife— understandably, since she was a daughter of Thomas Wriothesley, Earl of Southampton, who had been Barbara's longstanding foe as Lord High Treasurer. (The relationship between the two women can not have been helped by the fact that Barbara had taken for her family the two titles of Southampton and Northumberland which had been Elizabeth Wriothesley's.) However, the two women came together through their interest in a suitable marriage for their children, and Barbara marked the *détente* by having a liaison with husband Montagu.

It was not a particularly reprehensible union, for both partners were now so dissolute that the social impact was slight. But at least they could be viewed as striking a blow for England and English libertinism in foreign fields.

Already at home in London, after Barbara had been absent for less than a year, there was an almost nostalgic regret for her appealingly open bawdry. Portsmouth was outmarching her reputation for rapacity and Mazarin for sexual guile, but it was sensed that as an all-round punk of panache Barbara had never been beaten, and in some quarters it was, in tongue-in-cheek appeals to the King, declared shameful that he should have to rely on foreign whores when the native product was still the best:

To pay thy debts what sums canst thou advance
Now thy exchequer is gone into France
T'enrich a harlot all made up of French,
Not worthy to be call'd a whore, but wench?
Cleveland indeed deserv'd that noble name,
Whose monstrous lechery exceeds all fame.
The Empress Messalina tir'd in lust at least,
But you could never satisfy this beast.
Cleveland, I say, was much to be admir'd,
For she was never satisfi'd or tir'd.
Full forty men a day have swiv'd the whore,
Yet like a bitch she wags her tail for more.[20]

It is credible that even Charles was susceptible to this nostalgia, for when Barbara's amours of the spring of 1678 were maliciously drawn to his attention the response certainly indicated jealousy among other reactions of injured pride.

Towards the end of 1677 young Anne, now aged sixteen, quarreled so outrageously with her husband that the King sent her to Paris, where her mother put her in a religious house, the monastery of Conflans.[21] The restraint in this retreat was not so severe as might be imagined, for the wily Anne soon learned to bribe the abbess with presents so that she could come and go as she willed.[22]

At the same time the Duchess disposed of her youngest daughter—the five-year-old girl formally called the Lady Barbara Fitzroy, although she was never acknowledged by the King and never denied as the daughter of Churchill. She put the child in the English convent in Paris of the Order of the Conception, commonly called the Blue Nuns. She gave the convent £1,000 with which they immediately started building a new church: it is the only religious donation ever recorded of the Duchess of Cleveland.

She had a curious connection with this house. Its patron was the Abbé Walter Montagu, a kinsman of the Ambassador's. But also in this convent at the same time as little Barbara were two nieces of Roger Castlemaine, Jane and Barbara Darell. They were the daughters of Marmaduke Darell and Roger's sister, Catherine Palmer, and so were also the nieces of Henry Darell, who joined with Roger in underground activity against the Commonwealth and for the King in the months before the Restoration.*

Meanwhile, the Duchess of Cleveland had a double love affair on her mind and a double marriage on her hands.

In addition to Ralph Montagu, but unbeknown to him, she had accepted the advances—if she had not initiated them herself—of a young, handsome but indigent member of the French King's court, Alexis Marquis de Châtillon, First Gentleman of the Bedchamber to Louis XIV. But as a marriage broker she was in even greater intimacy with Montagu because she was devising a grand union between his family and hers by a dual link. Lady Betty Percy was no longer to be given to George Northumberland but to his elder brother, Henry, Duke of Grafton. George was to have Anne Montagu, the only daughter of the uneasy coupling between Ralph Montagu and the Dowager Countess of Northumberland. She was four years old and George was all of twelve, but there would be a reasonable age gap between husband and wife by the time she came to the age of consent—and in the meantime she was a

---

*See page 22. These nieces made their profession on January 25, 1667. One of them, Barbara, died in 1679. The other, Jane, continued at the convent and was abbess from 1723 to 1739, when she died at the age of eighty.[23] For Barbara Fitzroy's fate, see page 261.

great heiress, and should be shackled into a marriage contract quickly. The only apparent snag in this proposal was that Henry Grafton was already married. Before the King and Lord Arlington the Archbishop of Canterbury had joined him in matrimony to Isabella Bennet. Fortunately, little Isabella had not yet reached the age of twelve, when the vows had to be renewed for the marriage to be binding. Barbara Cleveland planned a speedy trip to England to break the Grafton/Arlington marriage and free handsome Henry, at the age of fourteen, for a brighter future.[24]

Politically, Ralph Montagu was now in the thickest of his intrigues. The proposal he had made earlier to Lord Treasurer Danby had at last germinated, and he was in possession of letters from Danby proposing a settlement between France on the one side and Holland and Spain and the Holy Roman Empire on the other, and naming, as the price of Charles's negotiation of this peace, a pension from Louis to Charles of six million livres [£500,000] a year for three years to support him until he could dare to meet Parliament again after this unpopular imposition.[25]

This was a purely adventurist policy of Montagu's which he was using for his own ends. He was aiming to secure the office of Secretary of State in London, for which he had offered the then holder, Henry Coventry, £10,000; but Danby had withheld his consent. The letters now in Montagu's cabinet could be used as blackmail to force Danby to yield this place when necessary.

Montagu's aim, as he frankly expounded it to his mistress, the Duchess of Cleveland, was to conspire for the extinction of Danby, to gain Secretary Coventry's place, to go on from there to take Danby's old post of Lord High Treasurer, and from this position to conciliate the King by finding a way "to furnish him so easily with money for his pocket and his wenches that we will quickly out Bab May and lead the King by the nose." As a preliminary to this project, he was sending to the English Court an astrologer for whom Charles had a great respect. This astrologer, Charles believed, had while the King was still in exile foretold his restoration even to the date of May 29, 1660, when he was to enter London. Montagu planned to bribe this astrologer to "foretell" to the King infallible ruin unless he rid himself of certain ministers who had an evil star, foremost among whom was the Earl of Danby. It is a measure of the indiscretion of Montagu, in spite of his long years as ambassador, that in his infatuation he confided all these plans to the Duchess of Cleveland, who was not the most reliable of conspirators.*

Montagu further complicated his plot by becoming furiously jealous of Barbara when he eventually found out that she was having a love affair with the Marquis de Châtillon. This disclosure occurred when Barbara was about to make her journey to England in order to break the Grafton/Arlington marriage, to get Charles to agree to the switch in Lady Betty Percy's bridegrooms, and to collect new rents now due to her after her appointment as Steward of Hampton Court and Ranger of Bushey Park.

Montagu had secured extremely compromising letters which Barbara had written to the Marquis, and he forwarded these to Charles while Barbara was making her journey. Consequently—and this is an indication of the surpris-

---

*The entire conspiracy, as the Duchess of Cleveland later disclosed it, is detailed in Barbara's letter to Charles, June 28, 1678, printed in the Appendix, page 267.

ing jealousy which Charles could still generate for Barbara —the Duchess of Cleveland received a remarkably cool reception when she arrived at Whitehall. One result of this was that the Grafton marriage was never broken.

But the direst blow was yet to fall. As soon as Montagu's mistress was out of France the Ambassador carried off her daughter Anne and seduced her, and there is no indication that the Countess of Sussex was unwilling. It was no clandestine affair. The liaison was the talk of Paris.[26]

Barbara therefore returned from London to Paris to face some highly undiplomatic conduct on the part of the English Ambassador.

In uncontrolled reaction she sat down to write one of the most amazingly forthright letters in the amalgam of fallible state policy and more fallible human emotion which makes up history. She told Charles that his daughter had left her monastery to stay repeatedly with Montagu until five in the morning. She admitted that Montagu had a hold on her by obtaining possession of a "foolish letter" she had sent her lover Châtillon, but claimed that he had forwarded it to the Court only in malice because she would not submit to his lust. She recounted the stages of Montagu's plot to "lead by the nose" the King, whom he despised and wished to send back on his travels—"for you were a dull governable fool, and the Duke [of York] a wilful fool. So that it was yet better to have you than him, but that you always chose a greater beast than yourself to govern you." She outlined the conspiracy with the astrologer, and Montagu's steps to take over the post of Lord High Treasurer. Admitting her affair with Châtillon, she pleaded: "All I have to say for myself is that you know as to love one is not mistress of one's self, and that

you ought not to be offended with me since all things of this
nature is at an end with you and I." The King of France,
she said, "could not imagine that you ought to be so angry,
or indeed be at all concerned; for that all the world knew
that now all things of gallantry were at an end with you and
I; that being so, and so public, he did not see why you
should be offended at my loving anybody."

In a final appeal she reminded him of his charge to her
when they had last met and he had revealed that he still
kept her letters: "You said, Madam, all that I ask of you for
your own sake is Live so for the future as to make the least
noise you can, and I care not who you love. Oh! this noise
that is had never been had it not been for the Ambassador's
malice. I cannot forbear once again saying I hope you will
not gratify his malice in my ruin."

Charles replied, in a letter which no longer exists, clearly
upholding Barbara in her tardy protection of their daughter,
and apparently making no reference to his intended treatment of Montagu. It was to be harsh, but it was not
woman's business. He enclosed a letter for Anne commanding her to submit to her mother.

Barbara replied with a letter of more domestic tone detail-
ing the strife which the wild Countess of Sussex was still
instigating. In this letter she made the forensically convincing claim that Anne, her first child, born exactly nine
months after the Restoration, really was the daughter of the
King, in spite of court gossip that she was Chesterfield's and
Roger Castlemaine's faint hope that she could be his:
"Though I am so good a Christian as to forgive her, yet I
cannot so far conquer myself as to see her daily; though
Your Majesty may be confident that, as she is yours, I shall

always have some remains of that kindness I had formerly, for I can hate nothing that is yours."

For the moment Charles confined his daughter to a stricter convent and poised to deal with Montagu. The Ambassador himself was behaving with the extreme reaction of panic. He sent an urgent letter to his sister, Lady Harvey, attempting to curry favor with the King by instructing her to hasten the match between George Northumberland and Lady Betty Percy through drafting a formal request from Charles to Montagu's wife.[27]

He traveled posthaste to England to make some personal explanation to the King, though this was a serious breach of duty since he had not been formally recalled. But he was dealing not only with a monarch's sense of protocol but also with a former lover's jealousy and with a possessive father's disgust at his sexual conduct.

Montagu was promptly deprived of all his offices, his privy councilorship, his post under Queen Catherine, and even the Mastership of the Royal Wardrobe for which he had paid £14,000. He was dismissed from his ambassadorship, and the Earl of Sunderland was sent to replace him, accompanied by Henry Savile, brother to the Marquis of Halifax, who was to sort out the tangled emotions of Barbara and her daughter Anne.*

As soon as he was convinced that he would remain in dis-

*Savile was perhaps an unfortunate choice. He had once attempted to rape Lady Northumberland, Montagu's wife, after midnight in her bedroom, was interrupted, and having escaped a hue and cry raised among the country house party they were both attending, was not wholly believed when he declared that Lady Northumberland must have seen a ghost. The summons to go to Paris came when he was sweating in the middle of the then fashionable mercury cure for venereal disease.[28]

grace as long as Lord Treasurer Danby was in power, Montagu approached Barillon, the French Ambassador in London, and negotiated a bargain under which he was to bring about the fall of Danby within six months. Montagu's price was 100,000 crowns down [£25,000] or a pension of 40,000 livres a year [over £3,000], and the deal was accepted, for the French wanted Danby out.[29] Montagu then got himself elected to the House of Commons in order to obtain parliamentary immunity from arrest in the struggle which lay ahead.

When the King and Danby moved against Montagu, therefore, they could only order the seizure of his papers and not his confinement.

In the House of Commons Montagu triumphantly produced the letters proving that Danby had ordered him to request Louis XIV for a six million livres pension for Charles as payment for not convening Parliament. Danby, impeached for high treason, dared not use the obvious defense that, if he was involved in a plot to purchase a shameful secret peace with France while still maintaining a standing army, Montagu was as equally involved, and had in fact instigated it. Belatedly, he tried to cover himself by getting the King to write on the drafts of the damning letters, "I approve of this letter," with his cipher.[30]*

In order to save Danby's neck Charles dissolved Parliament—it had sat for seventeen years, since 1661. Danby pulled every string to try and secure a more favorable Com-

---

*Thirty-two years later, when Danby, as Duke of Leeds, printed versions of these letters, he falsely published the endorsement as "This letter is writ by my order, C.R." The master-treatment of the subject is Andrew Browning: Thomas Osborne, Earl of Danby and Duke of Leeds 1632–1712, 3 vols., Glasgow, Jackson, 1944–1951.

mons in the new election, and failed. Trying to avoid a further impeachment, Charles granted Danby a pardon in advance. On a technical point the first impeachment was resumed.

Charles dared not face the publicity of a full trial, with the production of the documents of all his devious negotiations with France. He commanded Danby to go into hiding. Under pain of execution whenever he was discovered after a certain date, the Commons forced him into the open, and Danby went to the Tower for an indefinite period. Five years later he was released on bail.

A chief minister had fallen and an English standing army had been disbanded (which was exactly what French diplomacy wanted); a Parliament had been transferred into more reactionary hands; the King had been defeated in every move he had made to sustain his power and support his servants—all as a direct consequence of a sordid situation in Paris between a man, a mother and a daughter with an abundance of passion in each.

Sooner or later the stream of political events would have been swollen to race towards this particular cataract, and if it had not been this there might have been some other muddy froth on its surface. But without the interaction of the Duchess of Cleveland and Ambassador Montagu, and their separate influence on the King, the climax could have come later rather than sooner. Charles II might have staved off for much longer a political situation which weakened him if Barbara had not written her letter revealing the conspiracy, which prompted Montagu's powerful counterattack. And Barbara's letter would not have been written if she had not been in serious fear of her ruin through the evidence of

Charles's anger at her affair with the French Marquis. Charles, therefore, could have kept the dangerous situation at bay if he had more adequately repressed his jealousy, or had been serious when he told Barbara, "I care not who you love."

But, as it was, neither for love nor money could he shake himself free from her. A questing Barbara was bound for England again, seeking out treasure in Whitehall and trophies in Windsor. "His Majesty," said an amused observer, "gave the Commissioners of the Treasury fair warning to look to themselves, for that she would have a bout with them for money, having lately lost £20,000 in money and jewels in one night at play."[31]*

*The King could wryly warn his treasury commissioners, but he could not defend himself, and would not support his ministers when they tried to protect him against his former mistress. Barbara returned to England in the autumn of 1679 for the remarriage of Henry Grafton and Isabella Bennet which the King had commanded. She wheedled £25,000 out of Charles and sent to the Treasury for the money. The principal Commissioner of the Treasury—that is, the acting Lord High Treasurer in succession to Danby—was Arthur Capel, Earl of Essex. Essex stopped the payment of the £25,000 and told the King that he was following Charles's own request not to pay out money on accounts of this nature "while he was so much indebted to such as daily clamoured at their table for money." If the King wished the £25,000 to be paid, Essex said, then somebody else should do it, for he would rather surrender his office than pay it. Charles coldly replied, "I will take you at your word," and dismissed Essex, appointing Lawrence Hyde, who promptly paid the account. Hyde was the youngest son of former Chancellor Clarendon, and might have been expected to oppose his father's enemy, but "the Duchess was ever his friend and kept him in"—a revealing indication of the power Barbara still held."

CHARLES Stuart was in his fifties, and inclined to fall asleep after dinner. If he took off his wig to make himself easier he exposed a bald crown. When she felt mischievous, his daughter, Charlotte Lichfield, would tickle his pate. The King was relaxed now with Louise Portsmouth as the companion of his age, and the other idle ladies were memories or ambitions, provoking no more than a hand in the bosom. He enjoyed the family he had bred from his body and the families they were breeding for him.

"I must tell you I am glad to hear you are with child," he wrote to his dear Charlotte, "and I hope to see you here before it be long, that I may have the satisfaction myself of telling you how much I love you, and how truly I am your kind father, Charles Rex."[1]

Now all of Barbara's children were married except George Northumberland, the "tall black man" who most strongly resembled him. George was a good friend of the younger

boys, Nelly's Charles and Louise's Charles, the Dukes of St.
Albans and of Richmond. The King was glad he had been
able to raise George to his dukedom and give him his Garter
in time . . . in time.

Charles Stuart was on his deathbed, and in the exhaustion
of great pain he saw his sons kneel, one by one, before him.
Charles Plymouth, Charles Southampton, Henry Grafton,
George Northumberland, Charles Richmond, Charles St.
Albans—the King audibly blessed each in turn, seeming in a
state of great tenderness after his reception of the Holy
Communion according to the rites of the Church of Rome.
The Protestant bishops asked the King to bless his country
and his people. All the great concourse in the bedchamber
knelt. Charles found the strength to raise himself in his bed,
and asked those around him to forgive him for those actions
in which he had not been a good king, calling God's blessing
on them. He sank back, and sensing after a little the mood
of anticlimax among those who had been waiting four days
for his end, he said, in humorous apology, "I am sorry I am
so unconscionable a time a-dying." Then he called once
more for his brother and successor James, Duke of York,
who had already been the means of his final comfort by privately bringing to him Father Huddleston for reception by
his Church.

"He spake to the Duke," John Evelyn recorded, "to be
kind to his concubines the Duchess of Cleveland and,
especially, Portsmouth, and that Nelly might not starve."
"But I can never forget," the diarist interjected, "the
unexpressible luxury and profaneness, gaming and all dissolu-
tion and, as it were, total forgetfulness of God (it being
Sunday evening) which this day sennight I was witness of:

the King sitting and toying with his concubines Portsmouth, Cleveland and Mazarin, &c.; a French boy singing love songs in that glorious gallery, whilst about twenty of the great courtiers and other dissolute persons were at basset round a large table, a bank of at least 2000 in gold before them, upon which two gentlemen that were with me made reflections with astonishment, it being a scene of utmost vanity, and surely as they thought would never have an end. Six days after was all in the dust."[2]

It was impossible for Barbara not to be moved by the memories and implications of this good-natured reunion with Charles, albeit on terms of sophisticated, shared intimacy, just twenty-five years after they had first met. The love songs were never to be sung again for them in that glorious gallery. In understandably warm melancholy the Duchess of Cleveland was carried back from Whitehall Palace to her home at Cleveland House—where she was greeted by a swaggering, mouthing, pseudo-confident and not entirely clean tragedian, her lover Cardonell Goodman, known to his many enemies as "Scum."

She was devoted to him, as she was to all her fancy men as long as they fancied her. She was forty-four and he was ten years younger, with a career behind him which had started at Cambridge and the Court—he was expelled from both—and had progressed to the boards of Drury Lane, with highway robbery during resting periods.

They were not heroic figures. Her paint was smudged and his buckram was dented, and in Cleveland House there had been alternating scenes of passion and jealousy, culminating in the arrest of the actor on a charge of conspiring to hire a cook to poison Barbara's sons, the Dukes of Grafton and

Northumberland. It was all too theatrical to be true, and Goodman was not hanged. But he was found guilty and fined £1,000, which he procured by highway robbery, having a dispensation for this craft.*

Cardonell Goodman, long forgiven by Barbara, strutted from the criminal court to Drury Lane, where the Queen was to be in the audience to see him act. (His most famous roles were Othello and Alexander the Great.) As soon as the Queen arrived the usual practice was followed and the front stage curtain was raised. Goodman was discovered, center stage, sweeping the horizon of the boxes with hand-shaded eye. "What!" he entoned. "Is my Duchess come?" There was no sign of Barbara, but only an embarrassed indication that the Queen was present. "By God," said Goodman, with an additional selection of more terrible oaths, "the play does not start until my Duchess is come." At this moment Barbara came into the auditorium and relieved her lover of further *lèse-majesté*.[4]

With the accession of James II, who had been an open Roman Catholic for twelve years, the able Catholic Roger Castlemaine obtained royal recognition. He had come back to England in 1677 at an unfortunate time, just before the fabrication of the popish plot by Titus Oates, and for two years Roger was in and out of the Tower of London on fanciful charges of high treason.

King James now appointed him his Ambassador Extraordinary to Rome, and, although Roger's friends tried

*Goodman's influence, presumably exercised through Barbara, was strong enough to get him twice pardoned "for all robberies," in July, 1684 and November, 1685, although with one exception his are the only pardons for robbery noted in a House of Lords abstract of all pardons granted between 1681 and 1689. The pardons total about 220 and are typically for such upper-class offenses as dueling resulting in homicide.[8]

to dissuade him from accepting for fear of reprisals if a Protestant should later come to the throne,[5] the Earl of Castlemaine set out.

His exit from England was better timed than his previous return, for before he had reached Paris Barbara and her family were in the full blaze of scandal. Henry, Duke of Grafton, fought Jack Talbot, brother to the Earl of Shrewsbury, and killed him in a duel. He went into hiding immediately, and the only social effect of the duel was the cancellation of the Queen's Candlemas Ball that night, in which all Barbara's children had been invited to dance in different national costumes.[6]

A pardon was speedily obtained from King James, but as soon as Henry came out of concealment he learned that his brother George had contracted a clandestine marriage with a lady called Catherine Lucy, widow of a simple army captain and daughter of a poulterer. Henry, who had the affectations of the rest of the Court, objected strongly, holding with the Countess of Norton that the lady was "rich only in beauty, which though much prized will hardly maintain the quality of a Duchess."[7] King James was angry, perhaps with more reason for his frustration, since he had just negotiated to marry young George to a daughter of the Duke of Newcastle.*[8]

*She was the sister of the Earl of Ogle, at whom George had been pulling faces in Paris eight years previously for the love of Lady Betty Percy. Lady Betty soon afterwards was married to Ogle, but the boy died leaving her a virgin widow. Barbara Cleveland tried once more to gain her for George Northumberland, but her grandmother sold her in matrimony to the rich Thomas Thynne of Longleat, "Tom of Ten Thousand," who was shortly afterwards murdered by Count Coningsmark, also for love of Lady Betty. She finally married the Earl of Somerset, her third husband, at the age of fifteen.

Henry kidnapped the couple and browbeat George into shipping his new duchess to Flanders, where they put her into a convent at Ghent, and Henry came back to consult an ecclesiastical lawyer in Doctors Commons about the possibility of a divorce. This high-handed treatment of the new Duchess of Northumberland, who was a Catholic, further angered King James, who had accepted the marriage, once made. He sent the two brothers across the Channel again to bring the lady back and present her at Court.*⁹

Barbara, Duchess of Cleveland took no part in this commotion, being again parturient and in no condition to deal with her errant dukes, aged twenty-two and twenty. "In the meantime," a Town gossip reported to his country outlet, "their gracious mother is brought to bed of a son which the Town has christened Goodman Cleveland."¹⁰

Roger Castlemaine was not a success in Rome. Pope Innocent XI disliked his manner and would discuss nothing with him. When Castlemaine finally threatened to return to England, the Pope blandly recommended that he start early, since it was dangerous in Italy to travel in the heat of the day. Roger put his servants and his baggage (including four orange trees being consigned to the wife of Judge Jeffreys of the Bloody Assizes, now Lord Chancellor of England)¹¹ on

*She became an acceptable lady of the bedchamber. To complete her the marital adventures of Barbara's sons, Charles Southampton had been a childless widower since Mary Wood died in 1680 and he inherited her estates and a dozen years of lawsuits. He married again in 1694 and begot a son reputed to be "a greater fool than his father" but with the inestimable virtue of having estates worth over £100,000 a year. The story of how Lady Harriet Finch, sister of the Earl of Nottingham, was swept into marriage with this man, William, Duke of Cleveland and Southampton, by the mothers of the couple before the girl's brother could intervene to stop the "sacrifice" is entertainingly told in the Egmont Diary, January 26, 1732, HMC 63 I, p. 217.

the ship *Alexander* at Civita Vecchia. Fortunately he did not travel by her himself, for some leagues out at sea, she was captured by three Algerine pirates.[12]

Roger came home, was advanced to the Privy Council, and was mentioned for various offices including Lord Chancellor, Secretary of State, and Lord Lieutenant of Ireland. But in the Revolution which expelled James II, whereas Churchill and Grafton had a keen contest as to who should be first to desert the King who had greatly advanced them, Roger maintained his principles and his loyalty, and consequently was soon thrown into the Tower.*

For six years, from 1690 to 1696, the Earl of Castlemaine was alternately released and rearrested under a persecuting cat-and-mouse procedure, and spent much of his time in the Tower and even in Newgate.[14] Finally he went into exile at Saint-Germain in France and joined the court of his dethroned king.

The changes in the monarchy made little difference to the Duchess of Cleveland, who had still to exert herself

---

*Henry Grafton died shortly afterwards for King William and Queen Mary, being mortally injured when he was second in command to Churchill at the siege of Cork. In this Vicar-of-Bray period the most outstandingly regular turncoat was Ralph Montagu, who finally achieved a dukedom. His wife, Lady Northumberland, died in 1690 and he looked around for another fortune. He sighted Elizabeth Cavendish (another of the Newcastle/Ogle family), the dowager Duchess of Albemarle. She was extremely rich but even more eccentric, or perhaps more properly mad: she had declared that she would take no one for a second husband but a crowned head. Montagu therefore decked himself in Oriental costume, announced that he was the Emperor of China, and was accepted by the lady. Once he had got her £7,000 a year he kept her so secluded that it was rumored that she was dead but he dared not admit it because he would lose her income. However, she survived him by twenty-five years.[18]

periodically to get her pensions paid, but never had them totally withdrawn. She continued a long association with Goodman and yet was accepted at court. She fell into temporary disfavor by association when her youngest child Barbara, Churchill's daughter, herself bore an illegitimate child to James Douglas, Earl of Arran and later fourth Duke of Hamilton, a cousin of Barbara's old companion, Lady Anne Hamilton. Queen Mary II was so angered by news of this intrigue that she insisted that Lady Barbara Fitzroy should retire to another convent in France.*[15] Yet the Duchess of Cleveland rode out the storm and retained the tolerance of the Court despite the envy of other rejected royal mistresses.

There is a virulent letter from Catherine Sedley, Countess of Dorchester, to the Earl of Nottingham in which the former mistress of the deposed King James complains of being ostracized at Court "although it was the Queen's [Queen Mary II, daughter of James II and Anne Hyde] pleasure no wrong should be done me . . . I can add this to all the rest, that the Queen is obliged every day to admit of ladies I should be very sorry to be compared to, for instance the Duchesses of Mazarin and Cleveland, the Ladies Oxford, Fitzharding and Bellasis. The characters of every one of these must be so well known to you that converse freely in the world that I cannot be the least suspected

---

*Charles Hamilton, Barbara Fitzroy's son by this union, was a comfort to his grandmother Cleveland in her last years and became greatly loved by his father. He emerged as a historian of some distinction. Barbara Fitzroy died in 1734 at the age of forty-three, and was buried in the choir of the collegiate church of Manchester. A gentleman named William Dawson chose to be buried with her, "not only to testify his gratitude to a kind benefactress, but because his fate was similar to hers; for she was disowned by her mother, and he was disinherited by his father."[16]

of malice in naming them thus. I am sure it goes much against my stomach to name myself with them ... That jury might possibly acquit me that would whip every one of the ladies afore mentioned."[17]

Barbara, now aged fifty, smilingly declined to be whipped, and continued to pet Cardonell Goodman, until after six years he became engaged in a Jacobite conspiracy in which carbines and pistols were discovered in the Duchess's new home in Arlington Street, possibly planted in an attempt to incriminate her. Goodman escaped to France and Barbara went to Tunbridge.[18] She made her regular pilgrimage there, gambling against gentlemen only, and not always profitably.[19]

While she was there in 1705 she had news of the death of her husband, Roger, Earl of Castlemaine. He had slipped over from France to die in his mother's countryside among the Herberts and Powises of Wales, and there at last this wronged and rootless man expired at the age of seventy-one, and was buried at Welshpool, County Montgomery. His will made Anne, Countess of Sussex, not here claimed as his daughter, his trustee and principal legatee, passing much property to her, with all his plate, jewels and personalty. Anne had spent some years in France since the Revolution,[20] and Roger's old fondness for the child he had dandled had been cultivated.

The life of Barbara Duchess of Cleveland then progressed into farce. She was "free" after forty-six years, and so within four months she allowed herself to be courted, and was married again.

The victor was Robert Feilding, a self-styled major-general, commonly called "Handsome" Feilding or "Beau" Feilding, and declared to be "the universal flame of all the fair sex; innocent virgins sighed for him as Adonis; experienced widows as Hercules."[21] He was fifty-four years old and she was sixty-four.

So far Feilding had married one virgin, one widow and two fortunes, and having survived all four blessings he was now looking for a third wife and fortune. He was considering the siege of a young widow named Anne Deleau whose husband had left her £60,000—as Feilding checked by inspecting the will at Doctors Commons—when he heard of the death of Roger Castlemaine and paid more than usual attention to the circumstances of his titular widow. He was weighing in his mind whether to marry a block fortune or a high pension when it occurred to him that it might be possible to marry both.

He met a hairdresser called Charlotte Henrietta Villars who said she attended Mistress Deleau, and he promised her £500 if she would help him to bring off the marriage with the young widow. The hairdresser recognized that she had no influence with Mistress Deleau, but as she knew that Feilding had never seen his intended wife, but only the will that left her the money, she decided to introduce a substitute. Accordingly, one evening in early November, 1705, she brought to Feilding's lodgings a lady in widow's habit conveyed in a mourning coach whom she introduced as Mistress Deleau.

After a third clandestine meeting of this nature the couple were married by a Roman Catholic priest in these lodgings. The bride permitted the consummation of the marriage, but went away in the morning saying that the marriage must still be kept a secret until she had won her father round. She came back to sleep with Feilding at intervals, by arrangement with the hairdresser, and every time they met Feilding invested his supposed heiress-bride with money and gifts which he hoped soon to recoup from her fortune.

Unfortunately, the *soi-disant* Anne Deleau was a penniless adventuress recently out of Bridewell, named Mary Wadsworth. When Charlotte Villars asked for her £500 for having brought off the marriage Feilding asked her to wait for a few days and then gave her the money, having wheedled it from the Duchess of Cleveland whom he had married in the meantime.

Handsome Feilding had in fact been skilful enough to conduct two courtships simultaneously and to conclude two marriages in sixteen days, on November 9 and 25, 1705.

No sooner was he, however illegally, the lord and master of the Duchess of Cleveland than he began a course of swift extortion. Her Post Office pension of roughly £100 a week was coming in regularly at this time, and he got as much of it as possible into his own pocket. Then he began to dispose of her furniture. When she objected he locked her up and starved her. In order to get his hands on her money he beat her. Finally, Barbara conquered her pride sufficiently to tell her sons and grandsons what was happening. Feilding immediately threatened to kill her, broke open her closet and took £400, beat her until she cried "Murder!" from the window, whereupon he began shooting with a blunderbuss at people in the street. Barbara's sons got a warrant and brought Feilding before the Lord Chief Justice, who committed him to Newgate.

Amid the publicity aroused by this, Charlotte Villars and Mary Wadsworth, black and smarting with beatings they

themselves had recently received when Feilding discovered
that Wadsworth was not an heiress, came to the Duke of
Grafton, Barbara's grandson, and told him that Handsome
Feilding had been legally married to Mary Wadsworth a
fortnight before he married the Duchess of Cleveland. A
criminal charge of bigamy was brought against Feilding and
he was convicted, but Queen Anne pardoned him. It took
longer to establish a decree of nullity of marriage between
Robert Feilding and Barbara Duchess of Cleveland, but
when the lady was in her sixty-seventh year that, too, was
accomplished.[22]

She had two years to live. She moved out of London to
Chiswick Mall and was lovingly cared for by her grandson,
Charles Hamilton, Barbara Fitzroy's child. In the summer
of 1709 she developed a dropsy "which swelled her gradually
to a monstrous bulk and in about three months' time put a
period to her life."[23] She died on October 9, 1709.

While she was early laid on what became her deathbed,
Joseph Addison in *The Tatler* was writing a fanciful version
of the affair with the Beau. He recorded as the first greeting
given by Major General Feilding to the Duchess:
"Madam, it is not only that Nature has made us two the
most accomplished of each sex and pointed to us to obey her
dictates in becoming one; but that there is also an ambition
in following the mighty persons you have favoured. Where
kings and heroes as great as Alexander, or such as could per-
sonate Alexander,* have bowed, permit your General to lay
his laurels."[24]

*An allusion to Goodman, who was famous for his playing of Alexan-
der the Great.

It was gentle fun, and Barbara could find a smile for it. She had taken far harder literary knocks in her time, and much more venomous personal abuse. The eldest son of Chesterfield—of the Chesterfield with whom she had started her long course of love—sneered at the Beau and excoriated her with his reference to "a mad imaginary general who is so happy as to be fond of that which my father and all the world besides himself were weary of long ago. I think him a happy madman since he can at this time be pleased with Cleveland . . . without so much as calling back the idea of *quantum mutatus ab illo*." [25]

"*Quantum mutatus ab illo*": How changed from what I was. That was Wycherley's mournful text, which he insisted should be inscribed on the portraits painted in his youth. *Quantum mutatus ab illo* was Wycherley . . . was Churchill . . . was Charles . . . was Chesterfield. She had married none of them, yet had not been entirely barren. But Wycherley's song approved of that, and praised the offspring:

Great wits and great braves
Have always a punk for their mother.

"You! Wycherley!' she had shouted as she leaned out of her carriage to compliment him. "You are the son of a whore!"

And now, gross on her couch with the dropsy—*quantum mutata ab illa*—she was still of the spirit to lie back and shake with the resonance of that distant laughter.

# Appendix
## The Duchess of Cleveland's letters to
## King Charles II from Paris, 1678.

THESE unique letters are printed in full below. Apart from the factual evidence they offer on events preceding the downfall of Montagu and Danby, they present an unparalleled revelation of the difficulties affecting a king, his discarded mistress and their difficult, teenage child.

The letters are given in modernized spelling and punctuation. Barbara was an indifferent writer and an idiosyncratic speller. The third letter, printed as it was written, gives the modern reader an idea of the ordeal from which he has been spared. It is a highly characteristic begging letter from the Duchess of Cleveland to Lord Clifford of Chudleigh, Lord High Treasurer of England. It was written in June, 1673, in the days when the Test Act was coming into force. Lord Clifford was a (secret) Roman Catholic, and as soon as he should be required to take Holy Communion according to the Anglican rite, and sign a declaration denying the doctrine of transubstantiation in the Sacrament he would be in conscience bound to resign his office, as he did. There was a panic rush among his acquaintances to get him to sign their remittances before he departed.

*The Duchess of Cleveland to King Charles II, Paris, June 28, 1678.*

Paris, Tuesday 28 78
I was never so surprised in my whole lifetime as I was at my

coming hither, to find My Lady Sussex gone from my house and monastery where I left her, and this letter from her, which I here send you the copy of.

I never in my whole lifetime heard of such government of herself as she has had since I went into England. She has never been in the monastery two days together, but every day gone out with the Ambassador; and has often lain four days together at my house and sent for her meat to the Ambassador, he being always with her till five o'clock in the morning, they two shut up together alone, and would not let my maître d'hotel wait, nor any of my servants, only the Ambassador's.

This has made so great a noise at Paris that she is now the whole discourse. I am so much afflicted that I can hardly write this for crying, to see that a child that I doted on as I did on her should make so ill a return and join with the worst of men to ruin me. For sure never any malice was like the Ambassador's, that, only because I would not answer to his love and the importunities he made to me, was resolved to ruin me.

I hope Your Majesty will yet have that justice and consideration for me that, though I have done a foolish action, you will not let me be ruined by this most abominable man. I do confess to you that I did write a foolish letter to the Chevalier de Châtillon, which letter I sent enclosed to Madame de Pallas, and sent hers in a packet I sent to Lady Sussex by Sir Henry Tichborne; which letter she has either given to the Ambassador or else he had it by his man, to whom Sir Harry Tichborne gave it to, not finding My Lady Sussex. But as yet I do not know which of the ways he had it, but I shall know as soon as I have spoke with Sir Harry Tichborne. But the letter he has, and I doubt not but that he either has or will send it to you.

Now all I have to say for myself is that you know, as to love, one is not mistress of one's self, and that you ought not to be offended with me, since all things of this nature is at an end with you and I; so that I could do you no prejudice. Nor will you, I hope, follow the advice of this ill man, who in his heart, I know, hates you, and were it for his interest would ruin you, too, if he could.

For he has neither conscience nor honour, and has several

times told me that in his heart he despised you and your brother; and that for his part he wished with all his heart that the Parliament would send you both to travel; for you were a dull governable fool and the Duke a wilful fool. So that it was yet better to have you than him, but that you always chose a greater beast than yourself to govern you.

And when I was come over he brought me two letters to bring to you, which he read both to me before he sealed them. The one was a man's that he said you had great faith in, for that he had several times foretold things to you that were of consequence, and that you believed him in all things, like a changeling as you were. And that now he had writ you word that in a few months the King of France, or his son, were threatened with death, or at least a great fit of sickness in which they would be in great danger if they did not die; and that therefore he counselled you to defer any resolutions of war or peace till some months were past; for that if this happened it would make a great change in France.

The Ambassador, after he had read this to me, said "Now the good of this is," says he, "that I can do what I will with this man; for he is poor, and a good sum of money will make him write whatever I will." So he proposed to me that he and I should join together in the ruining My Lord Treasurer and the Duchess of Portsmouth, which might be done thus:

The man, though he was infirm and ill, should go into England and there, after having been a little time, to solicit you for money; for that you were so base that, though you employed him, you let him starve. So that he was obliged to give him £50, and that the man had writ several times to you for money. "Oh," says he, "when he is in England he shall tell the King things that he foresees will infallibly ruin him; and so wish those to be removed, as having an ill star, that would be unfortunate to you if they were not removed: but if that were done, he was confident you would have the gloriousest reign that ever was.

"This," says he, "I am sure I can order so as to bring to a good effect, if you will. And in the meantime I will try to get Secretary Coventry's place, which he had a mind to part with, but not to Sir William Temple, because he is the Treasurer's creature and he hates the Treasurer; and I have already employed my sister to talk with Mr. Cook and to send him to engage Mr Coventry not to part with it as yet, and he has assured My Lady Harvey he will not. And My Lord Treasurer's lady and Mr. Bertie are both of them desirous I should have it. And when I have it I will be damned if I do not quickly get to be Lord Treasurer; and then you and your children shall find such a friend as never was.

"And for the King, I will find a way to furnish him so easily with money for his pocket and his wenches that we will quickly out Bab May and lead the King by the nose."

So when I had heard him out I told him I thanked him but that I would not meddle in any such thing; and that for my part I had no malice to My Lady Portsmouth or the Treasurer, and therefore I would never be in any plot to destroy them; but that I found the character the world gave of him was true—which was that the Devil was not more designing than he was. And that I wondered at it; for that sure all these things working in his brains must make him very uneasy and would at last make him mad.

'Tis possible you may think I say all this out of malice. 'Tis true he has urged me beyond all patience, but what I tell you here is most true, and I will take the Sacrament of it whenever you please. 'Tis certain I would not have been so base as to have informed against him for what he said before me had he not provoked me to it in this violent way that he has. There is no ill thing that he has not done me, and that without any provocation of mine but that I would not love him.

Now as to what relates to my daughter Sussex and her behaviour to me I must confess that afflicts me beyond expression, and will do much more if what she has done be by your orders. For though I have an entire submission to your will, and will not complain whatever you inflict upon me, yet I cannot think you would have brought things to this extremity with me and not have it in your nature ever to do no cruel things to anything living. I hope therefore you will not begin with me, and if the Ambassador has not received his orders from you that you will severely reprehend him for this inhumane proceedings.

Besides, he has done what you ought to be very angry with him for: for he has been with the King of France and told him that he had intercepted letters of mine by your order, who had been informed that there was a kindness between me and the Chevalier de Châtillon, and therefore you bid him take a course in it and stop my letters; which accordingly he has done. And that upon this you ordered him to take my children from me and to remove My Lady Sussex to another monastery. And that you were resolved to stop all my pensions and never have any regard for me in anything. And that if he would oblige Your Majesty he should forbid the Chevalier de Châtillon ever seeing me upon the displeasure of losing his place and being forbid the Court; for that he was sure you expected this from him.

Upon which the King told him that he could not do anything of this nature, for that this was a private matter and not for him to take notice of. And that he could not imagine that you ought to be so angry or indeed be at all concerned; for that all the world knew that now all things of gallantry were at an end with you and I; that being so, and so public, he did not see why you should be offended at my loving anybody. That it was a thing so common nowadays to have a gallantry that he did not wonder at anything of this nature.

And when he saw the King take the thing thus he told him that if he would not be severe to the Chevalier de Châtillon upon your account he supposed he would be so upon his own, for that in the letters he had discovered he found that the Chevalier had proposed to me the engaging of you in the marriage of the Dauphin and Mademoiselle,* and that was my greatest business in England. That before I went over I had spoke to him of the thing and would have engaged him in it; but that he refused it, for that he knew very well the indifference you had whether it were or no, and how little you cared how Mademoiselle was married. That since I went into England 'twas possible I might engage somebody or other in this matter to press it to you, but that he knew very well that in your heart you cared not whether it was or no, that this business setting on foot by the Chevalier.

*Princess Marie Louise, daughter of Charles's dead sister Minette and the Duke of Orleans, brother to Louis XIV.

Upon which the King told him that if he would show him any letters of the Chevalier de Châtillon to that purpose he should then know what he had to say to him, but that till he saw those letters he would not punish him without a proof for what he did. Upon which the Ambassador showed a letter which he pretended one part of it was a double entendre. The King said he could not see that there was anything relating to it, and so left him, and said to a person who was there: "Sure the Ambassador was the worst man that ever was, for because My Lady Cleveland will not love him he strives to ruin her the basest in the world, and would have me sacrifice the Chevalier de Châtillon to his revenge, which I shall not do till I see better proofs of his having meddled with the marriage of the Dauphin and Mademoiselle than any yet that the Ambassador has showed me."

This methinks is what you cannot but be offended at, and I hope you will be offended with him for his whole proceeding to me, and let the world see that you will never countenance the actions of so base and ill a man.

I had forgot to tell you that he told the King of France that many people had reported that he made love to me, but there was nothing of it for he had too much respect for you to think of any such thing.

As for My Lady Sussex, I hope you will think fit to send for her over, for she is now mightily discoursed of for the Ambassador. If you will not believe me in this, make inquiry into the thing and you will find it to be true.

I have desired Mr Kemble to give you this letter and to discourse with you more at large upon this matter, to know your resolution and whether I may expect that justice and goodness from you which all the world does.

I promise you that, for my conduct, it shall be such as that you nor nobody shall have occasion to blame me; and I hope you will be just to what you said to me, which was at my house, when you told me you had letters of mine. You said "Madam, all that I ask of you, for your own sake, is live so for the future as to make the least noise you can, and I care not who you love." Oh, this noise that is had never been had it not been for the Ambassador's malice. I cannot forbear once again saying I hope you will not gratify his malice in my ruin.

*The Duchess of Cleveland to King Charles II, Paris, July, 1678.*

Paris, Friday, 3 o'clock in the afternoon
I received Your Majesty's letter last night with more joy than I can express, for this proceeding of yours is so generous and obliging that I must be the worst woman alive were I not sensible. No, Sir, my heart and soul is touched with this generosity of yours, and you shall always find that my conduct to the world and behaviour to your children shall always render me worthy of your protection and favour; this pray be confident of.

I did this morning send your letter to My Lady Sussex by my gentleman of the horse, who when he came to the gate asked for her. Her woman came and told him her lady was asleep. He said he would stay till she was awake, for that he had a letter to give into her own hands from the King, and that he would not deliver it but to herself.

Her woman went in to her and stayed above half an hour, which I believe was whilst she sent to the Ambassador, for he came in as Lachosse was there. Her woman came out and said that her lady had been ill two days and had convulsion fits and knew nobody: upon which Lachosse said that since she was in that condition he would carry back the letter to me. The woman answered that if he would leave the letter with her she would give it to her lady when she came to herself, but that now she knew nobody, and called all that were about her My Lord Ambassador and My Lady, and spoke of nothing but them.

As soon as I heard this I sent to the Archbishop of Paris to let him know that having sent to Belle Chasse to speak with my daughter and to send her a letter of concern from the King I heard that she was extreme ill and could not come to the parlour, wherefore I desired he would send to the Abbess to let one of my women go in to speak with her. He immediately writ, on which I sent Pigeon with. When she went to the Abbess she said that My Lady Sussex was not so ill as that there was a necessity of opening the doors of the monastery, and that if she would come at seven o'clock at night My Lady Sussex would be at the parlour, but that now she could not come because she had just been let blood, and that for coming in she would not permit her. Upon this I sent again to the Archbishop and sent your letter to him, which I made to be put into French that he might see why I pressed him so earnestly, and desired him to send a more positive command to the Abbess.

He read the letter and said he was very much surprised, but he would send a priest along with my woman and him to speak to the Abbess, but that priest should go in his coach. All this was to gain time that he might send, as I believe, to My Lady Sussex who he visits very often. And this monastery where she is is called the Bishop's Monastery, and has none of the best reputations.

When Pigeon came to the monastery the priest talked with the Abbess about half an hour, and then came to her and told her that My Lady Sussex was at the parlour. She went there and found My Lady Sussex sitting there with the Ambassador. She gave her the letter. The Ambassador turned to her and told her "Mistress Pigeon, the King has some of your letters." She made him a curtsey and said "Has he, My Lord? I am very glad of it."

My Lady Sussex said "Mistress Pigeon, if the King knew the reasons I have for what I have done he would be more angry with My Lady than with me, for that I can justify to the King and the world why I have done this, and though I have concealed it all this while out of respect to My Lady I will satisfy the King, and I doubt not but he will turn his anger from me to My Lady." Pigeon told her "These were things she did not enter into and that she had only orders from me to ask her for the letter when she had read it, that I might satisfy people that it was not by the King's order that she was there."

She said "No, she would not give the letter back." Upon which the Ambassador stood up and said "My Lady Sussex, do not give the letter back." "No, My Lord," says he, "I do not intend it." With that the Ambassador rise up and said "Mistress Pigeon, do you know who My Lady Sussex is that you should dare to dispute with her the delivering the letter?" She said "My Lord, I hope I have done nothing unbecoming the respect I ought to pay My Lady Sussex." "Yes," says he, "you see she is not well and you argue with her." "My Lord," says she, "I only ask her for the letter again as My Lady commandeth me." "The King," says he, "has letters both of yours and your lady's." "My Lord," says she, "what letters I have writ I do not at all apprehend the King's seeing, and for My Lady she is very well informed of all that is passed." "Mistress Pigeon," says he, "My Lady Sussex being the King's daughter it was not fit for her to live with My Lady Duchess who leads so infamous a life, and therefore she removed, and if anybody asks who counselled her to it you may tell them it was I."

" 'Tis enough, My Lord," says Pigeon, and so made a curse* and came away. This I thought fit to give you an account of with all speed that you may see how this ill man seeks to ruin her. He made her go to Court with My Lady Ambassadress, and she was at the hotel de ville of St John's Day at the fair and the supper, and has made a great many fine clothes and taken three women to wait on her, of the Ambassador's proffering, and a Swiss to stand at her parlour door, and there is furniture a-making for her apartment and she is taking more footmen, for as yet she has but one. I doubt not but that the Ambassador will invent a thousand lies for her and himself to write to you of me.

But believe me upon my word, if they tell truth they can have nothing to say of my conduct, for I have, both before I went into England and since I came back, lived with that reservedness and honour that, had you yourself marked me out a life, I am sure you would have ordered it so. And had it not been for that silly letter, his malice could not have had a pretension to have blasted me, and those letters can never be known but by him and My Lady Sussex. Pray, if Your Majesty has them, send them to me that I may see if they are all, and the originals. If

*It is tempting to retain this reading, but it is probably the Duchess's spelling of "curtsey."

not, I beg of you to oblige them to deliver them to you, for I know not what ill use they may make of them, or whether the Ambassador's malice may not forge letters I never writ. If you will let me see those you have, I will acquaint you whether or no they be all.

You are pleased to command My Lady Sussex to stay in the monastery at Conflans. I beg of Your Majesty not to command her that, for it must be very uneasy to her and me too, ever to live together after such a proceeding as she has had to me; and though I am so good a Christian as to forgive her, yet I cannot so far conquer myself as to see her daily, though Your Majesty may be confident that, as she is yours I shall always have some remains of that kindness I had formerly, for I can hate nothing that is yours.

But that which I would propose to you is that you would write a letter in French which may be showed to the Archbishop of Paris in which you desire that she may be put into the monastery of Port Royal at Paris, and that she may have two nuns given her to wait on her, and that she carries no servants with her, that she stirs not out nor receives no visits whatsoever without a letter from me to the Abbess. For where she is now all people visits her, and the Ambassador and others carries consorts of music every day to entertain her; so that the whole discourse of this place is nothing but of her, and she must be ruined if you do not tackle some speedy course with her. This Port Royal that I propose to you is in great reputation for the piety and regularity of it, so that I think it much the best place for her; and for Conflans, were it not for the reasons I have given before, that place would not be proper for her, for she has, by great presents that she has made the Abbess, gained her to say what she will. For when I came over she would have concealed from me My Lady Sussex's frequent going out of the monastery, but that it was so public she could not do it long. And when she saw that, she said that My Lady Sussex told her she went out for affairs of mine that I had ordered her to do in my absence. This being, Conflans is of all places the most unfit for her and would be the most uneasy to me; therefore I do most humbly beg of Your Majesty not to command her that place.

*The Duchess of Cleveland to Lord Clifford of Chudleigh, Lord High Treasurer, June, 1673.*

My Lord
I am aferd that the King wil not readyly consent to let me have this seven thousan pound nowe that he is to paye it himself owet of the exsise unles your lordship wil be so much my frind as to pres it to him & then I am confident I maye sucksed. I should not prese your lordship so earnestly in this but that tis of great consarne to me, for beleving myself sartan of this monny I have mayed expences in my houses of furnitur & plat which otherwayes I should not have done & nowe mising of this wil put me behind hand extremly; I wil not give your lordship anny furder trouble & this time but bege of you to beleve that non liveing is more sensible of your favors nor can be with more truth.

Your lordship
most faithful
humble sarvant
CLEVELAND

pray my Lord remember to make the report to the king of the to an twenty hunderd pound in disput between the Duke and me.

# References

## ʕɑ Abbreviations

Barbour = Violet Barbour: Henry Bennet, Earl of Arlington, Washington & Oxford, 1914.

BM = British Museum.

BM Add MSS = British Museum Additional Manuscripts.

Browning = Andrew Browning: Thomas Osborne, Earl of Danby, Duke of Leeds, 3 vols., Glasgow, 1951.

Burnet = Burnet's History Of My Own Time, 2 vols. edited Osmund Airy, Oxford, 1897, 1900: Supplement (termed Vol. III) ed. H. C. Foxcroft, Oxford, 1902.

Cal Clar S P = Calendar of the Clarendon State Papers, published by Oxford in four volumes with a fifth pending. (Through the courtesy of the keeper of Western MSS at the Bodleian Library, I have been able to consult and refer to the fifth volume in its proof form.)

Chesterfield = Letters of Philip Stanhope, second Earl of Chesterfield (including some short notes for my remembrance of things and accidents as they happened to me.) Manuscript by Chesterfield: BM Add MSS 19,253.

Clar Cont. = Continuation of the Life of Edward, Earl of Clarendon, 2 vols. London, 1827.

Clar Hist = Edward, Earl of Clarendon: The History of the

Rebellion and Civil Wars in England begun in the year 1641. (1702).
6-volume edition by W. Dunn Macray, Oxford, 1888. (references are not by volume and page but by the original book and paragraph number, and can be followed in any edition.)

Clar MSS = Clarendon Manuscripts in the Bodleian Library. (To verify, it is essential to couple the year and the volume number.)

Clar S P = State Papers collected by Edward, Earl of Clarendon, Oxford, 1786, 3 vols.

Corr Angleterre = Correspondence Politique, Angleterre; Archives des Affaires Etrangères, Paris.

CSPD = Calendar of State Papers (Domestic), Public Record Office.

Evelyn = E. S. de Beer, The Diary of John Evelyn, 6 vols., Oxford, 1955.

Forneron = Henri Forneron: Louise de Kéroualle, Duchess of Portsmouth, 1649-1734, Paris, Plon, 1886.

Gramont = Memoirs of the Comte de Gramont, trans. Peter Quennell, commentary by Cyril Hughes Hartmann, London, Routledge, 1930/1932.

HMC = Report of the Royal Commission on Historical Manuscripts. References use the conventional descriptions of the reports laid down by H. M. Stationery Office in their Guide and Index to HMC Reports, 1935: The number or nickname of the report, followed by the part or volume, if any, and the page number, sometimes marked into columns "a" and "b"—"n.s." = new series.

Jesse = John Heneage Jesse, Memoirs of the Court of England During the Reign of the Stuarts, 3 vols., London, Bohn, 1857.

Jusserand = J. J. Jusserand: A French Ambassador at the Court of Charles the Second, London, 1892.

Luttrell = Narcissus Luttrell: A Brief Historical Relation of State Affairs from September, 1678 to April, 1714. (Edition used: 6 vols., Oxford, 1857.)

MS Ashmole = Ashmole Manuscripts in the Bodleian Library.

MS Rawlinson = Rawlinson Manuscripts in the Bodleian Library.

POAS = Poems on Affairs of State, Augustan Satirical Verse

1660–1714, Yale University Press 1963– Vol. I, ed. George deForest Lord; Vol. II, ed. Elias F. Mengel Jr.; Vol. III, ed. Howard H. Schless; Vol. IV, ed. Gailbraith M. Crump.
Thurloe S P = Thurloe State Papers, 1714, 7 vols.

## ᛗ *Chapter 1*

1. Chesterfield f.8.
2. Chesterfield f.10.
3. Chesterfield f.12.
4. Chesterfield f.9.
5. Chesterfield f.9.
6. Chesterfield f.13.
7. Chesterfield f.14.
8. HMC 10 IV p.207.
9. At Mardyk, October 22, 1657. See Cal Clar S P, III, p.351, Clar Hist XV 132.
10. An Historical Poem, circ. 1678, line 12. H. M. Margoliouth printing the work (p.201) in The Poems and Letters of Andrew Marvell, 2 vols., 2nd. edition, Oxford, 1952, ascribes it to "author unknown" but Emile Lagouis in André Marvell: poète, puritain, patriote, Paris & London, 1928, p.300, partially disputes this. For an excerpt from the poem, see page 36.
11. Oldmixon: Critical History of England, London, 1730, II, p.276.
12. Cal Clar S P, III, p.73.
13. In 1653: Cal Clar S P, II, p.218.
14. Nicholas Papers, Camden Society, III, p.15.
15. Thurloe S P V, p.645.
16. The three comprehensive scriptures of pornography are discussed in D. F. Foxon's articles on Libertine Literature in England, 1660–1745, The Book Collector, Vol. 12, London, 1963.
17. Sprat, History of the Royal Society, 2nd ed., London, 1702, p.340.

18. Sprat, *ibid.* p.83.
19. Autobiography of Mary, Countess of Warwick, ed. T. Crofton Crocker, Percy Society, 1848.
20. The median age of menstruation dropped in a century from age 17 years in 1850 to age 13½ years in 1951. The assumption that this median age of sexual competence (not maturity) was not less than 17 in 1650 is borne out by the statistics of the age at which brides then married. Between 1619 and 1660 the mean age of brides in the diocese of Canterbury marrying for the first time was almost 24 [Peter Laslett: The World We Have Lost, London, Methuen, 1965, p. 83]. In the heart of the country it was far higher: at Colyton, in the Axe Valley in Devon, the mean age of the brides between 1630 and 1659 was almost 30 [E. A. Wrigley, Family Limitation in Pre-Industrial England, Economic History Review, Vol. XIX, No. 1, April 1966] but, as in modern Ireland, this may have been the outcome of a Malthusian form of population control in a poverty-ridden countryside.
21. James I to the Lords of the Council, 1617. See J. P. Kenyon: The Stuarts, London, Batsford 1958, Fontana, 1966, p.51.
22. Clar Hist VII 133.
23. Clar Hist *ibid.*
24. Clar Hist VI 67; Cheshire County Records.
25. HMC Ormonde n.s. II, p.376.
26. HMC 4, pp.33, 42, 279; HMC 5, p.20; HMC 6, p.916.
27. Abel Boyer: The History of the Life and Reign of Queen Anne, ed. of 1722, London, p.48 (Appendix).
28. Chesterfield f.204 verso.
29. Burnet: History of His Own Times; I, p.127.
30. Hester W. Chapman· The Tragedy of Charles II, 1630–1660, p.323, London, Cape, 1964.
31. Chesterfield f.204 verso.
32. Chesterfield *ibid.*
33. John Anderson, Memoirs of the House of Hamilton, Edinburgh, 1825.

34. Letters and Journals of Robert Baillie, 1658; ed. David Laing, Edinburgh 1841/2, Vol. III, p.387.
35. Chesterfield f.25.
36. Chesterfield f.29.
37. Chesterfield f.30.
38. Chesterfield f.204 verso.
39. Chesterfield f.4.
40. Chesterfield f.46.
41. John Evelyn, Diary, ed. E. S. de Beer, Oxford 1955, entry February 1, 1649.
42. Abel Boyer: reference 27 above.
43. Chesterfield f.15.
44. Chesterfield f.19.
45. Chesterfield f.16.
46. Cal Clar S P, IV, p.163.
47. CSPD 1660–1661, p.104.
48. Chesterfield f.203 verso.
49. The Letter-Book of John Viscount Mordaunt 1658–1660, ed. Mary Coate, Royal Historical Society, Camden Third Series, Vol. 69 (1945), p.165.
50. MS Rawlinson A 477.135; MS Ashmole 863 347–398.
51. Cal Clar S P, IV, p.527.
52. Rugge's Diurnal, BM Add MSS 10,116/7.
53. Chesterfield f.203 verso.
54. Samuel Pepys, Diary January 17, 1660.
55. The occasion and manner of Mr Francis Wooley's death ... by a gentleman of the Middle Temple, 1659 [1660].
56. Chesterfield f.48 verso.
57. Clar S P, III, p.665.
58. Clar MSS 1659–1660, Vol. 69, f.101.
59. Clar Hist XVI 138.
60. Clar MSS 1659–1660, Vol. 69, ff.129–130.
61. Hester W. Chapman; The Tragedy of Charles II, London, Cape, 1964, p.359.
62. Chesterfield f.49.
63. Chesterfield f.203 verso.
64. Hester W. Chapman; The Tragedy of Charles II, London, Cape, 1964, p.356.

64ᴬ Burnet I p. 538.

65. G. M. Trevelyan: England Under The Stuarts, London, Methuen, 1904 etc., ed. of 1965, p. 357.

65ᴬ Chesterfield, f.73.

66. Chesterfield f.20.

67. Chesterfield f.37.

68. Clar MSS 1660, Vol. 71, f.237.

69. BM Lansdowne MS 1236, f.124.

70. Sir Arthur Bryant (Charles II, revised ed. London, Collins, 1955, p.65) says the story that Charles spent his first night in Whitehall with Barbara Palmer "rests on the testimony of a footnote of Lord Dartmouth's, made in Burnet's History half a century later, and on the statement of the historian Oldmixon, who, writing in the reign of George I, is no more a first-hand authority on the Restoration than I should be on the Crimean War." If tardily recorded word-of-mouth traditions of this nature are completely excluded, many of Sir Arthur's beliefs must be rejected, including every statement in the four Gospels and many flying buttresses supporting the Conservative Party. The clearest indication that Charles II and Barbara Palmer were on fornicating terms in May, 1660, is that Charles accepted as his the girl Anne, born to Barbara in February, 1661, although word of mouth suggested she resembled Chesterfield. But see also pp. 250, 276.

71. HMC Le Fleming, p.25.

72. HMC 7, p.112b.

ᴅϞ *Chapter 2*

1. The number usually quoted as the total of Charles II's illegitimate children is 14 (as in The Complete Peerage, by G. E. C[ockayne] Vol. 6, Appendix F). But this list includes Barbara (Benedicta) Fitzroy, born July 16, 1672, the daughter of Barbara Villiers by John Churchill, later Duke of Marlborough. See pp. 231, 261.

2. Jesse, II, p. 470.

3. Jesse, II, p. 459; III, pp. 48, 49.
4. Charles, I, to Juxon. G. M. Trevelyan: England Under the Stuarts, London, Methuen, 1904, etc., ed. of 1965, p. 277.
5. Charles, II, to Parliament, December 24, 1660. Journal of the House of Lords 1660–1666, p. 236.
6. Charles, II, to Parliament, August 29, 1660. Journal of the House of Lords 1660–1666, p. 147.
7. D. H. Lawrence: Lady Chatterley's Lover, 6th par. from end.
8. For authorship see Chapter 1, note 10.
9. Pepys July 13, 1660.
10. Pepys June 6, 1660.
11. Jesse II, p. 41, Pepys September 16, 1660.
12. Pepys October 14, 1660.
13. Pepys October 7, 1660.
14. Burnet, I, p. 287.
15. Pepys June 22, 1660, August 14, 1660.
16. Clar cont., par. 89.
17. Jesse, III, p. 479.
18. Andrew Marvell, Last Instructions to a Painter, 1667, lines 62, 63.
19. At Hounslaerdike, August 9, 1659, according to the Duke of York's attestation Cal Clar S P, V, p. 80. Before this document was calendared the contract was thought to have been made on November 24, 1659, at Breda. But James was dim on dates, and could not himself precisely remember the date of his midnight wedding (see again Cal Clar S P, V, p.80).
20. Clar cont., par. 54.
21. Gramont, p.161.
22. Nancy Mitford: The Sun King, London, Hamilton, 1966, p. 55.
23. Cal Clar S P, IV, pp. 412, 441, 444.
24. Chesterfield f. 21.
25. Chesterfield f. 22.
26. W. D. Macray: Notes which passed at Meetings of the Privy Council between Charles II and the Earl of Clarendon, Roxburghe Club, 1896, p. 11.

27. Jesse, II, p. 383.
28. Pepys April 20, 1660.
29. Pepys April 23, 1661, Braybrooke's note.
30. David Ogg: England in the Reign of Charles II, 2nd ed., Oxford, 1956, p. 186.
31. Pepys August 17, 1661.
32. Pepys July 23, 1661.
33. Lennard (Dacre) Muniments, quoted G. S. Steinman: A memoir of Barbara, Duchess of Cleveland, privately printed Parker, Oxford, 1871–1878, p. 28.
34. Clar cont., par. 366.
35. Burnet, III, p. 65.
36. T. H. Lister: Life and Administration of the Earl of Clarendon, 3 vols., Oxford 1838 II, p. 394.
37. Clar cont., pars. 364, 371.
38. Evelyn January 6, 1662.
39. Pepys January 22, 1662.
40. Henriette Anne to Charles II, Paris January 4, 1662. Trans. C. H. Hartmann: The King My Brother, London, Heinemann, 1954, p. 38.
41. Elizabeth Frasier to Mrs Warmestry, London, February 10, 1662, HMC 8, p. 65.
42. Pepys February 5, 1662.
43. Elizabeth Frasier to Mrs Warmestry, London, February 14, 1662, HMC 8., p. 65.
44. Pepys April 13, 1662.
45. Pepys April 21, 1662.
46. Pepys April 6, 1662.
47. Pepys May 10, 1662.
48. Clar cont., par. 362.
49. Pepys May 18, 1662.
50. Macray, op cit. note 26, p. 69.
51. Charles II to Clarendon, Portsmouth, May 21, 1662. BM Lansdowne MSS 1236, f. 124.
52. Charles II to Henriette Anne, Portsmouth, May 23, 1662. C. H. Hartmann: The King My Brother, London, Heinemann, 1954, p. 39.
53. Pepys May 21, 1662.

54. Pepys May 31, 1662.
55. Burnet, I, p. 307.
56. Charles II to Clarendon, Portsmouth, May 21, 1662; May 25, 1662. BM Lansdowne MSS 1236 ff. 124, 130.
57. Clar cont., par. 359.
58. Clar cont., par. 364.
59. Chesterfield f. 51.
60. Memoirs of Sir John Reresby, ed. Andrew Browning, Glasgow, Jackson, 1936, p. 41.
61. Clar cont., par. 357.
62. Chesterfield f. 51.
63. Evelyn January 9, 1662.
64. Clar cont., par. 359.
65. Charles II to Clarendon, Portsmouth, May 25, 1662. BM Lansdowne MSS 1236, f.130.
66. Lord Cornbury to Marchioness of Worcester, Hampton Court, June 10, 1662. HMC 12 IX, p. 52.
67. Clar cont., par. 363. The narrative is related at length in Clar cont., pars. 357–392, which will not be minutely referred to here.
68. BM Lansdowne MSS 1236, f. 128.
69. Dorney Court Muniments. Quoted Steinman, *op cit.* note 33, p. 205.
70. Clarendon to Ormonde, July 17, 1662.
71. Clar cont., par. 391.
72. Clar cont., par. 392.
73. Lines 5–10, The Queen's Ball, circ. 1671, author unknown (slight attribution to Marvell). George deForest Lord, ed. Poems on Affairs of State 1660–1714, Yale U.P., Vol I, 1963, p. 421.

ᴆ *Chapter 3*

1. Pepys August 23, 1662.
2. *ibid.*
3. Pepys September 7, 1662.
4. Clarendon to Ormonde September 9, 1662.

5. Pepys September 7, 1662.
6. The patent of dukedom was granted February 14, 1663, but Monmouth had then used his title for three months: See Pepys November 17, 1662.
7. A short-lived son, James, born July 12, 1663.
8. Pepys September 7, 1662.
9. W. Denton to Sir Ralph Verney, London October 16, 1662, HMC 7, p. 463b.
10. Pepys October 17, 1662.
11. Pepys April 26, 1667.
12. Gramont: this author's translation.
13. POAS, II, p. 170.
14. Letter from Col. Richard Talbot, Dublin, September 30, 1662, HMC 4, p. 279; Letter November 20, 1662, *ibid.*
15. Gramont, p. 170.
16. Chesterfield, f. 40.
17. Grammont, p. 176.
18. Gramont, p. 181.
19. Pepys January 1, 1663.
20. George Fletcher to Sir Daniel Fleming December 30, 1662, HMC Le Fleming, p. 29.
21. Pepys January 5, 1663.
22. Pepys, December 31, 1662, heard or transcribed the tune as "Cuckolds All Awry," but it occurs often in the songbooks correctly as "Cuckolds All A-row." See W. Chappell, Popular Music of the Olden Time, pp. 340–342; POAS, Vol. I, p. 430, Vol. III, p. 9.
23. Pepys February 8, 1663.
24. Pepys February 17, 1663. It was not the only dissection the King conducted that year: see Pepys May 11, 1663.
25. Pepys January 1, 1663.
26. Pepys September 19, 1664.
27. Pepys February 8, 1663.
28. Pepys May 15, 1663.
29. Charles II to Princess Henriette Anne, Whitehall, February 16, 1663; Bryant, Letters of Charles II, London, Cassell, 1968, p. 139.
30. See Chapter 2, note 26. Clarendon to Charles II, November, 1662, Macray, p. 78.

31. Pepys February 23, 1663.
32. Pepys March 7, 1663.
33. Pepys April 25, 1663.
34. HMC 6, p. 473b.
35. POAS, II, p. 170.
36. Charles II to Princess Henriette Anne, Whitehall, April 20, 1663; Bryant *op cit.*, p. 141.
37. Pepys May 14, 1663.
38. Lord Chesterfield to Lord Cornbury, Bretby, May 16, 1663, Clar MSS Vol 79, ff. 237–238.
39. Pepys December 15, 1662.
40. Pepys July 4, 1663.
41. Jusserand, p. 213.
42. Gramont, p. 146.
43. Pepys July 13, 1663.
44. Pepys July 22, 1663.
45. Pepys August 11, 1663.
46. Jusserand, p. 89.
47. Jusserand, p. 94.
48. The Life and Times of Anthony Wood, antiquary of Oxford, 1632–1695, ed. Andrew Clark, 4 vols, Oxford, 1891, Vol I, p. 494.
49. Pepys October 13, 1663.
50. Gramont, p. 142.
51. Pepys October 26, 1663.
52. Pepys November 23, 1663.
53. Pepys November 9, 1663.
54. Pepys January 20, 1664.

## 🙢 Chapter 4

1. Pepys December 15, 1662.
2. Pepys July 31, 1663.
3. Pepys February 8, 1663.
4. De Wiquefort's dispatch of May 14, 1662, CSPD 1661-2 p. 371; see Burnet, I, p. 308.

5. Duke of Buckingham: Advice to a Painter, To Draw My Lord A——ton, Grand Minister of State.
6. Burnet, II, p. 300.
7. John Dryden: Absalom and Achitophel, 1681, lines 550, 563, 564.
8. Clar cont., par. 404.
9. Death Repeal'd by a Thankful Memoriall Sent from Christ-Church in Oxford, Celebrating the Noble Deserts of the Right Honourable Paule, Late Lord Vis-Count Bayning of Sudbury, Oxford, 1638.
10. D'Estrades to Louis XIV, August 29, 1661. Corr Angleterre Vol. 75, f. 132, quoted Barbour p. 53.
11. Barbour p. 54.
12. Barbour p. 55.
13. Clarendon to Ormonde October 25, 1662, Clar MSS 1662 vol. 78, f. 47.
14. Clar cont., pars 439, 440.
15. Pepys January 12, 1663, February 1, 1663.
16. Letters from Colonel Richard Talbot, Dublin, September 30, 1662; November 20, 1662, HMC 4, p. 279.
17. Letters, Duke of Ormonde to Earl of Clarendon, Dublin, September 29, 1662, October 4, 1662, November 12, 1662, Cal Clar S P, V, pp. 275, 276, 280.
18. Batailler to Louis XIV, London, December 4, 1662, quoted Jusserand, p. 31; Pepys November 24, 1662.
19. Cominges to Lionne, London, February 26, 1663, quoted Jusserand, p. 46.
20. Pepys November 10, 1662.
21. Bennet to Ormonde, November 22, 1662, Carte MS, f. 19, quoted Barbour, p. 61.
22. Clarendon to Ormonde, April 11, 1663: see Lister, Life of Clarendon, III, p. 244.
23. Charles II to Henry Bennet, December 22, 1654, Brown, Miscellanea Aulica, p. 109.
24. John Dryden: To Lady Castlemaine upon her encouraging his First Play (printed 1693).
25. Clar cont., par. 473.
26. Clar cont., par. 474.

27. Clar cont., par. 475.
28. Clar cont., par. 480.
29. Pepys November 6, 1663.
30. Cominges to Lionne, December 31, 1663, Corr Angleterre, quoted Jusserand, p. 224.
31. Oldmixon: Critical History of England, London, 1730, II, p. 276.
32. The Secret History of the Reigns of King Charles the Second and King James the Second, 1690, p. 141.
33. Quoted Barbour, pp. 42, 43.
34. Evelyn October 2, 1685.
35. Pepys December 22, 1663.
36. Charles II to Duchess of Orleans, Whitehall, January 4, 1664, quoted C. H. Hartmann, The King My Brother, Heinemann, London, 1954, p. 86.
37. Charles II to Duchess of Orleans, Whitehall, May 19, 1664, quoted *ibid*, p. 94.
38. Charles II to Duchess of Orleans, Whitehall, August 26, 1667, quoted *ibid*. p. 201. See page 183.
39. Pepys February 8, 1664.
40. Pepys February 22, 1664.
41. Pepys January 20, 1664.
42. Pepys February 1, 1664.
43. Pepys February 22, 1664. Pepys, who was uncertain of the number of Lady Castlemaine's children by the King, writes "nurses" plural and "child" singular.
44. Pepys May 31, 1664.
45. Pepys January 26, 1664.
46. Pepys January 24, 1664.
47. Pepys November 20, 1660; see also Pepys February 20, 1667.
48. Cominges to Lionne, April 17, 1664, Corr Angleterre, quoted Jusserand, p. 226.
49. Barbour, p. 81.
50. Clar cont., par. 179.
51. Downing to Bennet, The Hague, July 25, 1664, State Papers Holland, 171, pp. 25, 125.

52. Cominges to Lionne, London, September 15, 1664 (New Style Calendar, as always with the French, gap significant here.) Corr Angleterre, quoted Jusserand, p. 85.
53. Cominges to Lionne, London, October 2, 1664, Corr Angleterre, quoted Jusserand, p. 91.
54. G. S. Steinman: A Memoir of Barbara Duchess of Cleveland, privately printed Parker, Oxford, 1871, First addenda, 1874, p. 2.
55. Pepys March 25, 1664.
56. Charles II to Duchess of Orleans, Whitehall, December 26, 1664, Corr Angleterre, quoted C. H. Hartmann, The King My Brother, Heinemann, London, 1954, p. 135.
57. Clar cont., par. 603.
58. Thomas Salusbury to Earl of Huntingdon, Highgate, January 9, 1665, HMC 78 Hastings, II, p. 147.
59. Clar cont., par. 542.
60. George Walsh to Henry Slingesby, London, February 20, 1665, HMC 6, p. 337b.
61. Pepys February 3, 1665.
62. Charles II to Duchess of Orleans, Whitehall, February 9, 1665, quoted C. H. Hartmann, The King My Brother, Heinemann, London, 1954, p. 143.
63. Courtin to Lionne, London, July 9, 1665, Corr Angleterre, quoted Jusserand, p. 243.
64. *ibid.*
65. Burnet, I, p. 203.
66. The Three Ambassadors to Lionne, London, June 1, 1665, Corr Angleterre, quoted Jusserand, p. 237.
67. Baillol: Henriette Anne de France, Paris, 1886, p. 164, quoted Dictionary of National Biography, Barbara Villiers.
68. Andrew Marvell: Last Instructions to a Painter, 1667, lines 405–408.
69. Pepys March 19, 1665.
70. The marriage contract was signed July 5, 1664 (confounding the chronology of all extant commentators on Gramont) HMC 11, VI, p. 59.
71. Gramont, p. 184.

72. Sir Charles Sedley: To All You Ladies Now On Land, 1665.
73. Pepys June 3, 1665; John Dryden: Essay of Dramatick Poesie, London, 1668, first par.
74. Charles II to Duchess of Orleans, Whitehall, June 6, 1665, Corr Angleterre, quoted C. H. Hartmann, The King My Brother, Heinemann, London, 1954, p. 166.
75. Andrew Marvell: Second Advice to a Painter, April, 1666, lines 185–188, POAS, I, p. 44.
76. Pepys June 7, 1665.
77. Pepys June 28, 1665; see also July 20, 1665.
78. Pepys March 31, 1665, April 3, 1665.
79. Pepys August 26, 1667.
80. Bigorre to Lionne, London, July 9, 1665, Corr Angleterre, Quoted Jusserand, p. 243.
81. Courtin to Lionne, Kingston, July 16, 1665, Corr Angleterre, quoted Jusserand, p. 245.
82. *ibid.*
83. Duchess of Orleans to Charles II, St. Germain, June 22, 1665, translated C. H. Hartmann, The King My Brother, Heinemann, London, 1954, p. 171.
84. Jesse, III, p. 279; Chesterfield f. 204 verses.
85. Clar cont., par. 859.
86. Courtin to Lionne, Salisbury, August 30, 1665, Corr Angleterre, quoted Jusserand p. 249.
87. Clar cont., par. 726.
88. Gramont, p. 284; Pepys January 9, 1666; Jesse, III, p. 478.
89. Andrew Clark: The Life and Times of Anthony Wood, antiquary of Oxford, 4 vols., Oxford, 1891, II, p. 68.
90. Denis de Repas to J. R. M., London, March 8, 1666, HMC Portland, III, p. 293.
91. Jusserand, p. 178.
92. Pepys February 19, 1666
93. Pepys February 11, 1666.
94. CSPD May 23, 1666.
95. Anonymous (but by Lord Castlemaine): An Apology in behalf of the Papists, London, 1666.
96. Pepys December 1, 1666.

97. Charles II to Duchess of Orleans, Hampton Court, January 29, 1666, Corr Angleterre, quoted C. H. Hartmann, The King My Brother, Heinemann, London, 1954, p. 189.
98. "Dr Clerke telling me yesterday at Whitehall that he had had the membranes and other vessels in his hands which she had voided, and were perfect as ever woman's was that bore a child."
99. Clar cont., par. 857.
100. Work at Hampton Court, March, 1666, account endorsed by Christopher Wren, BM Harleian MS 1658, f. 139.
101. Ledger of Alderman Bakewell at Child & Company, Fleet Street bank, quoted G. S. Steinman, Memoir of Barbara Duchess of Cleveland, privately printed Parker, Oxford, 1871, first addenda, 1874, p. 3, second addenda, 1878, p. 4.
102. Pepys February 14, 1668.
103. Pepys May 1, 1667.
104. Pepys June 10, 1666.
105. Gramont p. 169. Song, BM Harleian MS 7332, quoted POAS, IV, p. 256.
106. Gramont, p. 262.
107. Pepys June 23, 24, 1667.
108. Pepys January 7, 1667.
109. Burnet, I, p. 406.
110. John Anderson: Memoirs of the House of Hamilton, Edinburgh, 1835.
111. Pepys reports the quarrel on June 10, 1666, but the reconciliation was made before June 7, 1666: see Sir Robert Paston to his wife at Oxnett, June 7, 1666, HMC 6 337b.
112. Pepys October 21, 1666. William Denton to Sir Ralph Verney, October 25, 1666, HMC 7, p. 485b.
113. Pepys October 21, 1666.
114. Domestic State Papers, V, f. 171, quoted Philip W. Sergeant: My Lady Castlemaine, Hutchinson, London, 1912, p. 136.
115. Pepys October 15, 1666.
116. Pepys November 22 ,1666.

117. Pepys November 15, 1666.
118. Pepys December 12, 1666.
119. David Ogg: England in the reign of Charles II, Oxford, 2nd edition, 1956, p. 331.
120. Dictionary of National Biography, William Chiffinch.
121. Pepys April 26, 1667.
122. Gramont, p. 316.
123. Burnet, I, p. 452.
124. Burnet, I, p. 453.
125. Charles II to Duchess of Orleans, Whitehall, August 26, 1667, quoted C. H. Hartmann, The King My Brother, Heinemann, London, 1954, p. 201.
126. C. H. Hartmann, note to Gramont, p. 369.
127. Pepys April 1, 1667.
128. Pepys April 26, 1667.
129. Signet Book Vol XVI, f. 102, Public Record Office, quoted G. S. Steinman, Memoir of Barbara Duchess of Cleveland, privately printed Parker, Oxford, 1871, p. 90.
130. Pepys July 7, 1667.
131. Pepys July 14, 1667.
132. Coke: A Detection of the Court and State of England, 1719, pp. 155–156, quoted Philip W. Sergeant: My Lady Castlemaine, Hutchinson, London, 1912, p. 144.
133. Jesse, III, p. 79 (quoting contemporary sources, reference mislaid )
134. Browning I, p. 42.
135. Browning I, p. 46.
136. CSPD 1666–7, pp. 532, 552, 560, quoted Burnet, I, p. 444
137. Browning, I, p. 46.
138. Pepys August 17, 1667. Jesse III p. 87.
139. Burnet I p. 448
140. Pepys June 21, 1667.
141. Anon: Fourth Advice to a Painter, 1667, lines 129–134, POAS, I, p. 146.
142. Pepys July 12, 1667
143. Mary de la Rivière Manley: Secret Memoirs . . . from the New Atalantis, 2 vols., 1716, I, p. 30.

144. Pepys July 30, 1667.
145. Gramont, p. 223.
146. Anon: The King's Answer to a Letter of the Duke of Monmouth, 1680, lines 23–25, POAS, II, p. 256.
147. Pepys July 30, 1667.
148. Pepys July 28, 1667.
149. Pepys July 29, 1667.
150. *ibid.*
151. Pepys August 7, 1667.
152. Pepys July 29, 1667.
153. *ibid.*
154. *ibid.*
155. Pepys July 25, 1667.
156. William Harris: An Historical and Critical Account of the Life of Charles the Second King of Great Britain, 2 vols., London, 1766, II, p. 297. Pepys, July 29, 1667, reports the income figure given by May as £300
157. Pepys July 29, 1667.
158. Clar cont., par. 1068.
159. Clar cont., par 1142. For "omitted" the text has "declined."
160. Clar cont., par. 1143.
161. Pepys August 27, 1667.
162. Lord Arlington to Sir Gilbert Talbot, August 29, 1667, Calendar of State Papers, VII, f. 425, quoted G. S. Steinman: Memoir of Barbara Duchess of Cleveland, privately printed Parker, Oxford, 1871, first addenda 1874, p. 3.
163. Clar cont., par. 1147; Pepys November 11, 1667.
164. Clar cont., par. 1117.
165. Clar cont., par. 1180.
166. Burnet, I, p. 445.
167. Evelyn December 9, 1667. (The entry is misdated by ten days.)
168. Clar cont., par. 1146.
169. Carte: History of the Duke of Ormonde, IV p. 52.
170. Pepys September 8, 1667.
171. Pepys August 27, 1667.
172. Burnet, I, p. 453.

173. Pepys March 27, 1667, December 21, 1667.
174. Pepys July 29, 1667.
175. Pepys July 30, 1667.
176. Pepys September 1, 1667.
177. Pepys September 10, 1667.
178. Pepys July 29, 1667.
179. Burnet, I, pp. 166–167.
180. Anon: Nell Gwynne, 1669, POAS, I, p. 420.

Dξ *Chapter 5*

1. Clar cont., par. 970. Jesse, III, p. 89.
2. William Denton to Sir Ralph Verney, July 25, 1667, HMC 7, p. 458b. Newsletter July 23, 1667, reporting events of July 20, 1667, HMC Le Fleming, p. 51. Pepys July 22, 1667.
3. Charles II to Duchess of Orleans, Whitehall, 1667, quoted C. H. Hartmann, The King My Brother, Heinemann, London, 1954, p. 202.
4. Jesse, III, p. 95.
5. Pepys January 17, 1668.
6. *ibid.*
7. Jesse, III, pp. 95–96. Pepys May 19, 1669. Viscountess Camden to Lord Roos, December 11, 1667. HMC Rutland, II, p. 43.
8. Ruvigny to Lionne, London, February 10, 1668, Corr Angleterre Vol. XCI, quoted Hartmann *op. cit.*, p. 216.
9. Pepys March 26, 1668.
10. Burnet, I, pp. 474–475. Pepys January 11, 1668.
11. Luttrell, July, 1679.
12. Philalethes: Remarks Upon Bishop Burnet's Posthumous History, London, 1724, p. 56, quoted Burnet, I, p. 475.
13. Pepys January 14, 1668.
14. Pepys May 31, 1668.
15. Pepys April 7, 1668.
16. Gramont, p. 252.

17. Andrew Marvell: Last Instructions to a Painter, 1667, lines 79–102. This is the only reference to Lady Castlemaine's liaison with a running footman. But Marvell, although he made in this poem one political error which was not righted until original sources were uncovered in the twentieth century, has had no other major inaccuracy of statement or innuendo traced to him in this remarkably sustained and comprehensive work.
18. Gramont, p. 252.
19. Dictionary of National Biography: Jacob Hall.
20. Pepys September 21, 1668.
21. Gramont, p. 112.
22. Dictionary of National Biography: Jacob Hall.
23. Pepys July 29, 1667.
24. On the 13th of October, 1667. Dictionary of National Biography: Barbara Villiers.
25. Dr. Thomas Wood, quoted POAS, III, p. 535.
26. Pepys November 12, 1666.
27. B M Stowe MS 1055, f. 15.
28. Evelyn February 4, 1668.
29. Pepys February 14, 1668.
30. B M Add MSS 36916, f. 62.
31. Pepys March 25, 1968.
32. Pepys March 24, 1668.
33. Impartial Protestant Mercury, No. 64, November 29 to December 2, 1681.
34. Pepys March 25, 1668.
35. The Poor Whores Petition . . . London, 1668.
36. Pepys April 6, 1668.
37. The Gracious Answer of the most illustrious Lady of Pleasure, the Countess of Castlem . . . to the Poor Whores Petition, London, 1668.
38. Andrew Marvell: Last Instructions to a Painter, 1667, lines 955–960.
39. Treasury Books July 7, 1668.
40. Ruvigny to Louis XIV, May 21, 1668, quoted Dalrymple, Memoirs of Great Britain, 2 vols. 1773, Appendix, p. 10.

41. Forneron, pp. 139–140. POAS, III, p. 170.
42. HMC 63 Egmont Diary II, p. 32.
43. Charles II to Duchess of Orleans, Whitehall January 27, 1668, quoted Hartmann, *op cit.*, p. 209.
44. Pepys May 19, 1668.
45. Burnet, I, 452n.
46. Pepys August 18, 1668.
47. Pepys December 21, 1668.
48. Pepys May 1, 1667.
49. Lives of the Most Celebrated Beauties, London, 1715, quoted POAS, II, p. 230.
50. Cunningham, Story of Nell Gwyn, London, 1892, p. 167.
51. Case of Her Grace the Dutchess of Cleveland, the Dukes of Grafton and Northumberland, touching an Annuity of 4,700l. per annum payable out of the Post Office, . . . London, 1696.
52. Pepys January 16, 1669.
53. *ibid.*
54. Pepys April 28, 1669.
55. Lionne to Colbert, Paris, April 3, 1669, Corr Angleterre LXXXIV, quoted Mignet: Négociations rélatives à la succession d'Espagne sous Louis XIV, Paris, Imprimerie Royale, 1842, III, p. 84.
56. J. S. Clarke: The Life of James the Second . . . collected out of Memoirs writ with his own hands, London, 1816, I, p. 442.
57. Charles II to Duchess of Orleans, Whitehall, January 20, 1669, quoted Hartmann *op cit.*, p. 237.
58. Pepys April 28, 1669.
59. Louis XIV to Colbert February 9, 1669, quoted Forneron p. 16.
60. See Colbert to Lionne, February 9, 1669, Corr. Angleterre, XCIV, quoted J. J. Jusserand: Instructions données aux ambassadeurs et ministres de France, XXV, Angleterre, tome II 1666–1690, Paris, Boccard, 1929, p. 98.
61. Colbert to Lionne, February 14, 1669, quoted Forneron, p. 16.
62. Lionne to Colbert, February 16, 1669. Corr Angleterre.

63. Charles II to Duchess of Orleans, Whitehall, March 22, 1669, quoted Hartmann *op cit.*, p. 250.
64. Lionne to Colbert, April 23, 1669, Corr Angleterre XCIV, f. 169.
65. Lionnel to Colbert, April 23, 1669, Corr Angleterre XCIII, f. 322.
66. Colbert to Lionne, April 29, 1669, Corr Angleterre XCIV, f. 169.
67. HMC Buccleuch I, Montagu-Arlington letters May 3, 1669, p. 422. Colbert to Louis XIV, May 25, 1669, Corr Angleterre XCIV, f. 196.
68. Louis XIV to Colbert, May 25, 1669, Corr Angleterre, XCIV, f. 347.
69. Colbert to Louis XIV, May 25, 1669, Corr Angleterre, XCIV, f. 196.
70. Charles II to Duchess of Orleans, Whitehall, June 7, 1669, quoted Hartmann, *op cit.*, p 265.
71. Pepys April 28, 1669.
72. Pepys January 15, 16, 1669.
73. Pepys May 5, 1668.
74. Colbert to Lionne, February 28, 1669, quoted Forneron, p. 17.
75. Pepys January 16, 1669.
76. Charles II to Duchess of Orleans, Whitehall, June 6, 1669, quoted Hartmann, *op. cit.*, p. 262.
77. T. Carte: History of James, Duke of Ormonde, 6 vols, 1851, II, p. 276.
78. Chesterfield, f. 37.
79. Anon: The Town Life, Poems on State Affairs, 1703–1707, I, p. 122.
80. Pope: A Sermon Against Adultery; or Sober Advice from Horace. (Works, ed. Warton), 1797, VI, p. 45.
81. Andrew Marvell: Letter to a Friend in Persia, August 9, 1671 (Marvell ed. H. M. Margoliouth) 2 vols., Oxford, 1952, II, p. 310.
82. Patent, August 3, 1670.
83. Sir John Clayton to Sir Robert Paston, July 16, 1670, HMC 6, p 367b.

84. Anon: Old Rowley the King, 1684, lines 1–9, POAS, III, p. 479.
85. Richardsonia, quoted Notes & Queries, 12th series, IX, p. 135.

D₹ *Chapter 6*

1. Dr William Fenton to Sir Ralph Verney, April 6, 1671, HMC 7, p. 489a.
2. John Evelyn October 17, 1671.
3. Dr. William Fenton to Sir Ralph Verney, May 4, 1671, HMC 7, p. 489a.
4. G. S. Steinman: Memoir of Barbara Duchess of Cleveland, privately printed Oxford, Parker, 1871–8, p. 237.
5. Lady Mary Bertie to Katherine Noel, Westminster, January 17, 1671; February 23, 1671, HMC Rutland II, pp. 22–23.
6. Marquis de Saint-Maurice to Duke Charles Emmanuel II of Savoy, Paris, September 19, 1671, quoted in Jean Lemoine: Letters sur la Cour de Louis XIV, 1667–1670.
7. Jesse, III, p. 96.
8. Colbert to Pomponne, October 8, 1671, Corr Angleterre, Vol. CI, ff. 66–68, quoted Barbour, p. 181.
9. Colbert to Louvois, September 21, 1671, quoted Forneron, p. 47.
10. Louvois to Colbert, September 29, 1671, Corr Angleterre Vol. CII, f. 283.
11. John Evelyn October 16, 1671.
12. John Evelyn October 9, 1671.
13. Colbert to Louis XIV, December 12, 1670, quoted Forneron, p. 45.
14. Colbert to Louvois, September 21, 1671, quoted Forneron, p. 46.
15. Clar Hist, V, p. 232.
16. Ormonde to Charles II, May 13, 1660, Clar MSS, Vol. 76 ff. 245–246.
17. POAS, I, p. 107n.

18. Andrew Marvell: Last Instructions to a Painter, 1667, lines 163–168.
19. The Complete Peerage, edited G. E. Cockayne, revised Vicary Gibbs, London, 1910, entry: Cleveland.
20. *ibid.*
21. John Aubrey: The Natural History of Wiltshire, ed. John Britton, London, Nichols, 1847.
22. H o L MSS December 19, 1689, HMC 12 VI H.L., pp. 783–785. H o L MSS November 17, 1692, HMC 14 VI H.L., pp. 112–114. BM Harleian MSS 5277, ff. 89, 90. Proceedings in Parliament: The Case of Mrs Mary Wood, an Infant . . . no date (British Museum).
23. HMC 78 Hastings II p. 315 for January 18, 1670. Ashmole MSS 1139, ff. 309–321 for November 21, 1674.
24. Privy Seal Docquet Book July 29, 1679, HMC Hodgkin p. 14.
25. MacPherson: Original Papers containing the Secret History of Great Britain from the Restoration to the Succession of Hanover, 2 vols, London, 1775, I, p. 67.
26. W. D. Christie: Letters to Sir Joseph Williamson 1673, 1674, Derham to Williamson November 5, 1673, 2 vols, Camden Society, London, 1874.
27. 11 (written ii) August, 1674. MSS Ashmole 837, f. 214.
28. Secret Service Expenses of Charles II and James II, July 19, 1684; December 24, 1684, Camden Society (Old Series) Vol. 52, pp. 87, 91, 96, 97, 99.
29. Ashmole MSS 1134, f. 190b.
30. William Fall to Sir Ralph Verney August 5, 1675; August 11, 1675, HMC 7, p. 465b.
31. Humphrey Prideaux to John Ellis, September 17, 1674, Letters of Humphrey Prideaux, Camden Society (New Series) Vol. 15.
32. London Museum *ad hoc* caption at Nonsuch Exhibition, 1970.
33. Andrew Marvell: Letter to a friend in Persia, August 9, 1671, works ed. Margoliouth, II, p. 75.
34. Case of Her Grace, the Dutchess of Cleveland, the Dukes of

Grafton and Northumberland, touching an annuity of 4,7001, per annum, payable out of the Post Office, British Museum, no date, probably 1696.

35. Deed quoted G. S. Steinman; Memoir of Barbara Duchess of Cleveland, privately printed Oxford, Parker, 1871–1878, p. 134.
36. Letter to Williamson August 25, 1673, ref. note 26.
37. Patents 26 Car. II, p. 7, n. 13/19.
38. BM Add MSS 28078, f. 69.
39. Duchess of Cleveland to Lord High Treasurer Clifford,– June, June 16, 1673, Treasury Books, 1672–5, p. 175.
40. Derham to Williamson, November, 1673, ref. note 26.
41. HMC 63 Egmont Diary, I, p. 217.
42. Duchess of Cleveland to Charles II, June 28, 1678, BM Harleian MSS 7006, ff. 171–176. Fully quoted in Appendix.
43. Dennis: Familiar Letters, London, 1721, pp. 216–217.
44. Leigh Hunt: The Dramatic Works of Wycherley, Congreve, Vanbrugh and Farquhar, London, Moxon, 1851, p. 11.
45. William Wycherley: The Country Wife, Act I, scene 1, page 71 in above reference.
46. 4th Lord Chesterfield: Letters to His Son, November 18, 1748.
47. Garnet, Lord Wolseley: Life of John Churchill, Duke of Marlborough to the Accession of Queen Anne, London, Bentley, 1894, p. 68.
48. Mary de la Rivière Manley: Secret Memoirs . . . from the New Atalantis, London, 1709.
49. Burnet, I, p. 476. Corr Angleterre, Vol. CXXXVII, f. 403.
50. 4th Lord Chesterfield: Letters to His Son, November 18, 1748.
51. Mary de la Rivière Manley: Secret Memoirs . . . from the New Atalantis, London, 1709.
52. 4th Lord Chesterfield: Letters to His Son, November 18, 1748.
53. Abel Boyer: The History of the Life and Reign of Queen Anne, London, 1722.

54. Alexander Pope: A Sermon Against Adultery; or Sober Advice from Horace. (Works, ed. Warton, London, 1797, VI, p. 45.)
55. Courtin to Louvois, November 16, 1676, quoted Forneron, p. 47.
56. Lady Mary Hastings to Earl of Huntingdon, ?Spring, 1676? HMC 78 Hastings II, p. 169.
57. Courtin to Lionne, December 17, 1676, quoted Forneron, p. 47.
58. Ruvigny to Pomponne, May 14, 1674, quoted Forneron, p. 47.

ᏦᏩ  *Chapter 7*

1. Rawlinson MSS D260, f. 35b.
2. See The Haymarket Hectors, written very early in 1671, lines 20, 21, POAS, I, p. 169.
3. See particularly Dialogue, written well after January, 1676, line 6; and A Satyr on Charles II, written before January 20, 1674, lines 23–27. Both in David M. Vieth: The Complete Poems of John Wilmot, Earl of Rochester, Yale University Press, 1968, pp. 129 & 60, respectively.
4. John Wilmot, Earl of Rochester: A Satyr on Charles II, probably 1673, lines 28–32: in work quoted above.
5. Ruvigny to Pomponne, January 2, 1676, Corr Angleterre, Vol. CXVII, f. 132.
6. Courtin to Louis XIV & Pomponne, July 9, 1676, Corr Angleterre, Vol CXXA, f. 143.
7. Andrew Marvell to Sir Henry Thompson, Westminster, December 19, 1674, HMC 6, p 473b.
8. C. H. Hartmann: The Vagabond Duchess, London, Routledge, 1926, p. 186.
9. Courtin to Louis XIV, August 3, 1676, Corr Angleterre, Vol CXIX, f. 79.
10. Lady Chaworth to Lord Roos, November 2, 1676, HMC Rutland, II, p. 34.

11. Courtin to Louvois, November 30, 1676, Corr Angleterre, Vol CXX, f. 227.

12. Lady Chaworth to Lord Roos, December 25, 1676, HMC Rutland II, p. 34.

13. Lady Chaworth to Lord Roos, January 19, 1677, January 28, 1677, HMC Rutland, II, p. 36.

14. On February 20, 1677. Edward Smith to Lord Roos, February 22, 1677, HMC Rutland, II, p. 40.

15. Humphrey Prideaux to John Ellis, February 2, 1677, Letters of Humphrey Prideaux, Camden Society (new series) Vol. 15.

16. Montagu to Lord Treasurer Danby, Paris, March 1, 1677, Danby, II, p. 260.

17. *ibid*.

18. Ralph Montagu to Lord Treasurer Danby, Paris, April 4, 1677, Browning, II, p. 262–263.

19. Reference as for note 15.

20. John Lacy: Satire, 1677, lines 41–52; POAS, I, p. 427.

21. Lady Chaworth to Lord Roos, December 18, 1677, HMC Rutland, II, p. 43.

22. Duchess of Cleveland to Charles II, Paris, July, 1678, BM Add MSS 21505. Printed in full here in Appendix, page 268.

23. Archaeologia, Vol XXVIII, 1839, p. 196.

24. Lady Chaworth to Lord Roos, December 18, 1677, HMC Rutland II, p. 43.

25. Lord Treasurer Danby to Ralph Montagu, March 25, 1678, BM Add MSS 38849, quoted in Danby II, pp. 346–349.

26. Duchess of Cleveland to Charles II, Paris, June 28, 1678, BM Harleian MSS 7006, ff. 171–176. Printed in full here in Appendix, page 273.

27. Ralph Montagu to Lady Harvey, Paris, July 5, 1678, quoted Browning, II, pp. 362–363.

28. Unsigned letter in Finch collection, September 12, 1673, HMC 7 513a. J. P. Kenyon: Robert Spencer, Earl of Sunderland, 1641–1702, London, Longmans, 1958, p. 19.

29. DNB entry Ralph Montagu. Barillon to Louis XIV, October 24, 27; November 3, 14, 1678.

30. Lord Treasurer Danby to Montagu, January 17, 1678; March 25, 1678, BM Add MSS 38849, f. 130, f. 140.
31. Edward Pyckering to Lord Montagu, July 31, 1679, HMC Buccleuch I, p. 331.
32. John Verney to Sir Ralph Verney, November 27, 1679, HMC 7 Appendix, p. 477b.

## ℔ Chapter 8

1. Charles II to Countess of Lichfield, Whitehall, October 20, 1682, Archaeologia, London, Vol LVIII, Part 1, p. 176.
2. John Evelyn February 6, 1685.
3. HMC 12 VI H.I.,
4. Oldmixon: History of England during the Reign of the House of Stuart, London, 1730, II, p. 576.
5. Dr Owen Wynne to Sir William Trumbull, Whitehall, December 16, 1685; February 1, 1686, HMC 75 Downshire, I, p. 72, p. 113.
6. Peregrine Bertie to Countess of Rutland, February 2, 1686, HMC Rutland, II, p. 102.
7. Letter from the Countess of Norton, March 13, 1686, HMC Rutland, II, p. 106.
8. John Tucker to Sir William Trumbull, Whitehall, March 15, 1686, HMC Downshire 75, p. 135.
9. Various letters of March 23, 25, 29; April 4, 17, 18; May 7, 13, 19, 1686, HMC Downshire 75, pp. 135–169.
10. Peregrine Bertie to Countess of Rutland, April 3, 1686, HMC Rutland II, p. 107.
11. Sir William Trumbull to Lord Chancellor Jeffreys, Leghorn, June 9–19, 1687, HMC 75 Downshire, I, p. 247.
12. Newsletter ibid., p. 247.
13. DNB: Entries Ralph Montagu, Henry Fitzroy.
14. Daniel Bret to Earl of Huntingdon, July 7, 1696, HMC 78 Hastings, II, p. 264.
15. DNB: Entry Charles Hamilton, 1691–1754.
16. Archaeologia, London, Vol. XXVIII, 1839, p. 196.

17. Catherine Sedley, Countess of Dorchester to Earl of Nottingham, 1690 or 1691, HMC 71 Finch, III.
18. Daniel Bret to Earl of Huntingdon, September 3, 1696, HMC 78 Hastings, II, p. 281.
19. Stanley West to Robert Harley, Tunbridge Wells, August 29, 1704, HMC Portland, IV, p. 118.
20. Henry Crymes to Sir William Trumbull, December 21, 1696, HMC 75 Downshire, I, p. 717.
21. Joseph Addison: The Tatler, No. 50, August 4, 1709.
22. HMC Hodgkin, p. 255, pp. 344–345. The Duchess of Cleveland's evidence against Mr Feilding, in Memoirs of the Life of Barbara Duchess of Cleveland, divorced wife of Handsome Feilding, London, Smith, 1709; Luttrell July 25, 27; September 3; October 5, 24; December 6, 1706.
23. Abel Boyer: History of the Life & Reign of Queen Anne, London, 1722, entry for 1709.
24. Joseph Addison: The Tatler, No. 50, August 4, 1709.
25. Lord Stanhope to Dr Atterbury, December 17, 1705, Atterbury's Correspondence, II, p. 31.

*These references could never have been made and checked in the efficient ambience of my own study without the skilled service of the staff of the comparatively small public library of the London Borough of Ealing. Without any pressure or cajoling they produced rare old books from all over Great Britain for my perusal at home in their pursuance of a valuable and unsung public service.*

Addison, Joseph, 265
Albany, N.Y., 112
Albemarle, Elizabeth Cavendish, Duchess of, 260
Albemarle, George Monck, 1st Duke of, 131
Albemarle, 2nd Duke, 157
Alexander, 115, 257, 265
*Alexander*, ship, 260
Anne, Princess later Queen, 118, 140, 203, 265
Aretino, Pietro, 84, 111-113, 116, 119, 126, 129, 141
Arlington, Henry Bennet, 1st Baron, 1st Earl of, 95-103, 107, 146-148, 156, 158, 165, 180, 185, 186, 190, 192, 196, 206-209, 217, 219, 223, 246
Arlington, Isabella Bennet, Countess of; *see* Grafton, Isabella, Duchess of
Arran, James Douglas, Earl of, 261
Arran, Richard Butler, Earl of, 41, 78
Arras, 102
Arundell of Wardour, Lord, 186
Ashley, 1st Baron; *see* Cooper, Anthony Ashley, 1st Baron Ashley, 1st Earl of Shaftesbury
Aubrey, John, 212

Bagot, Mary, Countess of Falmouth, 152, 223, 261
Bakewell, Edward, 131, 180
Barillon, Ambassador, 251
Barn Elms, 167
Bartholomew Fair, 173
Bayning, Mary; *see* Viscountess Grandison, later Countess of Anglesey
Bayning, Paul, 2nd Viscount, 96
Beauclerc, Charles; *see* St. Albans, Charles, Duke of
Bellasis, Lady, 261
Bennet, Sir Henry; *see* Arlington
Bennet, Isabella; *see* Grafton
Berkeley, Sir Charles, 1st Viscount Fitzharding, 1st Earl of Falmouth, 42, 43, 62, 82, 94, 96, 102, 109, 112, 113, 116, 123, 125, 132, 164, 223
Berkeley of Stratton, Lord, 198
Berkshire, Earl of, 13, 170, 180

Berkshire House, St. James's, 155, 180-182, 184, 196, 214, 216
Bernard, Edward, 240, 242
Bertie, Mr., 270
Berwick, James, Duke of; *see* Stuart, James
van Beuninghen, 115
Boleyn, Anne, 164
Bourbonne-les-Bains (Bourbon), 26, 28, 29
Bow Street, 228
Boyer, Abel, 230
Boyle, Mary, 6, 7, 12
Boys, Thomas, 175
Brandenburg, 143
Breughel, Pieter, 16
Bridewell, 264
Bristol, George Digby, 2nd Earl of, 103-106
Brodrick, Sir Allan, 20, 22, 23, 30, 68
Brounker, Henry, 121, 122, 133
Brudenell, Anna Maria; *see* Shrewsbury, Countess of
Brudenells, Earls of Cardigan, 148
Buccleuch, Earl of, 75
Buckingham, George Villiers, 1st Duke of, 8
Buckingham, George Villiers, 2nd Duke of, 8, 12, 51, 89, 95, 106, 113, 142, 143, 146-151, 154, 158, 160, 165-170, 185, 196, 205, 207, 210, 218, 228
Buckingham Palace, 218
Burnet, Gilbert, 28
Butler, Lady Elizabeth, Countess of Chesterfield, 44, 78-82, 87, 125
Butler, James; *see* Ormonde, Marquis of
Butler, Richard; *see* Arran, Earl of

Calais, 26, 100, 206
Canterbury, Archbishop of; *see* Sheldon, Gilbert
Capel, Arthur; *see* Essex, Earl of
Carlos, Don; *see* Plymouth, Charles, Earl of
Carnegie, Lady; *see* Hamilton, Lady Anne
Carnegie, Lord, later Robert, Earl of Southesk, 134
*Cataline*, 193

Catherine of Braganza, Queen, 47, 50-72, 74-76, 79, 85, 86, 88-92, 97, 106-108, 110, 117, 130-132, 136, 139, 142, 164, 165, 171, 176, 182, 205, 212, 238, 250.

Cavalier Parliament, 47, 100

Cavendish, Elizabeth, Duchess of Albemarle, Duchess Montagu; *see* Albemarle

Cavendish, Henry; *see* Newcastle, Duke of

Chaillot, 216

Champvallon, François de Harley; *see* Paris, Archbishop of

Charles I, King, 9, 13, 16, 24, 34, 77, 211

Charles II, King, Begging letter, 4; behavior in Paris and Brussels, 5; match with Frances Cromwell, 12; letter to Roger Palmer, 23; familiar with Barbara, 23; pardons Chesterfield, 24, 25; and Henriette Anne, 25; best ovation, 31-33; intention to survive, 34; and Parliament, 35, 101; promiscuity, 36; and James's marriage, 41-43; energy, 45; as gambler, 49; and Catherine, 52-53; Bedchamber crisis, 61-72; pleads with Queen to live, 91; an executive King, 102; his Catholicism, 107; host at Barbara's, 113; war and masquerades, 117; mourns Berkeley, 123; and Catherine's miscarriage, 131; broken by Frances Stuart, 142; and Buckingham, 147-151; itch, 162-165; turns to actresses, 170; removes Barbara from Whitehall, 180; resumes passion for Frances, 182; absolute power, 186-188, 195; Treaty of Dover, 198; and Louise de Kéroualle, 200, 205-210; and Mazarin, 234-239; deathbed, 255

Chatham, 145

Châtillon, Alexis, Marquis de, 245-248, 268-272

Chester, Sir Henry, 214

Chester, Lady, 214, 215

Chesterfield, Philip Stanhope, 2nd Earl of, 1-3, 11-15, 18-23, 25-29, 33, 44, 55, 56, 60, 78-82, 87, 134, 197, 203, 249, 266

Chichester, Earl of; *see* Southampton, Charles Fitzroy, Duke of

Chiffinch, Will, 137-139

Chiswick Mall, 265

Churchill, Arabella, 127, 202, 232

Churchill, John, later Duke of Marlborough, 127, 201, 203, 216, 228-232, 244, 260, 266

Clarendon, Edward Hyde, Earl of, 9, 23, 24, 38-44, 46, 48, 53-55, 58, 59, 85, 87, 94-101, 103-105, 111-113, 115, 116, 126, 127, 130, 140, 141, 145-147, 149, 151, 154-160, 162, 180, 184, 192, 211, 253

Clarendon Code, 100

Clarendon House, 116, 145, 155-158

Cleveland, Duchess of; *see* Villiers, Barbara

Cleveland, Earl of, 10, 33, 222

Cleveland, Goodman, 258

Cleveland House, 196, 228, 256

Cleveland, William Fitzroy, 2nd Duke of, 224, 259

Clifford, Sir Thomas, Lord Clifford of Chudleigh, 95, 112, 113, 186, 267, 277

Colbert de Croissy, Charles, Marquis de, 188-192, 194, 195, 207-210

Colbert, Jean-Baptiste, 191

Coleraine, Henry Lord, 175

College of Heralds, 125

Cominges, Ambassador, 110, 113

Commons, House of, 100, 104, 112, 116, 117, 130, 147, 154, 155, 157, 199, 215, 224, 251, 252

Coningsmark, Count, 258

Cooper, Anthony Ashley, 1st Baron Ashley, 1st Earl of Shaftesbury, 95, 113, 196

Corey, Mistress, 193, 194

Cornaro, Andrea, 120

Cornbury, Lord; *see* Hyde, Edward, Lord Cornbury, 2nd Earl of Clarendon

Corneille, Pierre, 176

Cornwall, Duchy of, 224

Courtin, Ambassador, 231, 232, 236, 238

Coventry, Dr Thomas Wood, Bishop of, 174, 214, 215

Coventry, infant "Earl" of, 169

Coventry, Henry, 246, 264-270
Coventry, Sir William, 112, 113
Cowper, Lady, 212
Cresswell, Madam, 177, 178
Crofts, James; see Monmouth, James, Duke of
Cromwell, Frances, 12
Cromwell, Mary; see Falconberg, Lady
Cromwell, Oliver, 4, 12, 15, 20, 46, 99, 212
Cromwell, Richard, 20
Customs and Excise, 163, 223, 277

Dacre, Thomas Lennard, 15th Lord, Earl of Sussex, 219, 238, 239, 244
Danby, Thomas Osborne, Earl of, 235, 241, 242, 246, 247, 250-252; 267-270
Darell, Barbara, 245
Darell, Henry, 22, 245
Darell, Jane, 245
Darell, Marmaduke, 245
Davis, Moll, 170, 171, 181, 183, 184
Dawson, William, 261
Declaration of Indulgence, 101, 103, 104
Deleau, Anne, 263, 264
Denham, Sir John, 133, 134
Denham, Margaret Brooke, Lady, 133, 134
Deptford, 32
Derby, 15
Dieppe, 206
Digby, George; see Bristol, 2nd Earl
Doctors Commons, 259, 263
Dorchester, Catherine Sedley, Countess of, 202, 261
Douglas, James; see Hamilton, 1st Duke
Douglas, James; see Arran, Earl of
Douglas, William; see Hamilton, 2nd Duke
Dover, Earl of; see Jermyn, Harry
Dover, Treaty of, 25, 188, 198, 217
Downing, Sir George, 112
Drogheda, Countess of, 227
Dryden, John, 14, 103, 122
"Dunkirk House;" see Clarendon House

Edgehill, 9, 24

Edward IV, King, 114
Ellis, John, 197, 230
Essex, Arthur Capel, Earl of, 253
Essex, Elizabeth Percy, Countess of, 14
d'Este, Maria Beatrice (Queen Mary), 236, 258
Euston, Earl of; see Grafton, Henry Fitzroy, Duke of
Evelyn, John, 138, 176, 204, 208-210, 255

Fairfax, Thomas, 3rd Baron, 12, 168
Fairfax, Mary, Duchess of Buckingham, 12, 148, 168
Falconberg, Mary Cromwell, Lady, 46
Falmouth, Earl of; see Berkeley, Sir Charles
Falmouth, Countess of; see Bagot, Mary
Falmouth, Viscount; see Northumberland, George Fitzroy, Duke of
Feilding, Robert, 262-265
Finch, Lady Harriet, 259
Fire of London, 136, 155, 174, 181
Fitzcharles; see Plymouth, Charles, Earl of
Fitzharding, Viscount; see Berkeley, Sir Charles
Fitzroy, Anne; see Sussex, Countess of
Fitzroy, Lady Barbara (Benedicta), 231, 244, 261, 265
Fitzroy, Charles; see Southampton, Duke of
Fitzroy, Charlotte; see Lichfield, Countess of
Fitzroy, George; see Northumberland, Duke of
Fitzroy, Henry; see Grafton, Duke of
Fitzroy, William; see Cleveland, 2nd Duke
Four Days Battle, 130, 136
Frazier, Sir Alexander, 83
French Ambassadors; see Barillon, Colbert, Cominges, Courtin, Ruvigny

Gerard, Charles, Lord, later Earl of Macclesfield, 81, 85, 86
Gerard, Jane de Civell, Lady, 81, 83, 85, 86

Glemham, Dr. Henry, Bishop of St. Asaph, 174

Gloucester, Duke of; *see* Stuart, Henry

Godfrey, Mrs., 228

Goodman, Cardonell "Scum," 256-259, 261, 262, 265

Grafton, 51, 223

Grafton, Henry Fitzroy, Duke of, 90, 106, 127, 164, 216-219, 221-223, 231, 239, 245-248, 253, 255, 256, 258, 260

Grafton, Isabella Bennet, Duchess of, 217-219, 245-248, 253

Gramont, Comte, 77, 83, 86, 88, 90, 92, 93, 237

Grandison, George Villiers, 4th Viscount, 69, 99, 126, 144, 159, 184

Grandison, Mary Baynham, Viscountess, Countess of Anglesey, 8, 10, 17, 212

Grandison, William Villiers, 2nd Viscount, 8-10, 38, 48

Grenville, Sir John, 21

Guildford, 53

Gwyn, Nell, 125, 161, 169, 171, 183, 184, 206, 208, 221, 234, 255

Hackney, 10

Halifax, George Savile, Marquis of, 229

Hall, Jacob, 173, 184, 198

Hamilton, Anne Duchess of, 13

Hamilton, Lady Anne, 1-3, 13, 121, 134, 135, 261

Hamilton, Charles, 261, 265

Hamilton, 1st Duke, James Douglas, 13

Hamilton, 2nd Duke, William Douglas, 13, 135

Hamilton, Elizabeth, 90, 93

Hamilton, George, 90, 92, 109

Hamilton, James, 78, 80, 81, 90, 92, 109, 125

Hampton Court Palace, 7, 52, 58-63, 70, 74, 125, 131, 219, 247

Hart, Charles, 125, 170, 171, 173

Hart, William, 171

Harvey, Anne Montagu, Lady, 153, 181, 182, 193, 194, 235, 243, 250, 270

Harvey, Sir Daniel, 153, 181

Hazelrigg, 76

Henri IV, King, 57, 62

Henry II, King, 115

Henriette Anne, Princess; *see* Orleans, Duchess of

Henrietta Maria, Queen, 11, 22, 24-26, 40-43, 75, 167, 192, 211, 216

Herbert, Catherine; *see* Palmer, Lady

Herbert, William, 1st Baron Powis, 16, 262

*Horace*, 176

Hounslaerdyke, 41

Howard, Lady Elizabeth, 13, 14, 21

Howard, Philip, 21

Howard of Castle Rising, Baron, 204

Huddlestone, Father, 255

Hungerford, Sir Edward, 230

Huntingdonshire, 224

Hurstmonceux Castle, 239

Hyde, Anne; *see* Duchess of York

Hyde, Edward, 1st Baron Hyde, 1st Earl of Clarendon; *see* Clarendon

Hyde, Edward, Lord Cornbury, 2nd Earl of Clarendon, 59, 141

Hyde, Lawrence, later Earl of Rochester, 253

Hyde Park, 80, 88, 89, 121

Innocent XI, Pope, 259

James I, King, 62, 137

James II, King; *see* York, James, Duke of

Jeffreys, Justice George, later Lord Chief Justice, 259

Jermyn, Harry, later Earl of Dover, 42, 43, 62, 75, 77, 78, 82, 109, 151, 152, 171-173

Jermyn, Henry; *see* St Albans, Earl of

Jewel House, 144, 156

Kemble, Mr., 272

Kéroualle, Louise de; *see* Portsmouth, Duchess of

Killigrew, Harry, 62, 135, 149, 166-169

Killigrew, Tom, 42

Lachosse, 273

Lauderdale, John Maitland, 2nd Earl, 1st Duke, 96, 113, 120, 195, 196

Lee, Sir Edward Henry; see Lichfield, Earl of
Leeds, Duke of; see Danby, Thomas Osborne, Earl of
Lely, Sir Peter, 90, 226
Lennard, Thomas; see Dacre, Lord
Lennox, Charles Stuart, 6th Duke, 137-141, 157, 165, 183, 220
Lennox, Esme Stuart, 4th Duke, 10, 13, 33, 137
Leroy, John, 131
Lichfield, Bishop of; see Coventry, Bishop of
Lichfield, Dean of; see Coventry, Bishop of
Lichfield, Earl of, 220, 221, 239
Lichfield, Charlotte Fitzroy, Countess of, 113, 216, 219, 220, 239, 240, 254
Life Guards, 46, 53, 101, 176
Limerick, Lord, Charles Fitzroy; see Southampton, Duke of
London, Bishop Braybrooke of, 174
London, Lord Mayor of, 118
Lords, House of, 10, 33, 105, 147, 199, 257
Louis XIV, King, 5, 25, 28, 47, 77, 92, 97, 100, 111, 113, 115, 118, 120, 129, 136, 143, 163, 185-192, 200, 206, 211, 232, 237, 241, 245, 249, 251, 269, 272
*Love in a Wood*, 226
Lowestoft, Battle of, 122, 123, 132, 133
Lucy, Catherine, Duchess of Northumberland, 258-259
Ludgate Hill, 3, 11, 16

Madrid, 96
Magdalen College, Oxford, 129
Maitland, John; see Lauderdale
Mancini, Hortensia; see Mazarin, Duchess of
Marie Louise, Princess, 271, 272
Marlborough, Duke of; see Churchill, John
Marston Moor, 25
Marvell, Andrew, 4, 123, 179
Mary, Princess Royal, Princess of Orange, 5, 11, 40-43
Mary, Princess and Queen of Great Britain, 140, 203, 260,

261
Mary of Modena, Queen; see d'Este
Matted Gallery, 134
May, Baptist, 121, 123, 126, 135, 138, 139, 144, 154, 156, 195, 247, 270
Mazarin, Hortensia, Duchess of, 234-239, 243, 256, 261
Medway, Battle of, 145, 149, 150
Merton College, Oxford, 120, 130, 216
Middleton, Charles, 87
Middleton, Jane, 77, 78, 86, 87, 90, 236, 237
Molina, Conde de, 119
Monck, George; see Albemarle
Monmouth, James, Duke of, 74, 87, 164, 190, 219, 220
Montagu, Abbé Walter, 245
Montagu, Anne, infant, 245
Montagu, Anne; see Harvey, Lady
Montagu, Edward, Earl of Manchester, 193
Montagu, Edward, 1st Earl of Sandwich, 37, 87, 89, 109
Montagu, Ralph, later Duke Montagu, 87, 192, 193, 206, 235-237, 240-252, 260, 267, 276
Montespan, Athènais de, 28
Mordaunt, Lord, 21
Morrice, Sir William, 99
Mountbatten, Prince Philip, 165
Muskerry, Lord, 132

New Amsterdam, 112
New Dunkirk; see Clarendon House
New Netherlands, 112
Newcastle, Henry Cavendish, Duke of, 241, 258
Nicholas, Sir Edward, 97, 98
Nicholls, Captain, 112
Nonsuch, 223
Nonsuch, Baroness; see Villiers, Barbara
Norfolk, Duke of, 204
Norton, Countess of, 258
Northumberland, Earls of, 11, 218, 223, 241
Northumberland, Elizabeth Howard, Countess of, 241

Northumberland, Elizabeth Wrio-
thesley, Countess of, 236, 237,
241, 245, 250, 260
Northumberland, George Fitzroy,
Duke of, 128, 129, 213, 216-
218, 221, 239-241, 245, 250,
254, 255, 257-259
Norwich, Earl of, 5
Norwich, Viscount; see Grafton,
Duke of
Nottingham, 15
Nottingham, Earl of, 259, 261

Oates, Titus, 257
Ogle, Lord, 241, 258
Old Rowley, 200
Oldmixon, 4
Orleans, Henriette Anne, Duchess
of, 24-28, 42, 43, 50, 53, 112,
118, 125, 141, 167, 187, 189,
198-200, 205, 217, 236, 271
Orleans, Philippe, Duke of, 25,
28, 43, 54, 271
Ormonde, Marquis of, 41, 44, 78,
99, 196, 198, 211
Osborne, Thomas; see Danby
Oxford, Bishop Fell of, 204, 219,
229
Oxford, Lady, 261

Page, Damaris, 177, 178
Palais Royal, Paris, 24
Pallas, Madame de, 268
Palmer, Anne; see Sussex, Count-
ess of
Palmer, Catherine, 22, 245
Palmer, Catherine Herbert
Vaughan, Lady, 16
Palmer, Charles; see Southamp-
ton, Duke of
Palmer, Charlotte; see Lichfield,
Countess of
Palmer, George; see Northumber-
land, Duke of
Palmer, Henry; see Grafton, Duke
of
Palmer, Roger, 1st Earl of Castle-
maine, 15, 16, 17, 20, 22, 30,
37, 45, 48, 60, 68, 69, 73, 74,
76, 120, 121, 130, 137, 181,
183, 215, 216, 245, 249, 257,
260, 262, 263
Paris, Archbishop of, 242, 273-
276
Pegge, Catherine, 240
Pepys, Samuel, 21, 37, 54, 82, 91,
102, 122, 123, 129, 138, 154,
159, 168, 173, 174, 178, 183,

192, 194, 195
Percy, Lady Anne, 11
Percy, Lady Betty, 218, 223, 236,
240, 241, 243, 245, 250, 258
Phoenix Park, 196, 197
Piccadilly, 116, 155, 180
Pigeon, Mistress, 273-275
Plymouth, Charles, Earl of, 240,
241, 255
Pointoise, 216
Pope, Alexander, 198, 231
Portsmouth, Louise, Duchess of,
165, 205-210, 221, 223, 224,
232, 234, 235, 238, 243, 254-
256, 269, 270
Powis, Lord; see Herbert, William
Pratt, Roger, 116
Pregnani, Abbé, 189, 190
Price, Goditha, 133
Prideaux, Humphrey, 212, 240
Privy Council, 43, 53, 149, 169,
181, 260
Privy Garden, 200
Privy Purse, 126, 144, 147
Pulteney, Catherine; see Lucy

Regiment Royal-Anglois, 232
Reresby, Sir John, 55
Rich, Charles, Earl of Warwick,
6, 12
Rich, Robert, 12
Richmond, 1st Duke of; see Len-
nox, Esme Stuart
Richmond, 3rd Duke of; see Len-
nox, Charles Stuart
Richmond, Charles, Duke of (son
of Louise de Kéroualle), 221,
222, 231, 255
Richmond, Mary Villiers, Duchess
of, 50, 51, 137, 222
Richmond Palace, 69, 70, 89, 105
Richmond Park, 89
Roberts, Jane, 170
Rochester, John Wilmot, Earl of,
234
Rochester, Lawrence, Earl of; see
Hyde, Lawrence
Rosamund (Fair), 115
Royal African Company, 111
*Royal Charles* ship, 122, 123, 145
Royal Society, 6, 36
Rupert, Prince, 9, 83, 131, 219
Ruvigny, Ambassador, 181

St. Albans, Henry Jermyn, Earl of,
192
St. Albans, Charles Beauclere,
Duke of, 255

St. Asaph, Bishop of; *see* Glemham, Dr. Henry
St. Germain's Fair, 85
St. Gregory by St. Paul's, 17
St. James's Fight, 136
St. James's Palace, 180, 196, 226
St. James's Park, 37, 78, 114, 133, 239
St. John, Lord, 13
St. John's College, Oxford, 240
St. Margaret's Westminster, 9, 61
St. Martin-in-the-Fields, 12, 45
St. Paul's Cathedral, 32, 174
Sandwich, Earl of; *see* Montagu, Edward
Savile, George; *see* Halifax
Saville, Henry, 250
Schelling, 145
Scott, Lady Anne, 75, 87, 150
Scotts; *see* Buccleuch, Earls of
Sealed Knot, 20
Sedley, Catherine; *see* Dorchester, Countess of
Sedley, Sir Charles, 122, 160, 170
Shaftesbury, Earl of; *see* Cooper
Shakespeare, Joan, 171
Shakespeare, William, 125, 171
Sheldon, Gilbert, Archbishop of Canterbury, 159, 160, 179, 215, 218, 246
Sheldon, Ralph, 117
Sheldonian Theatre, Oxford, 167
Shore, Jane, 51, 114, 115
Shrewsbury, Anna Maria Brudenell, Countess of, 148, 166-169, 206-210
Shrewsbury, Francis, 11th Earl of, 167, 169
Sidney, Harry, 127, 128
Somerset, Earl of, 258
Somerset House, 75, 183, 238
Southampton, Thomas Wriothesley, 4th Earl of, 41, 48, 111, 116-118, 126, 222, 243
Southampton, Countess of; *see* Villiers, Barbara
Southampton, Earl of, later Duke of, Charles Fitzroy, 48, 60, 61, 74, 127, 211-217, 220, 222, 231, 239, 255, 259
Spanish Ambassador; *see* Molina
Spencer, Robert, Earl of Sunderland, 250
Stanhope, Lady Gertrude, 126
Stanhope, Philip; *see* Chesterfield, Earl of
Stillingfleet, Edward, 106

Stuart, Anne; *see* Anne
Stuart, Charles; *see* Charles I
Stuart, Charles; *see* Charles II
Stuart, Charles; *see* Lennox
Stuart, Esme; *see* Lennox
Stuart, Frances, 50, 76, 79, 80, 83, 85, 88, 89, 92, 103, 105-107, 119, 125, 132, 136-142, 146, 157, 164, 165, 169, 170, 182, 183, 200, 223
Stuart, Henry, Duke of Gloucester, 37, 83
Stuart, James; *see* James I
Stuart, James; *see* York, James, Duke of
Stuart, James, Duke of Berwick, 232
Stuart, Mary; *see* Mary, Princess
Suffolk, Barbara Villiers, Countess of, 59, 61, 89
Suffolk, Earl of, 69, 126
Sunderland, Earl of; *see* Spencer
Sussex, Earl of; *see* Dacre
Sussex, Anne Fitzroy, Countess of, 45, 74, 216, 219, 220, 237-239, 244, 248-250, 262, 268-276
Sussex, Anne Villiers, Countess of, 45, 223

Talbot, Francis; *see* Shrewsbury, Earl of
Talbot, Jack, 258
Talbot, Richard, 42
*Tatler, The*, 265
Temple, Sir William, 269
Temple Bar, 32, 131
Texel, 121, 122
*The Country Wife*, 228
Thynne, Thomas, 258
Tichborne, Sir Henry, 268

Valliere, Louise de la, 28
de Vere, Aubrey, 20th Earl of Oxford, 61
Verney, Sir Edmund, 9
Villars, Charlott Henriette, 263-269
Villiers, Anne; *see* Sussex, Countess
Villiers, Barbara, in love with Chesterfield, 1, 2; letters to Chesterfield, 2, 3, 17, 18; war baby, 7; ancestry, 8; early poverty, 10; marries Roger Palmer, 17, 18, 19; joins Charles II, 22-25; called "gay," 30; conceives Charles's child, 33; promiscuity, 36; flirts with

dukes, 37; and Chesterfield's remarriage, 44; bears Anne, 45; receives title, 48, 49; clash with Mary Villiers, 51; Bedchamber crisis, 56-71; bears Charles, 61; leaves Roger, 69; final parting, 74; patronage of Frances Stuart, 84; her cabal, 85; gambling losses, 85; demonstrations of strength, 86, 89; bears Henry, 90; a cultivated geisha, 103; received by Roman Church, 107; asserts public precedence, 109; cabal re-formed, 113; bears Charlotte, 113; abused as Jane Shore, 114; courted by ambassadors, 119; nominates to Privy Purse, 126; procures estates, 126; bears George, 128; reprimanded by Charles, 132; final settlement with Roger, 137; betrays Frances Stuart, 137-141; her turbulent summer 1667, 146-155; and fall of Clarendon, 155-161; coarser lovers, 171-174; Poor Whores' Petition, 177-179; enters Berkshire House, 180; assault on Treasury, 184; and French alliance, 188-193; and John Churchill, 201-203; 229-232; financial coups, 211-224; her profligacy as a female rake, 225; and Wycherley, 225-228; sole prostitution, 230; bears Barbara, 231; scandalous life in Paris, 242-253, 267-276; and Cardonell Goodman, 256-262; and Beau Feilding, 263-266; dies, 266; begging letter, 277

Villiers, Barbara; *see also* Suffolk, Countess

Villiers, Charles, 2nd Earl of Anglesey, 10, 17, 45, 223

Villiers, Christopher, 1st Earl of Anglesey, 8

Villiers, Colonel Edward, 69, 89, 144, 184

Villiers, George, 1st Duke of Buckingham; *see* Buckingham

Villiers, George, 2nd Duke of Buckingham; *see* Buckingham

Villiers, George, 4th Viscount Grandison; *see* Grandison

Villiers, John, 1st Viscount Purbeck, 8

Villiers, Mary; *see* Richmond, Duchess

Villiers, William, 2nd Viscount Grandison; *see* Grandison

Wadsworth, Mary, 264, 265

Walters, Lucy, 75

Webb, Colonel William, 16

Wells, Winifred, 76, 77, 82, 83, 117, 142

Westminster Abbey, 46, 169

Westminster Hall, 37, 145, 159

Whalley, Captain John, 15

Whitehall Chapel, 38, 114, 153, 173

Whitehall Palace, 30, 33, 37, 41, 43, 46, 53, 68, 73, 75, 77, 82, 86, 87, 93, 102, 109, 114, 131, 141, 162, 176, 178, 180, 194, 248, 253, 256

William III, King, 11, 260

Wilmot, John; *see* Rochester, Earl of

Wilson, waiting woman, 144, 194

Winchester, Bishop of, 42

Windsor, 3, 13, 16, 30, 87, 219, 220, 253

Wolley, Francis, 21

Wolley, Dr., 21

Wood, Antony, 127, 128, 175

Wood, Sir Henry, 211-214, 226

Wood, Mary, 211-216, 222, 259

Wood, Dr. Thomas; *see* Coventry, Bishop of

Worcester, Marchioness of, 59

Worcester House, Strand, 40, 68, 116

Wriothesley, Henry; *see* Southampton, Earl of

Wycherley, William, 198, 225-229, 266

York, Anne Hyde, Duchess of, 38-43, 47, 75, 87, 90, 94, 114, 118, 127, 128, 140, 184, 192, 202-204, 261

York, James, Duke of, later James II, 30, 37, 38, 46, 51, 53, 75-82, 85, 92, 94, 109, 112, 113, 121-123, 126-128, 132-135, 143, 155, 177, 180, 184-186, 192, 202-204, 209, 219, 220, 224, 236, 255, 257-261, 269, 277

*CAROBALJO made this index*